4

Grammar Connection

STRUCTURE THROUGH CONTENT

SERIES EDITORS

Marianne Celce-Murcia

M. E. Sokolik

Noël Houck

Sharon Hilles

HEINLE
CENGAGE Learning™

Australia • Brazil • Japan • Korea • Mexico • Singapore • Spain • United Kingdom • United States

HEINLE
CENGAGE Learning

Grammar Connection 4:
   Structure Through Content
Noël Houck, Sharon Hilles

Series Editors: Marianne Celce-Murcia, M. E. Sokolik

Publisher: Sherrise Roehr

Acquisitions Editor, Academic ESL: Tom Jefferies

Senior Development Editor: Michael Ryall

Editorial Assistant: Cécile Bruso

Product Marketing Manager: Katie Kelley

Senior Content Project Manager:
   Maryellen Eschmann-Killeen

Manufacturing Buyer: Betsy Donaghey

Production Project Manager: Chrystie Hopkins

Production Services: InContext Publishing Partners

Index: Alexandra Nickerson

Cover and Interior Design: Linda Beaupre

Cover Image: Karin Slade/Taxi/Getty Images

Credits appear on page 304, which constitutes a continuation of the copyright page.

Library of Congress Control Number: 2008920430

ISBN 13: 978-1-4130-0845-6

ISBN 10: 1-4130-0845-3

International Student Edition
ISBN 13: 978-1-4130-1756-4
ISBN 10: 1-4130-1756-8

Heinle
25 Thomson Place
Boston, Massachusetts 02210
USA

Cengage Learning products are represented in Canada by Nelson Education, Ltd.

Visit Heinle online at **elt.heinle.com**

Visit our corporate website at **cengage.com**

Printed in the United States of America.
1 2 3 4 5 6 7 8 9 10 — 12 11 10 09 08

Contents

Using language grammatically and being able to communicate authentically are important goals for students. My grammar research suggests that students' mastery of grammar improves when they interpret and produce grammar in meaningful contexts at the discourse level. *Grammar Connection* connects learners to academic success, allowing them to reach their goals and master the grammar.

— Marianne Celce-Murcia

"Connections" is probably the most useful concept in any instructor's vocabulary. To help students connect what they are learning to the rest of their lives is the most important task I fulfill as an instructor. *Grammar Connection* lets instructors and students find those connections. The series connects grammar to reading, writing, and speaking. It also connects students with the ability to function academically, to use the Internet for interesting research, and to collaborate with others on projects and presentations. — M. E. Sokolik

Dear Instructor,

With experience in language teaching, teacher training, and research, we created *Grammar Connection* to be uniquely relevant for academically and professionally oriented courses and students. Every lesson in the series deals with academic content to help students become familiar with the language of college and the university and to feel more comfortable in all of their courses, not just English.

While academic content provides the context for this series, our goal is for the learner to go well beyond sentence-level exercises in order to use grammar as a resource for comprehending and producing academic discourse. Students move from shorter, more controlled exercises to longer, more self-directed, authentic ones. Taking a multi-skills approach, *Grammar Connection* includes essential grammar that students need to know at each level. Concise lessons allow instructors to use the material easily in any classroom situation.

We hope that you and your students find our approach to the teaching and learning of grammar for academic and professional purposes in *Grammar Connection* effective and innovative.

Marianne Celce-Murcia
Series Editor

M. E. Sokolik
Series Editor

Welcome to Grammar Connection

■ **What is *Grammar Connection*?**

Grammar Connection is a five-level grammar series that integrates content with grammar instruction in an engaging format to prepare students for future academic and professional success.

■ **What is the content?**

The content in *Grammar Connection* is drawn from various academic disciplines: sociology, psychology, medical sciences, computer science, communications, biology, engineering, business, and the social sciences.

■ **Why does *Grammar Connection* incorporate content into the lessons?**

The content is used to provide high-interest contexts for exploring the grammar. The charts and exercises are contextualized with the content in each lesson. Learning content is not the focus of *Grammar Connection*—it sets the scene for learning grammar.

■ **Is *Grammar Connection* "discourse-based"?**

Yes. With *Grammar Connection,* learners go beyond sentence-level exercises in order to use grammar as a resource for comprehending and producing academic discourse. These discourses include conversations, narratives, and exposition.

■ **Does *Grammar Connection* include communicative practice?**

Yes. *Grammar Connection* takes a multi-skills approach. The series includes listening activities as well as texts for reading, and the production tasks elicit both spoken and written output via pair or group work tasks.

■ **Why are the lessons shorter than in other books?**

Concise lessons allow instructors to use the material easily in any classroom situation. For example, one part of a lesson could be covered in a 50-minute period, allowing instructors with shorter class times to feel a sense of completion. Alternatively, a single lesson could fit into a longer, multi-skills class period. For longer, grammar-focused classes, more than one lesson could be covered.

■ **Does *Grammar Connection* include opportunities for students to review the grammar?**

Yes. A Review section is included after every five lessons. These tests can also be used by instructors to measure student understanding of the grammar taught. In addition, there are practice exercises in the Workbook and on the website (elt.thomson.com/grammarconnection).

■ **Does *Grammar Connection* assist students in learning new vocabulary?**

Yes. The Content Vocabulary section in each lesson of *Grammar Connection* incorporates academic vocabulary building and journaling. In Book 1 this takes a picture dictionary approach. In later books words from the Academic Word List are used. This, along with the content focus, ensures that students expand their vocabulary along with their grammatical capability.

A **picture-based vocabulary** section in lower levels familiarizes students with the content-based academic vocabulary that is used in the lesson. At higher levels, students are introduced to words from the **Academic Word List.**

Thought-provoking **discussion questions** activate students' knowledge of the content area. The questions can also be used as **diagnostic tests** to assess students' mastery of the grammar before it is taught.

Grammar Connection is organized into thirty concise lessons, each containing two or three parts of connected grammar points. Every lesson follows a unique pedagogical approach.

The grammar in each lesson is **contextualized** with topics from different **academic disciplines.**

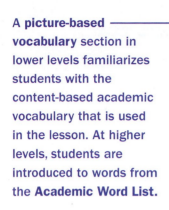

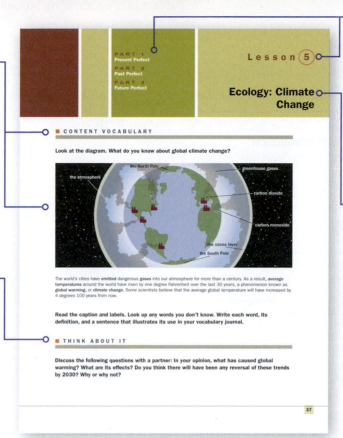

PART 1
Present Perfect

PART 2
Past Perfect

PART 3
Future Perfect

Lesson 5

Ecology: Climate Change

■ CONTENT VOCABULARY

Look at the diagram. What do you know about global climate change?

The world's cities have **emitted** dangerous **gases** into our atmosphere for more than a century. As a result, **average temperatures** around the world have risen by one degree Fahrenheit over the last 30 years, a phenomenon known as **global warming**, or **climate change**. Some scientists believe that the average global temperature will have increased by 4 degrees 100 years from now.

Read the caption and labels. Look up any words you don't know. Write each word, its definition, and a sentence that illustrates its use in your vocabulary journal.

■ THINK ABOUT IT

Discuss the following questions with a partner: In your opinion, what has caused global warming? What are its effects? Do you think there will have been any reversal of these trends by 2030? Why or why not?

37

An integrated **audio program** allows students to listen to the content readings and dialogues.

Content readings and dialogs present the grammar in a meaningful and interesting way.

Contextualized grammar charts provide **easy-to-understand** clear explanations of grammar form as well as notes on usage.

PART ONE   Present Perfect Progressive

■ GRAMMAR IN CONTENT

A Read and listen to the following article about English.

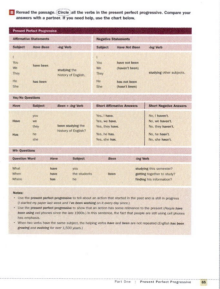

Students move from a **variety** of controlled exercises to more self-directed ones enabling students to become comfortable using the grammar.

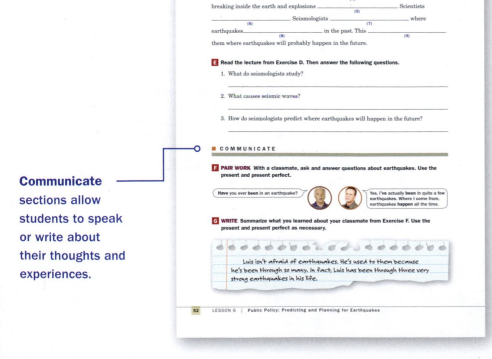

PART THREE   Adjective Sequences

■ GRAMMAR IN CONTENT

A Reread the passage on page 102. Put a wavy line under all the adjectives of measurement, size, and length. Compare your answers with a partner. If you need help, use the chart below.

Adjective Sequences

Adjectives preceding a noun usually follow this sequence:
1. **quality:** beautiful, classic
2. **measurement, size, length:** large, long
3. **age:** old, modern
4. **shape:** round, triangular
5. **condition:** chipped, perfect
6. **color:** beige, navy
7. **origin, material:** French, cotton, wool
8. **noun modifier:** fashion (as in fashion show)
Examples:
the **beautiful long beige** coat (quality, length, color)
a pair of **traditional navy wool** slacks (age, color, material)

B Fill in the blanks, putting the adjectives in parentheses in the correct order.

Sergio is visiting New York for a job interview with a major fashion house. He is carrying a ___heavy black leather___ (leather/heavy/black) folder that is full of his
(1)
latest designs. The interview is in a _____ (brick/tall) building
(2)
close to his hotel, but it's on a _____ (dirty/long) street. The
(3)
_____ (cotton/trendy/blue) shirt that he bought especially for
(4)
the interview no longer looks so chic, but it's too late to change. He walks through a
_____ (modern/red) door, and the receptionist greets him warmly.
(5)
She shows him into the interview room. He shakes hands with the three interviewers,
sits down at a _____ (polished/large/wooden) table, and opens his
(6)
folder. The interview has begun.

C Look at the following pictures of models in a show. Write a description of each model in the space provided. Use complete sentences and a variety of adjectives in your description.

Naomi _____

Kika _____

Reiko _____

Sasha _____

D Listen to the lecture. Fill in the blanks while you listen. Listen again to check your work.

CD1,TR16   People _have always had a personal interest_ in earthquakes, but the scientific study of
(1)
earthquakes _____ . Scientists who _____
(2)   (3)
are called seismologists. Seismic waves _____ Rocks
(4)
breaking inside the earth and explosions _____ Scientists
(5)
_____ . Seismologists _____ where
(6)   (7)
earthquakes_____ in the past. This _____
(8)   (9)
them where earthquakes will probably happen in the future.

E Read the lecture from Exercise D. Then answer the following questions.

1. What do seismologists study?
_____

2. What causes seismic waves?
_____

3. How do seismologists predict where earthquakes will happen in the future?
_____

■ COMMUNICATE

Communicate sections allow students to speak or write about their thoughts and experiences.

F PAIR WORK With a classmate, ask and answer questions about earthquakes. Use the present and present perfect.

Have you ever **been** in an earthquake?

Yes, I've actually **been** in quite a few earthquakes. Where I come from, earthquakes **happen** all the time.

G WRITE Summarize what you learned about your classmate from Exercise F. Use the present and present perfect as necessary.

Luis isn't afraid of earthquakes. He's used to them because he's been through so many. In fact, Luis has been through three very strong earthquakes in his life.

At the end of each lesson, students are encouraged to put together the **grammar and vocabulary** from the lesson in a productive way.

Interesting projects allow students to put newly learned grammatical forms and vocabulary to use in ways that encourage additional independent reading, **research**, and/or communication. Many of these activities are group activities, further requiring students to put their language skills to work.

Internet activities encourage students to connect the grammar with online resources.

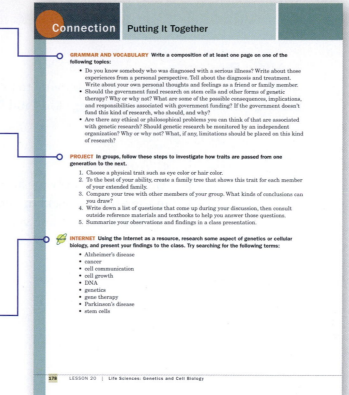

Connection Putting It Together

GRAMMAR AND VOCABULARY Write a composition of at least one page on one of the following topics:

- Do you know somebody who was diagnosed with a serious illness? Write about those experiences from a personal perspective. Tell about the diagnosis and treatment. Write about your own personal thoughts and feelings as a friend or family member.
- Should the government fund research on stem cells and other forms of genetic therapy? Why or why not? What are some of the possible consequences, implications, and responsibilities associated with government funding? If the government doesn't fund this kind of research, who should, and why?
- Are there any ethical or philosophical problems you can think of that are associated with genetic research? Should genetic research be monitored by an independent organization? Why or why not? What, if any, limitations should be placed on this kind of research?

PROJECT In groups, follow these steps to investigate how traits are passed from one generation to the next.

1. Choose a physical trait such as eye color or hair color.
2. To the best of your ability, create a family tree that shows this trait for each member of your extended family.
3. Compare your tree with other members of your group. What kinds of conclusions can you draw?
4. Write down a list of questions that come up during your discussion, then consult outside reference materials and textbooks to help you answer those questions.
5. Summarize your observations and findings in a class presentation.

INTERNET Using the Internet as a resource, research some aspect of genetics or cellular biology, and present your findings to the class. Try searching for the following terms:

- Alzheimer's disease
- cancer
- cell communication
- cell growth
- DNA
- genetics
- gene therapy
- Parkinson's disease
- stem cells

178 LESSON 20 | Life Sciences: Genetics and Cell Biology

A **Review** section after every five lessons helps assess and reinforce language learning.

A **Learner Log** encourages students to reflect on what they have learned and enhances learner independence.

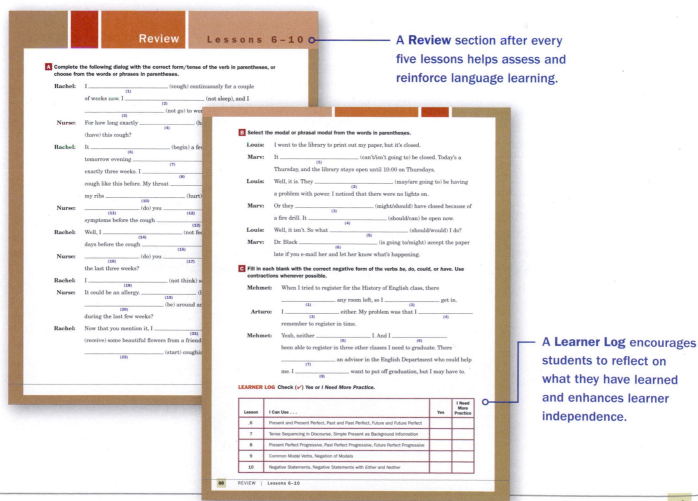

Review Lessons 6–10

A Complete the following dialog with the correct form/tense of the verb in parentheses, or choose from the words or phrases in parentheses.

Rachel: I _____ (cough) continuously for a couple of weeks now. I _____ (not sleep), and I _____ (not go) to wor...

Nurse: For how long exactly _____ (h... (have) this cough?

Rachel: It _____ (begin) a few tomorrow evening _____ exactly three weeks. I _____ cough like this before. My throat my ribs _____ (hurt)

Nurse: _____ (do) you symptoms before the cough _____

Rachel: Well, I _____ (not fee... days before the cough _____

Nurse: _____ (do) you the last three weeks?

Rachel: I _____ (not think) s...

Nurse: It could be an allergy. _____ (_____ (be) around an during the last few weeks?

Rachel: Now that you mention it, I _____ (receive) some beautiful flowers from a friend _____ (start) coughin...

B Select the modal or phrasal modal from the words in parentheses.

Louis: I went to the library to print out my paper, but it's closed.

Marv: It _____ (can't/isn't going to) be closed. Today's a Thursday, and the library stays open until 10:00 on Thursdays.

Louis: Well, it is. They _____ (may/are going to) be having a problem with power. I noticed that there were no lights on.

Marv: Or they _____ (might/should) have closed because of a fire drill. It _____ (should/can) be open now.

Louis: Well, it isn't. So what _____ (should/would) I do?

Marv: Dr. Black _____ (is going to/might) accept the paper late if you e-mail her and let her know what's happening.

C Fill in each blank with the correct negative form of the verbs *be, do, could,* or *have.* Use contractions whenever possible.

Mehmet: When I tried to register for the History of English class, there _____ any room left, so I _____ get in.

Arturo: I _____ either. My problem was that I _____ remember to register in time.

Mehmet: Yeah, neither _____ I. And I _____ been able to register in three other classes I need to graduate. There _____ an advisor in the English Department who could help me. I _____ want to put off graduation, but I may have to.

LEARNER LOG Check (✔) *Yes* or *I Need More Practice.*

Lesson	I Can Use . . .	Yes	I Need More Practice
6	Present and Present Perfect, Past and Past Perfect, Future and Future Perfect		
7	Tense Sequencing in Discourse, Simple Present as Background Information		
8	Present Perfect Progressive, Past Perfect Progressive, Future Perfect Progressive		
9	Common Modal Verbs, Negation of Modals		
10	Negative Statements, Negative Statements with *Either* and *Neither*		

88 REVIEW | Lessons 6–10

Supplements

■ Audio Program

Audio CDs and Audio Tapes allow students to listen to every reading in the book to build listening skills and fluency.

■ Workbook

The Workbooks review and practice all the grammar points in the Student Book. In addition each workbook includes six Writing Tutorials and vocabulary expansion exercises.

■ Website

Features additional grammar practice activities, vocabulary test items, and other resources: elt.heinle.com/grammarconnection.

■ Annotated Teacher's Edition with Presentation Tool CD-ROM

Offers comprehensive lesson planning advice and teaching tips, as well as a full answer key. The Presentation Tool CD-ROM includes a PowerPoint presentation for selected lessons and includes all the grammar charts from the book.

■ Assessment CD-ROM with *ExamView*® Test Generator

The customizable generator features lesson, review, mid-term, and term-end assessment items to monitor student progress.

Grammar Connection is based on scientific research on the most effective means of teaching grammar to adult learners of English.

■ Discourse-based Grammar

Research by Celce-Murcia and Olshtain (2000) suggests that learners should go beyond sentence-level exercises in order to use grammar as a resource for comprehending and producing academic discourse. *Grammar Connection* lets students move from controlled exercises to more self-expressive and self-directed ones.

■ Communicative Grammar

Research shows that communicative exercises should complement traditional exercises (Comeau, 1987; Herschensohn, 1988). *Grammar Connection* balances effective controlled activities, such as fill-in-the-blanks, with meaningful interactive exercises.

■ Learner-centered Content

Van Duzer (1999) emphasizes that research on adult English language learners shows that "learners should read texts that meet their needs and are interesting." In *Grammar Connection* the content readings are carefully selected and adapted to be both high-interest and relevant to the needs of learners.

■ Vocabulary Development

A number of recent studies have shown the effectiveness of helping English language learners develop independent skills in vocabulary development (Nation, 1990, 2001; Nist & Simpson, 2001; Schmitt, 2000). In *Grammar Connection,* care has been taken to introduce useful academic vocabulary, based in part on Coxhead's (2000) work.

■ Using Background Knowledge

Because research shows that background knowledge facilitates comprehension (Eskey, 1997), each lesson of *Grammar Connection* opens with a "Think About It" section related to the lesson theme.

■ Student Interaction

Learning is enhanced when students work with each other to co-construct knowledge (Grennon-Brooks & Brooks, 1993; Sutherland & Bonwell, 1996). *Grammar Connection* includes many pair and group work exercises as well as interactive projects.

■ References

Celce-Murcia, M., & Olshtain, E. (2000). *Discourse and Context in Language Teaching.* New York: Cambridge University Press.

Comeau, R. Interactive Oral Grammar Exercises. In W. M. Rivers (Ed.), *Interactive Language Teaching* (57–69). Cambridge: Cambridge University Press, 1987.

Coxhead, A. (2000). "A New Academic Word List." *TESOL Quarterly,* 34 (2), 213–238.

Eskey, D. (1997). "Models of Reading and the ESOL Student." *Focus on Basics 1 (B),* 9–11.

Grennon-Brooks, J., & Brooks, M. G. (1993). *In Search of Understanding: The Case for Constructivist Classrooms.* Alexandria, VA: Association for Supervision and Curriculum Development.

Herschensohn, J. (1988). "Linguistic Accuracy of Textbook Grammar." *Modern Language Journal 72(4),* 409–414.

Nation, I. S. P. (2001). *Learning Vocabulary in Another Language.* New York: Cambridge University Press.

Nation, I. S. P. (1990). *Teaching and Learning Vocabulary.* Boston: Thomson Heinle.

Nist, S. L., & Simpson, M. L. (2001). *Developing Vocabulary for College Thinking.* Boston: Allyn & Bacon.

Schmitt, N. (2000). *Vocabulary in Language Teaching.* New York: Cambridge University Press.

Sutherland, T. E., & Bonwell, C. C. (Eds.). (1996). "Using Active Learning in College Classes: A Range of Options for Faculty." *New Directions for Teaching and Learning, Number 67,* Fall 1996. San Francisco, CA: Jossey-Bass Publishers.

Van Duzer, C. (1999). "Reading and the Adult Language Learner." *ERIC Digest.* Washington, D.C.: National Center for ESL Literacy Education.

To Marianne.

— *Noël Houck and Sharon Hilles*

The authors, series editors, and publisher wish to thank the following people for their contributions:

Susan Alexandre
Trimble Technical High School
Fort Worth, TX

Joan Amore
Triton College
River Grove, IL

Cally Andriotis-Williams
Newcomers High School
Long Island City, NY

Ana Maria Cepero
Miami Dade College
Miami, FL

Jacqueline Cunningham
Harold Washington College
Chicago, IL

Kathleen Flynn
Glendale Community College
Glendale, CA

Sally Gearhart
Santa Rosa Junior College
Santa Rosa, CA

Janet Harclerode
Santa Monica College
Santa Monica, CA

Carolyn Ho
North Harris College
Houston, TX

Eugenia Krimmel
Lititz, PA

Dana Liebowitz
Palm Beach Central
  High School
Wellington, FL

Shirley Lundblade
Mt. San Antonio College
Walnut, CA

Craig Machado
Norwalk Community College
Norwalk, CT

Myo Myint
Mission College
Santa Clara, CA

Myra Redman
Miami Dade College
Miami, FL

Eric Rosenbaum
BEGIN Managed Programs
New York, NY

Marilyn Santos
Valencia Community College
Valencia, FL

Laura Sicola
University of Pennsylvania
Philadelphia, PA

Barbara Smith-Palinkas
University of South Florida
Tampa, FL

Kathy Sucher
Santa Monica College
Santa Monica, CA

Patricia Turner
San Diego City College
San Diego, CA

America Vasquez
Miami Dade College,
  Inter-American Campus
Miami, FL

Tracy von Mulaski
El Paso Community College
El Paso, TX

Jane Wang
Mt. San Antonio College
Walnut, CA

Lucy Watel
City College of Chicago -
  Harry S. Truman College
Chicago, IL

Donald Weasenforth
Collin County Community
  College
Plano, TX

Lesson ①

Psychology: Personality and Occupation

■ CONTENT VOCABULARY

Look at the pictures. What would be an ideal job for each of these people, based on their personality types?

Oscar likes people. He is an **extrovert**. He is **confident** and **friendly**. He has an **outgoing personality**.

Ms. Jenkins is a good **listener**. She is not **judgmental**. She doesn't like to **argue**. She **empathizes** with other people.

Layla is **shy**. She is an **introvert**. She doesn't like to **take risks**. She doesn't like parties. She enjoys time alone.

Mr. Jones is **organized** and **reliable**. He is **conscientious**. He **pays attention** to details.

Read the description below each picture. Look up any words you don't know. Write each word, its definition, and a sentence that illustrates its use in your vocabulary journal.

■ THINK ABOUT IT

What jobs are good for extroverts? What kind of job would an introvert like? Discuss these questions in a group. When you are finished, record your ideas in your writing journal.

■ GRAMMAR IN CONTENT

A Read and listen to this dialog between a student and his advisor.

A Different Kind of Test

Advisor:	What **can I do** for you?
Student:	Well, I'm not sure what to major in, and I **have to** declare a major next month.
Advisor:	I **think** I **can help** you with that. What **are** you interested in?
Student:	That's the problem. **I don't know.** I'm going to work at a newspaper this summer. Maybe I'll like journalism, but maybe **I won't.** When I **was** young, I always **had** trouble making up my mind. When my friends and I **got** together after school, I **could** never **decide** between football and baseball. In high school I **wanted** to do too many things, so I **didn't do** anything well. I'm afraid the same thing **is going to happen** again as soon as I **declare** a major.
Advisor:	I **know** something that **might help.** I'm going to make an appointment for you with Ms. Smith down at the testing center.
Student:	Not another test!
Advisor:	I **think** you're going to like this one. It'll give us a personality profile. Then we'll match your profile with compatible majors and careers. For example, if you **are** organized and **enjoy** math, you **will** probably **like** accounting. That's a good major for a career as a CPA.
Student:	That **sounds** great, but I'm afraid I **won't pass. Is** the test hard? **Will** I **have to** study for it?
Advisor:	Don't worry. You **don't have to** study for this test. There **are** no right or wrong answers. It'll be fun.
Student:	OK. I'll do it.

an accountant: a person who keeps financial records

compatible: capable of working or living well together

to declare a major: to state formally one's primary subject of study in college

a CPA: Certified Public Accountant

journalism: the gathering and reporting of news

a profile: a group of characteristics, especially of a person

B Reread the dialog. (Circle) all the verbs in the present tense. Check your answers with a partner's answers.

Present Tense			
Affirmative Statements		**Negative Statements**	
I We You They	**work** ——————— hard.	I We You They	**do not/don't** ——————— **work** at night.
He She	**works**	He She	**does not/doesn't**

Yes/No Questions with Do			Short Affirmative Answers	Short Negative Answers
Do	I we you they	work on the weekend?	Yes, I **do**. Yes, we **do**. Yes, they **do**.	No, I **don't**. No, we **don't**. No, they **don't**.
Does	he she		Yes, he **does**. Yes, she **does**.	No, he **doesn't**. No, she **doesn't**.

Wh- Questions			Answers
When do	I we you they		I **work** during normal office hours. They **work** all the time.
Where does	he she	work?	He **works** at a university. She **works** at home.
How does	it		It **works** with a battery.

Notes:

- Use the present tense to express habitual or repeated actions that you do not think of as changing: *Jeff **does** his homework every night after dinner.*
- The present tense shows present emotions, states, or perceptions that you think aren't necessarily going to change: *He **doesn't like** math.*
- The present tense describes actions or states not connected to a specific time to make a factual report: *An individual's personality **changes** over time.*
- Use the present tense in time clauses for future sentences and in *if*-clauses for future possible conditionals: *After he **takes** the test tomorrow, he will meet with his counselor. If you **take** the test, you are going to discover some interesting things.*

C **Work with a partner. Fill in the blanks with the correct present tense form of the verb.**

Personality tests _____are_____ (be) fun and helpful. They _____ (can)
(1)   (2)

tell you a great deal about your personality. There _____ (be) no
(3)

right or wrong answers, but people _____ (have to) be honest when
(4)

they take the test. "The Big Five" _____ (be) a popular personality
(5)

test that you _____ (can take) online. It is called "The Big Five"
(6)

because it _____ (test) for five basic personality components. Many
(7)

career centers _____ (have) other kinds of personality tests as well.
(8)

D Work with a partner. Listen to Kristy's comments about her friend, Walter. Fill in the blanks as you listen.

CD1,TR2

My friend, Walter, _has an appointment on Monday_ for a personality test. After he
                    (1)

_____ a career counselor will interpret the results. Walter
            (2)

_____ what he is going to do after he graduates. He always
            (3)

_____ interested in anything. He _____
            (4)   **(5)**

or a career. If Walter _____, the counselor will be able to match
                                    (6)

Walter's personality with suitable careers. According to Ms. Smith from the Campus

Career Center, if you _____ your career goal, the center
                                (7)

_____ the appropriate major.
            (8)

■ **COMMUNICATE**

E **PAIR WORK** Take turns. Tell your partner about the personality of several people you know and each person's occupation and goals. Choose from the personality traits listed below to help guide your description.

My friend Abir **handles stress very well**, and **she's very organized** too.

What does she do?

Sounds like a good match.

She's still in school, but she **wants to be an accountant.**

Personality Traits

- handles stress very well
- likes to take risks
- is self-confident and outgoing
- likes to read and watch movies
- has a great sense of humor
- is very opinionated
- pays attention to details

- gets overwhelmed very easily
- doesn't like to take risks
- is shy and introverted
- prefers social activities
- is serious most of the time
- usually agrees with other people
- sees the big picture

F **WRITE** Write a paragraph about somebody you know. Describe his or her personality and occupation. How well do they match?

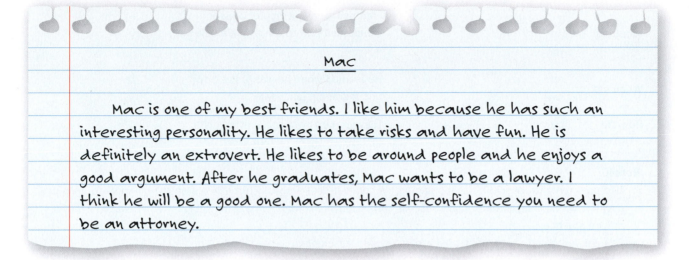

Mac

Mac is one of my best friends. I like him because he has such an interesting personality. He likes to take risks and have fun. He is definitely an extrovert. He likes to be around people and he enjoys a good argument. After he graduates, Mac wants to be a lawyer. I think he will be a good one. Mac has the self-confidence you need to be an attorney.

PART TWO	Past Tense Review

■ GRAMMAR IN CONTENT

A Reread the dialog on page 2. Underline all the verbs that are in the past tense. If you need help, use the chart below.

Past Tense	
Affirmative Statements	**Negative Statements**
I We You They learned a new song. He She	I We You They did not/didn't learn the dance. He She

Yes/No Questions with *Do*		**Short Affirmative Answers**	**Short Negative Answers**
Did	I we you learn the song? they he she	Yes, I **did**. Yes, we **did**. Yes, you **did**. Yes, they **did**. Yes, he **did**. Yes, she **did**.	No, I **didn't**. No, we **didn't**. No, you **didn't**. No, they **didn't**. No, he **didn't**. No, she **didn't**.

Past Tense

Wh- Questions			Answers
What did	I we you	learn?	I **learned** a new computer program. We **learned** how to assemble a new circuit.
When did	he she		He **learned** when he was just a boy. She **learned** it last year.
How did	they		They **learned** by studying every night.

Notes:
- Use past tense to describe actions and states completed at a specific time in the past; time markers may or may not be explicitly stated: *Juan's success* **came** *after many years of hard work. Last year he* **started** *his own private practice.*
- Regular verbs add *-ed* to make past tense: *learned, assembled, created,* and so on.

B **Work with a partner. Fill in the correct past tense of the verb.**

Several years ago, Juan ___*took*___ (take) a personality test. He
(1)
_____ (discover) several important things about himself, even
(2)
though he already _____ (know) most of those things. For
(3)
example, he _____ (test) high on extroversion. The test results
(4)
also _____ (reveal) that he is organized and pays attention to
(5)
details. Before taking the test, he _____ (be) already interested
(6)
in nursing, and the test _____ (confirm) that people with his
(7)
personality type are suited to a career in nursing. Juan _____
(8)
(enroll) in a nursing program, and a year later he _____ (become)
(9)
a certified nursing assistant. He _____ (start) work at a small
(10)
hospital, and two years later he _____ (get) an even better job.
(11)
He says the personality test _____ (give) him the confirmation he
(12)
_____ (need) to pursue his goals.
(13)

C Read the following e-mail. Circle the correct form of each verb.

Yesterday our professor writes /(wrote) something interesting on the board:
_____ (1)
"opposites attract / attracted." Do / Did you think that's true? I guess I think / thought he's
_____ (2)   _____ (3)   _____ (4)
right. I mean, there's this woman, Gwendolyn, who lives / lived in my dorm, and she
                                                    _____ (5)
is really outgoing and friendly. She is / was totally an extrovert. Her boyfriend, Bob, on the
                               _____ (6)
other hand, is / was a real introvert. They meet / met last year in Dr. Sanchez's Psych 102.
_____ (7)   _____ (8)
They sit / sat next to each other. Bob was so shy that he said / says nothing for 10 weeks.
_____ (9)   _____ (10)
When he finally gets / got up the courage to speak to Gwendolyn, he said, "I
_____ (11)
think / thought I'm going to throw up." He was so nervous that he makes / made himself
_____ (12)   _____ (13)
sick. Once Bob breaks / broke the ice, Gwendolyn takes / took over. They
_____ (14)   _____ (15)
start / started talking that day, and they are getting married next year.
_____ (16)

■ COMMUNICATE

D **GROUP WORK** Listen to Professor Sanchez's lecture and take notes. Then work together to answer the questions.

CD1, TR3

1. How did researchers originally collect their data?

   Researchers surveyed thousands of people from all over the world.

2. How was the data analyzed?

   _____

3. What did they find out about the components of human personality?

   _____

   _____

E **PAIR WORK** Describe someone you have known since you were a child. Use the past tense. Then describe the person's personality today using the present tense.

■ GRAMMAR IN CONTENT

A Reread the passage on page 2. Put a <u>broken line</u> under all the future forms in the reading.

| Future Tense | | | | | | |

Will and Be Going To			Will and Be Going To			
Affirmative Statements			**Negative Statements**			

I	am going to		I	am not going to		
You	are going to		You	aren't going to		
We			We			
They		start soon.	They	will not/won't		start
He	will		He			immediately.
She			She			
It	is going to		It	is not going to		

Yes/No Questions with Will			Short Answers	Yes/No Questions with Be Going To			Short Answers
	I		Yes, I **will**.	Am	I		No, I'm **not**.
	you		Yes, you **will**.		you		No, you **aren't**.
	we		No, we **won't**.	Are	we	going to	Yes, we **are**.
Will	he	start again?	No, he **won't**.		they	start all	Yes, they **are**.
	she		Yes, she **will**.		he	over?	No, he **isn't**.
	it		No, it **won't**.	Is	she		Yes, she **is**.
	they		Yes, they **will**.		it		No, it **isn't**.

Wh- Questions with Will			Wh- Questions with Be Going To			
	I	learn?	What am	I		do?
What will	you	discover?	What are	you		get?
	we	see?	What are	we		stop?
	he					
When will	she	change?	When is	he	going to	
	it			she		listen?
				it		
How will	they	know?	How are	they		survive?

Notes:
- *Be going to* and *will* can be used for plans/intentions, predictions, and decisions.
- *Will* is used for offers, promises, agreements, and refusals.
- In general, introduce a plan or prediction with **be going to**. Continue with **will**; for example: *I think **it's going to** rain. It **won't rain** for very long, though.*

B Fill in the blanks with the future form of the verb. More than one form may be possible. In the blank space after the sentence, tell whether the sentence gives a plan, intention, prediction, decision, offer, promise, agreement, or refusal.

1. Martha's parents told her today that they have chosen a man for her to marry. She said that she __won't marry__ (not marry) him. **Function:** ___Refusal___

2. Our friends Susan and Malcolm _____ (get) married as soon as they finish college. **Function:** _____

3. I _____ (run) to the store if you want me to and get some more sugar so we can finish making cookies. **Function:** _____

4. John has thought about it for a long time, and he's finally decided that he _____ (change) majors. **Function:** _____

5. I'm so sorry. I promise you that I _____ (never do) that again. **Function:** _____

6. OK. I agree. I _____ (do) it, but I _____ (not like) it. **Function:** _____

7. I'm going to help you finish this report. In fact, I _____ (pick up) that book you wanted from the library. **Function:** _____

8. **Juan:** _____ you _____ (be) available to help me on Friday?

   Susan: Sure. I _____ (see) you then. **Function:** _____

■ **COMMUNICATE**

C **PAIR WORK** Talk to a classmate about your educational goals. What degrees do you intend to get? What will you do after graduation? Use *will* and *be going to.* Explain why these goals are compatible with your personality.

> What's your major?

> What **are you going to do** after you graduate?

> I'm majoring in education.

> I'm going to get a teaching certificate, because I love working with children. I think I'll **teach** preschool.

GRAMMAR AND VOCABULARY Write a paragraph in the past tense describing your personality as a child. Then write three sentences in the present tense that describe your personality today. Conclude with three sentences that tell about your plans for the future.

PROJECT Discuss various jobs and the kinds of people that are suited for them.

1. In a group, look at the following list of careers and occupations:

   - construction worker
   - secretary
   - veterinarian
   - doctor
   - accountant
   - lawyer
   - teacher
   - engineer

   - counselor
   - journalist
   - nurse
   - musician
   - politician
   - security guard
   - police officer
   - salesclerk

   - software designer
   - restaurant server
   - bus driver
   - house cleaner
   - fashion designer
   - meteorologist
   - banker
   - film director

2. Talk about three or four of these jobs. What are the duties and responsibilities of each one? What kind of person would do well in that occupation? Take notes during your discussion.
3. Summarize your discussion for the rest of the class.

 INTERNET Do a search online using the keywords "personality" and "test." Find an online test that looks interesting. Take the test and tell the class what you found out. Do you agree with the results? Why or why not?

PART 1
Present Progressive

PART 2
Past Progressive

PART 3
Future Progressive

Lesson ②

Nursing: Careers in Nursing

■ CONTENT VOCABULARY

What's happening in each picture? Read the captions, paying attention to the verb forms.

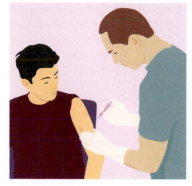

The **nurse** is giving the **patient** an injection.

The nurse was **conducting** a **lab test**. Now he is **sterilizing** his hands.

The patient is going to be getting a new **prescription**. The nurse is explaining the effects of the new **medication**.

Look up any words you don't know. Write each word, its definition, and a sentence that illustrates its use in your vocabulary journal.

■ THINK ABOUT IT

Imagine a hospital scene. What are the nurses doing? What about the doctors and patients? What are they doing? In your writing journal, write for five minutes.

■ GRAMMAR IN CONTENT

CD1,TR4

A Read and listen to the following information about a registered nurse.

an allergy: an unusually high sensitivity and reactions to substances such as certain plants, chemicals, foods, animals, or dust

a clinic: a health center, small hospital

to diagnose: to identify a disease, ailment, or injury

licensed: having a permit given by an official institution

a registered nurse: a nurse who has a degree and has passed a state examination for nurses

a treatment: medical attention

Becoming a Nurse Practitioner

Last summer Maria received her degree as a registered nurse (RN) from Lincoln University. She **is** currently **working** at Mercy Hospital and **living** in a small apartment near her job. Soon she's **going to be working** in an allergy clinic. She'll **be giving** injections and **testing** patients with allergies and other complaints.

Yesterday Maria **was talking** to another nurse about her work last year and her plans for the future. Last year she **was working** during the day as a licensed practical nurse (LPN) and **attending** classes four evenings a week. She **was living** at home and **looking** for an apartment in her free time. At work, Maria **was assisting** a doctor and **performing** simple lab tests. Maria's position this year involves more responsibility, and she **is enjoying** her job. However, she wants even more independence.

For this reason, Maria **is considering** a special program at the state college. She **is hoping** to become a nurse in a private clinic. In this position, she will have even more responsibility. In three years, she **will be treating** patients, **diagnosing** their problems, **planning** their treatment, and **prescribing** medication. It's going to be a lot more work, but Maria **is looking** forward to the challenge.

B Reread the passage. (Circle) six present progressive verbs (including contractions). If you need help, use the chart below.

Present Progressive					
Affirmative Statements			**Negative Statements**		
Subject	**Be**	**-ing Verb**	**Subject**	**Be + Not**	**-ing Verb**
I	am		I	am not	
He			He		
She	is	considering a career in nursing.	She	is not (isn't)	going to night school.
You			You		
We	are		We	are not (aren't)	
They			They		
Yes/No Questions			**Short Affirmative Answers**		**Short Negative Answers**
Are you **taking** any medication?			Yes, I **am**.		No, I'm not.
Is the medication **working**?			Yes, it **is**.		No, it **isn't**.

Wh- Questions	Answers
What **are** you **studying?**	I **am getting** a degree in pharmacology.
Where **is** Diego **working?**	He's **working** at the Mayo Clinic.
How **are** they **diagnosing** patients?	They **are using** X-rays.

Notes:
- Use the present progressive to talk about an activity that is in progress and therefore incomplete: *Maria is giving an injection. She'll be finished in a minute.*
- Use the present progressive to talk about events in the near future: *We are taking a test on Friday.*
- Stative verbs (for example, *like, understand, know, need, contain, have*) don't usually take the progressive form.
- When two verbs in the same sentence have the same subject, it is not necessary to repeat the auxiliary verb: *Maria is working at a clinic and is living at home.*

C Choose the correct verb and use the present progressive form to complete the passage below. Discuss your choice with a partner.

| go | stay | ~~take~~ | count | watch | relax | lie |

Pearl _____*is taking*_____ (1) her brother Peter to work at the hospital. Peter

_____ (2) the minutes because he is late. The streets are wet, and

Pearl _____ (3) very slowly. I _____ (4) at

home today and _____ (5). My brother David is at home too. He

_____ (6) on his bed and _____ (7) television.

D Choose simple present or present progressive. Remember that stative verbs do not usually occur in the progressive. Explain your choices to a partner. Take turns reading the passage aloud when you are finished.

Jorge _____*is working*_____ (1) (work) with Dr. Abbott today. So far, he

_____*likes*_____ (2) (like) the doctor. At the moment Jorge _____ (3)

(help) Dr. Abbot with an operation. He _____ (4) (hold) a bottle. The bottle

_____ (5) (contain) oxygen. Maria _____ (6) (also work) with

Dr. Abbot today. She _____ (7) (enjoy) the work and _____ (8)

(hope) to stay on this team for a while. Doctor Abbot _____ (9) (operate

on) Sonia Johannsen's father today. Sonia's mother _____ (10) (stay) at the

hospital, so Sonia _____ (11) (take care of) the rest of the family.

E Listen to the following informal conversation and fill in the blanks. Check your work with a partner.

Jose: Hey, Jake, _____how's it going?_____
(1)

Jake: Pretty good. What's up with you?

Jose: _____ nights at Mercy Hospital, but
(2)

_____ a job with St. Anthony's.
(3)

Jake: Why _____ at Mercy anymore?
(4)

Jose: I like the place, but St. Anthony's _____ better work
(5)

hours.

Jake: And _____ more money?
(6)

Jose: Yeah, but I really don't need the money. _____ to an
(7)

occasional free evening.

■ **COMMUNICATE**

F **PAIR WORK** Do the following role-play with a partner. One student is a nurse and the other is a patient. Using the words and phrases below, the nurse asks the patient questions about his or her personal habits and lifestyle. When you are finished, switch roles.

Are you **sleeping well?**

Are you **drinking a lot of caffeine?**

You might want to cut out the coffee after dinner.

No, I'm not **sleeping well** at all these days.

Yes, I drink coffee all day long.

Personal Habits and Lifestyle

- sleep well
- drink a lot of caffeine
- consume a lot of sugar
- drink a lot of water
- take any medication

- stay up very late
- take vitamins
- eat fresh fruits and vegetables
- experience a lot of stress
- exercise on a regular basis

■ GRAMMAR IN CONTENT

A Reread the passage on page 12. <u>Underline</u> seven boldfaced past progressive verbs. If you need help, refer to the chart. Include conjoined verbs where the auxiliary verb is used once.

Past Progressive						
Affirmative Statements				**Negative Statements**		
Subject	*Was/Were*	*-ing* **Verb**		**Subject**	*Was/Were*	*-ing* **Verb**
I He She	was	checking a patient's temperature.		I He She	was not (wasn't)	reading the patient's chart.
You We They	were			You We They	were not (weren't)	

Yes/No Questions					
Was/Were	**Subject**	*-ing* **Verb**		**Short Affirmative Answers**	**Short Negative Answers**
Were	you	**going**	to the lab?	Yes, I was.	No, I wasn't.
Was	the doctor	**working**	late?	Yes, he was.	No, he wasn't.
Were	they	**admitting**	patients?	Yes, they were.	No, they weren't.

Wh- Questions				
Wh-		*Was/Were*	**Subject**	*-ing* **Verb**
Why		were	you	**working** so late?
How		was	the patient	**doing**?

Notes:
The past progressive describes or talks about:
- an activity in progress at a certain time in the past: *She **was drawing** blood yesterday afternoon.*
- an action in the past that was interrupted by another action of a shorter duration: *Twelve patients **were waiting** when Maria arrived.*
- a temporary or extended situation in the past: *She **was living** at home last year.*
- two actions in the past that occurred simultaneously: *Maria **was living** with her aunt while she **was attending** nursing school.*

B Listen to the passage about Florence Nightingale, and then answer the questions, based on the passage. Use the past progressive in your answers.

1. Why was Turkey at war?

   It was defending itself against the Russian Empire.

2. What were conditions like at the British military hospital?

   _____

3. What was Nightingale's role during the Crimean War?

   _____

4. In what ways do you think conditions during the American Civil War resembled those of the Crimean War?

   _____

C Complete this imaginary interview with Florence Nightingale. Use the words in parentheses, and put the verbs in the past progressive.

Interviewer: What _____*were you doing*_____ (do) when you
                                               (1)
decided to become a nurse?

Nightingale: I _____ (study) mathematics.
                                  (2)

Interviewer: Where _____ (work) when the Crimean War
                                        (3)
started?

Nightingale: At a hospital in London.

Interviewer: What did you find when you arrived at the British hospital in Turkey?

Nightingale: The soldiers _____ (contract) fatal diseases.
                                              (4)
They _____ (not die) from their injuries—they
                    (5)
_____ (die) from the unsanitary conditions at
              (6)
the hospital.

Interviewer: In other words, you mean that receiving medical treatment

_____ (kill) them?
              (7)

Nightingale: Exactly. They _____ (come) to the hospital
                                              (8)
because of their injuries. But they _____ (get)
                                                           (9)
sick from infections. Of course, we didn't know that at the time. We've

learned a lot since then.

D **PAIR WORK** Tell a classmate about a time when you were sick or injured. Who treated you? What were they doing for you? Use the past progressive.

Once I was in the hospital for three days with pneumonia.

Why were you in the hospital for so long?

Because I had a high fever and I **was losing** consciousness.

PART THREE	Future Progressive

■ GRAMMAR IN CONTENT

A Reread the passage on page 12. Draw a ☐box☐ around seven verbs. Remember to include contractions and conjoined verbs where the future auxiliary is used only once. If you need help, use the chart below.

Future Progressive with *Be Going To*		
Affirmative Statements		**Negative Statements**	

I	am	going to be studying late tonight.	I	am	not going to be studying very late tonight.
He	is		He	is	
We	are		We	are	

Yes/No Questions		**Short Affirmative Answers**	**Short Negative Answers**

Is	she	going to be graduating this year?	Yes, she **is**.	No, she **isn't**.
Are	you		Yes, I **am**.	No, I'm not.

Future Progressive with *Will*		
Affirmative Statements	**Negative Statements**

We	will be assisting the doctor tomorrow.	We	won't be assisting the doctor tomorrow.
They		They	

Yes/No Questions		**Short Affirmative Answers**	**Short Negative Answers**

Will	you	be checking my temperature later on?	Yes, I **will**.	No, I **won't**.
	he		Yes, he **will**.	No, he **won't**.

Wh- Questions with *Be Going To* and *Will*	Answers
When are you **going to be graduating?**	I'll **be graduating** in June.
When will he **be finishing** the lab test?	He'll **be finishing** the test in about an hour.

Notes:
- Use the future progressive to tell about an activity that will be in progress in the future: *Juan* **will be assisting** *Dr. Wong in surgery for the next three weeks.*
- *Be going to* is common in informal conversation; *will be* is used in more formal situations.
- In a sentence with a *when* clause, you can often use the future progressive with the main clause: *When we arrive at the clinic, Suzi* **will be waiting** *for us.*
- Some stative verbs such as *want* and *need* can occur in the future progressive. Don't say ~~I am needing more towels~~; you can say *I will be needing more towels.*

B Take turns reading the following conversation with a classmate. Use the appropriate form of the future progressive verb in parentheses to reflect the informality of the conversation.

Thuy: I'm graduating in June. How about you?

Suzi: Yes, I _____'ll be graduating_____ (graduate) in June too. As soon as I
(1)

graduate, I'm going to look for a job. I _____ (need)
(2)

some money for my own apartment.

Thuy: _____ (you move out of) your parents' place? I didn't
(3)

know that.

Suzi: Yeah. I _____ (need) more privacy.
(4)

Thuy: I envy you. I _____ (still live) with my parents next
(5)

year.

Suzi: Well, there are some disadvantages. I _____ (spend) a
(6)

lot more money on food and rent.

Thuy: But you _____ (make) more money.
(7)

Suzi: Yeah, and it'll be worth it because I _____ (not share)
(8)

a bathroom with my brothers and sisters.

C Suzi's mother, Mrs. Olsen, is writing an e-mail to her sister about Suzi's move. She has made seven errors in verb forms that take the future progressive form. Correct the errors.

Jennie,

I have terrible news. My dear little Suzi is going to get her own apartment this summer.

~ing

She's go to be living alone in a strange part of town all by herself. She isn't even going be coming

home for dinner. She certainly won't eating right. You know she hates to cook. On top of that,

she's going to be work nights at the hospital in Lincoln, so she'll getting home late. I not

be sleeping well. Call me. I'm going to be need your advice this summer.

Bonnie

■ **COMMUNICATE**

D **PAIR WORK** Fill out the daily planner to show what you will be doing tomorrow. Tell a classmate about three different times in your schedule. Use the informal *be going to.*

At 8:00 A.M. **I'm going to be sleeping. I won't be getting** up until 9:00.

Lucky you. At 8:00 A.M. **I'm going to be driving** to class.

Daily Planner	
8:00 a.m. _____*sleep*_____	3:00 p.m. _____
9:00 a.m. _____	4:00 p.m. _____
10:00 a.m. _____	5:00 p.m. _____
11:00 a.m. _____	6:00 p.m. _____
12:00 noon _____	7:00 p.m. _____
1:00 p.m. _____	8:00 p.m. _____
2:00 p.m. _____	9:00 p.m. _____

GRAMMAR AND VOCABULARY Fill in the blanks while you listen to the conversation. Check your work with a partner and then practice reading the dialog aloud. Take turns reading the two parts.

CD1,TR7

Carmen: Hey, Stan, _____how're you doing?_____
(1)

Stan: Pretty good. How about you?

Carmen: OK. _____ at Valley Hospital.
(2)

Stan: _____ the night shift
(3)

_____ at University Hospital pretty soon.
(4)

Carmen: I thought _____ as a nurse practitioner?
(5)

Stan: Yeah, but at University Hospital _____
(6)

the doctors with _____. How about you?
(7)

_____ these days?
(8)

Carmen: Well, _____ but I went back to school last fall.
(9)

_____ my B.A. in June.
(10)

PROJECT Research and make predictions about the treatment of a disease.

1. With classmates, form a group. Choose a disease you would like to research and talk about in class, such as polio or a type of cancer. You could also decide to find out about a mental health condition such as depression or post-traumatic stress disorder.

2. Use encyclopedias and online resources to find out about the history of the disease and its treatment. How were doctors diagnosing and treating patients in the past? Make some predictions about the future, too. How will doctors be treating this disease in the future? Use the past progressive, present progressive, and future progressive in your description.

3. When you are finished, have one member of the group present the group's findings to the class.

INTERNET Create a glossary of terms related to nursing and health care. You can generate a list of terms by doing a search on the Internet. Use the search terms "health care + vocabulary." Visit any resulting websites that seem useful. Write the new words you discover along with their meanings in your vocabulary journal.

PART 1
Present Tense vs. Present Progressive

PART 2
Past Tense vs. Past Progressive

PART 3
Adverbs of Frequency

Lesson ③

Engineering: Building Bridges

■ CONTENT VOCABULARY

These students are in an engineering class. Each team is designing a different kind of bridge. How are these bridges different?

These students are at a **field site.** They are examining the **construction** of a **beam bridge.**

This group chose to **design** a **suspension bridge.** They are drafting a **model** of it.

Another group is working on a **truss bridge.** They are studying their **blueprint.**

Read the captions and look up any words you don't know. (You can also check the glossed words on the next page for some of these terms.) Write each word, its definition, and a sentence that illustrates its use in your vocabulary journal.

■ THINK ABOUT IT

In your writing journal, draw a picture of a bridge that you are familiar with. Show it to a partner. Talk about the similarities and differences between your drawings. Then, in your journal, write a description of the bridge you drew.

■ GRAMMAR IN CONTENT

CD1, TR8

A **Read and listen to the following passage about an engineering class.**

Designing a Bridge

Engineers **design** different types of bridges for different purposes. A beam bridge **is** the simplest, least expensive type of bridge. It **consists** of a single horizontal beam. Vertical columns, or pilings, **support** the beam at each end. Beam bridges **are** short, so engineers **often choose** a suspension bridge when they **need** to span a large body of water. Large cables **suspend** the bridge. This **allows** suspension bridges to be much longer.

The students in Professor Chu's civil engineering class **are designing** bridges for an assignment. The Red Team **is examining** the construction of a beam bridge. The Blue Team **is building** a three-dimensional model of a suspension bridge. The Green Team **is drafting** a diagram for a truss bridge.

The Red Team **began** their project last week, but they **didn't agree** on the design. When Professor Chu **joined** their group, the members **were arguing**. Franz **was advocating** a beam bridge and Jose and Amir **were arguing** against that design. The professor **reminded** the team that their bridge **needed** to cross a river that was 1,000 feet wide. Beam bridges **rarely span** more than 250 feet; suspension bridges **are** very expensive and vary in length from 2,000 to 7,000 feet. Even the classic arch bridge **is generally** only about 800 feet long. When the professor **left** the group, the members **were** still **talking** about the advantages of an extended beam bridge versus the advantages of a truss bridge.

a cable: many wires twisted together

an arch bridge: a bridge shaped like an arch

a truss bridge: a bridge made from a framework of beams

to span: to connect two points with something; to extend across

B **Reread the passage.** (Circle) **11 verbs in the present tense and 4 verbs in the present progressive. Remember to include contractions. If you need help, use the chart below.**

Present Tense vs. Present Progressive	
Affirmative Statements	**Negative Statements**
Engineers **design** bridges. The team **is designing** a bridge.	The bridge **doesn't cross** the Hudson River. We **aren't working** at the same site anymore.

Yes/No Questions	**Short Answers**	*Wh- Questions*
Does the design work? **Is** Ian coming?	Yes, it **does**. No, he **isn't**.	What **do** I **need** for the project? What kinds of materials are they using?

Notes:
- Use present tense to express habits (We **study** every evening), statements of fact (Beam bridges **are** short), and states (Dr. Willis probably **has** the flu).
- Use present progressive to express actions in progress at the moment (I'm **studying** now) and temporary situations (Franz **is living** in the dorm this term).
- If two verbs in present progressive are connected by *and*, you do not need to repeat the auxiliary verb: *Each team **is designing** and ~~is~~ **building** a bridge.*

C **In this dialog, Professor Chu is questioning the Red Team about their design. Read the dialog with a partner and fill in the blanks with the appropriate form of the verb in parentheses (simple present or present progressive).**

Chu: _____*Is*_____ (be) a beam bridge the best possible choice for
(1)
this river?

Jose: I _____ (not think) so.
(2)
Engineers _____ (begin) to use suspension bridges
(3)
more frequently these days.

Chu: But they _____ (not use) them for small projects like
(4)
this one.

Franz: They're too expensive. A nice beam bridge _____
(5)
(cost) much less.

Chu: Right, but beam bridges usually only _____ (span)
(6)
up to 250 feet.

Jose: So we _____ (need) something longer. What
(7)
_____ (do) engineers _____
(8)   (9)
(use) to span 1,000 feet nowadays?

Chu: They often _____ (connect) several beams to span
(10)
that distance.

Jose: How about a truss bridge?

Chu: My engineering friends _____ (not build)
(11)
many truss bridges at the moment. Maybe that type of bridge
_____ (become) less popular.
(12)

D PAIR PRACTICE Tell your partner about something you are doing or wearing today. Have your partner ask whether that is what you normally do or wear. Use the present or present progressive, as appropriate. Reverse roles after answering several questions.

PART TWO	Past Tense vs. Past Progressive

■ GRAMMAR IN CONTENT

A Reread the passage on page 22. <u>Underline</u> six verbs in the simple past and four verbs in the past progressive. If you need help, use the chart below.

Past Tense			Past Progressive	
Affirmative Statements				
The architect **drew** a set of plans this morning. A group of engineers **visited** the site last week.			The secretary **was talking** on the phone when I walked in. Mr. Diaz **was expecting** me at 9 A.M.	
Negative Statements				
The bridge **didn't withstand** the earthquake. The cable **wasn't** strong enough.			The traffic **wasn't moving**. I **wasn't paying** attention.	
***Yes/No* Questions**	**Short Answers**		***Yes/No* Questions**	**Short Answers**
Did you **go** to class yesterday? **Was** Isabel on time?	Yes, I **did**. No, she **wasn't**.		**Were** you **following** directions? **Were** they **working** carefully?	Yes, I **was**. Yes, they **were**.
***Wh-* Questions**				
How **did** they finally **solve** the problem? Which materials **worked** best?			What **were** you **doing** last summer? What **was** the class **waiting** for?	

Notes:
- Use the simple past tense to tell about a completed past action (*I **studied** last night*), a situation from the past of long duration (*Martha **lived** in Ohio in 2004*), and past states or personal conditions (*He probably **had** the flu*).
- Use the past progressive to tell about an action that was in progress when another action happened (*I **was studying** when you called*) and temporary situations in the past that are in contrast to present conditions (*Franz **was living** in the dorm last year, but this year he's living in an apartment*).

B Listen and fill in each blank with the correct form of the verb in parentheses.

The Collapse of the Tacoma Narrows Bridge

Sometimes bridges develop unexpected problems. A famous case ___occurred___ (occur) with the Tacoma
(1)
Narrows Bridge in Washington state. On November 7, 1940, four months after the bridge _____ (open),
(2)
something unexpected _____ (happen).
(3)
On that day, a strong wind _____ (blow). The bridge suddenly
(4)
_____ (begin) to move. Cars _____ (cross)
(5)   (6)
the bridge at the time. By coincidence, a group of engineers _____
(7)
(meet) near the bridge. When they _____ (see) the movement
(8)
of the bridge, they _____ (be) horrified. They immediately
(9)
_____ (close) the bridge and _____
(10)   (11)
(call) the fire department. When they _____ (return), the bridge
(12)
_____ (sway) and _____ (bend). Motorists
(13)   (14)
_____ (leave) their cars and _____ (crawl)
(15)   (16)
to the bridge tower. Finally, the bridge _____ (snap) in the middle
(17)
and _____ (fall) into the water below.
(18)

C Listen to the recording and then answer the questions in complete sentences.

1. What did engineers at the Tacoma Narrows Bridge first notice?

   _____

2. What did they do about it?

   _____

3. What did Professor Farquharson's students do?

   _____

4. What did Professor Farquharson tell people he was doing at the bridge?

   _____

5. After Professor Farquharson made his recommendations, why was he still worried?

   _____

D Read this imaginary interview with Dr. Farquharson, an actual engineer who studied the Tacoma Narrows Bridge and its collapse. Fill in the blanks with the correct form of the verb in parentheses and practice the dialog with a partner.

Interviewer: Good afternoon, Dr. Farquharson, and welcome to our studio. When

_____*did you begin*_____ (begin) work on the Tacoma Narrows Bridge?
(1)

Farquharson: In the spring of 1940.

Interviewer: What _____ (happen)?
(2)

Farquharson: The bridge _____ (sway) back and forth.
(3)

Interviewer: What _____ (recommend)?
(4)

Farquharson: Initially, I _____ (recommend) temporary cables.
(5)

Interviewer: Did the cables help stabilize the bridge?

Farquharson: Yes, they helped a little, but we still _____
(6)

(notice) some movement. In particular, we _____
(7)

(see) some movement in the middle of the bridge.

Interviewer: _____ (worry) about that?
(8)

Farquharson: No, we _____ (not worry) too much at first.
(9)

Interviewer: What _____ (be) your biggest concern?
(10)

Farquharson: Under certain conditions, the bridge _____
(11)

(twist) and _____ (turn).
(12)

Interviewer: What _____ (cause) the problem?
(13)

Farquharson: Strong winds. I _____ (suspect) the
(14)

bridge was in danger of collapsing but it was too late. The bridge

_____ (collapse) five days later.
(15)

■ COMMUNICATE

E **WRITE** Write a summary of the interview with Dr. Farquharson. You might begin as follows:

Dr. Farquharson began working on the bridge in the spring of 1940.

■ **GRAMMAR IN CONTENT**

A **Reread the passage on page 22. Put a ~~wavy line~~ under three adverbs of frequency in the text. If you need help, use the chart below.**

Adverbs of Frequency						
With *Be*				**With Other Verbs**		
I	am	always usually		You	always usually	arrive on time.
He	is	often sometimes	punctual.	He	often sometimes	finishes early.
We	are	rarely never		It	rarely never	starts on time.

Notes:
- Adverbs of frequency usually occur with simple tense.
- Some adverbs of frequency such as ***usually, sometimes,*** and ***often*** can also occur at the beginning of a sentence (***Usually*** he **works** alone).
- Sometimes adverbs of frequency occur with the progressive. In those cases the adverb of frequency comes between the auxiliarly verb and main verb (He **is always arguing**).
- Frequency expressions such as ***every day*** and ***all the time*** appear after the main verb or the complement to the verb: He **works** ***all the time*** (She **drives** to work ***every day***).
- Adverbs that indicate a finite period of time (***once a week, yesterday***) are used with simple tense. Adverbs that indicate the time of the action (***at the moment, for the time being***) are usually used with progressive forms.

B **Look at the boldfaced adverbs and adverbial phrases in the following sentences. (Circle) "S" if the adverb usually occurs within a simple tense; (circle) "PROG" if the adverb usually occurs with a progressive. Then read the correct form of each sentence aloud to your partner.**

1. S (PROG) **At the moment** Amir (work) on his team's model bridge.

2. S PROG He (work) on it **for an hour** yesterday.

3. S PROG He **usually** (study) his engineering notes before he goes to class.

4. S PROG **For the time being** he (focus) intensely on his project with the Red Team.

5. S PROG **Once a week** Amir (provide) lunch for his team.

6. S PROG The team members (see) each other **every day.**

7. S PROG The Green Team (meet) with Dr. Chu **yesterday.**

8. S PROG The team (discuss) Dr. Chu's suggestions **at the moment.**

C In each blank, insert an appropriate adverb or adverbial phrase from the boldfaced adverbs in Exercise B.

Amir is very busy. This morning he had classes, and _____*at the moment*_____
                                                        (1)
he is meeting with other members of his team. The team meets for several hours

_____. They _____ meet at Franz's house,
          (2)   **(3)**
but Franz's father is painting the dining room, so _____ they are
                                                          (4)
meeting at the library. _____ all the members meet with Dr. Chu in
                               (5)
his office to discuss their progress. _____ they are working on the
                                             (6)
model. This evening they will write a report for their meeting with Dr. Chu tomorrow.

■ **COMMUNICATE**

D **WRITE** Write about one thing that you do every day, one thing that you sometimes do, and one thing that you never do. Share your answers with a partner.

Connection Putting It Together

GRAMMAR AND VOCABULARY Write four short paragraphs containing the following: (1) two sentences in the simple present; (2) two in the simple past; (3) two in the present progressive; (4) and two in the past progressive. Use the following vocabulary: *bridge, build, collapse, construction, design, engineer, field site, model.*

PROJECT In teams of two or three, interview an engineer or an advanced engineering student. Ask him or her to tell you the story of a famous engineering failure in the past. Ask him or her what engineers are doing now to avoid these problems. If you can't find an engineer or engineering student to interview, try to find an account of such a failure in a book or on the Internet. Prepare a written summary, underlining every verb in the present tense, past tense, present progressive, and past progressive.

 INTERNET Search the Internet for the Brooklyn Bridge, Golden Gate Bridge, Oakland Bay Bridge, Royal Gorge Bridge, Chesapeake Bay Bridge-Tunnel, Tacoma Narrows Bridge, or the London Millennium Bridge. In some cases, you may be able to find video or images of earthquakes or other disasters that have damaged some of these bridges. Take notes on what you learn, and present your findings to your class or group.

Sociology: Marriage Customs and Trends

■ CONTENT VOCABULARY

Marriage is a very special kind of relationship that exists in most cultures and countries around the world. What are some of the steps and rituals associated with marriage?

Mrs. Mori is going to **arrange** a meeting between Reiko and Kenchi. They will get to know each other better in the coming months, a period of time known as **courtship**.

Raul **proposed** to Claudia, and now they are **engaged**. They will be **getting married** in May.

James and Chantal are **newlyweds**. They will be spending their **honeymoon** in Hawaii.

Read the captions. Look up any words you don't know. Write each word, its definition, and a sentence that illustrates its use in your vocabulary journal.

■ THINK ABOUT IT

In your writing journal, write about marriage customs in your home country or culture. How do people choose a marriage partner? What happens at a wedding ceremony? What kinds of places do newlyweds visit on their honeymoon?

■ GRAMMAR IN CONTENT

CD1,TR11

A Read and listen to the following interviews from a campus newspaper.

Campus Talk
By Josh Markam

Today's Interview Question:

When choosing a marriage partner, what role should parents play?
Are your parents going to help you find a mate?

"In Korea, parents choose marriage partners for their children, and I think it's a good system. I know my parents **will arrange** a good marriage for me, and I trust their judgment. They **will** always **know** more about life than I do because they **will** always **be** older and **have** more experience. I'**ll learn** to love the person they choose, and I know I'**ll be** happy. Maybe that sounds old-fashioned to you, but I'm very traditional."

Young Soon
Sophomore, Computer Science

"I think people should choose for themselves. I'**m going to live** with that person for the rest of my life, aren't I? Well then, I should choose. Oh sure, I'**ll ask** my parents for their opinion. There **won't be** any problems as long as they agree with me, and I'm sure they **will**. They brought me up to make decisions for myself."

Brittany Roberts
Freshman, Statistics

"Actually, I **am getting** married next month. My parents introduced me to my fiancée last year, and they **are coming** all the way from India for the wedding. They'**ll be staying** with us from June until September. My friends think I'm crazy, but that's totally normal where I come from."

Ashok Patel
Senior, Linguistic Anthropology

---

a fiancée: an engaged woman   old-fashioned: no longer in common use, out-of-date

30   LESSON 4 | *Sociology: Marriage Customs and Trends*

B **Reread the passage. Look at all the verbs in future time. What are the rules for making statements about the future?**

Future with *Will*

Affirmative Statements			**Negative Statements**		
Subject	***Will***	**Base Form of Verb**	**Subject**	***Won't***	**Base Form of Verb**
I She They	will	**get** married in October.	You He We	won't	**get** married until next year.

Yes/No Questions

Will	**Subject**	**Base Form of Verb**	**Short Affirmative Answers**	**Short Negative Answers**
Will	you they	**invite** everybody you know?	Yes, I **will.** Yes, they **will.**	No, I **won't.** No, they **won't.**

Notes:

Use *will* + **base form** to tell about:

- plans and intentions (We*'ll* **be** there on time.)
- offers (I*'ll* **close** the window for you.)
- promises (*I will* **stay** with you forever.)
- agreements and refusals (*I'll* **talk** to him if you want me to; I'm sorry, *I* **won't be able** to help you.)
- hypotheses and predictions (*People who marry for the wrong reasons* **will be** disappointed.)

Future with *Be Going To*

Affirmative Statements			**Negative Statements**		
Subject	***Be***	***Going To* + Base Form of Verb**	**Subject**	***Be***	***Not + Going To* + Base Form of Verb**
I You He	am are is	**going to attend** the ceremony.	I You He	am are is	**not going to bring** a camera.

Yes/No Questions

Be	**Subject**	***Going To* + Base Form of Verb**	**Short Affirmative Answers**	**Short Negative Answers**
Are Is	you she	**going to stay** for the reception?	Yes, I **am.** Yes, she **is.**	No, I'm **not.** No, she **isn't.**

Notes:

Use *be going to* + **the base form of a verb** to tell about:

- plans and intentions (*He's* **going to propose** to her tonight.)
- predictions (*I'm sure she's* **going to accept** his proposal.)
- events in the near future (*We're* **going to dance** after the wedding vows are exchanged.)

Future Statements in the Present Progressive	Future Statements in the Present
I'm **leaving** for the party in an hour. We're **spending** our honeymoon in Mexico. He **isn't coming** tonight.	The plane **leaves** in a few minutes. The guests **arrive** at 5:00. Tom **gives** a speech when everyone is seated.

Notes:

1. The present progressive is commonly used when talking about the future. Use the present progressive to tell about:
   - plans (*I'm having a party this weekend.*)
   - recurring, scheduled events (*I'm working every other Saturday this month.*)
2. The simple present tense is more formal than the present progressive when talking about the future. It is usually used to tell about travel plans and timetables (*Our plane leaves at noon*).

C Hans, a visitor to the United States, is attending a wedding ceremony. His friend Michael is explaining the ceremony to him. Read the dialog and complete each statement using the verb in parentheses. Use *will, be going to,* or the present progressive, as appropriate. In many cases, more than one verb form is possible.

Hans: What _____ *will happen* _____
(1)
(happen) first?

Michael: They _____ (exchange) their wedding vows.
(2)

Hans: _____ (exchange) rings during the ceremony?
(3)

Michael: Yes, they _____ (will). After the ceremony
(4)

they _____ (leave) the church. They
(5)

_____ (have) a reception outside in the garden.
(6)

Hans: I suppose the bride and groom _____ (have) the
(7)

first dance?

Michael: That's right. While the bride is dancing, the guests

_____ (pin) money to her dress. It means the bride
(8)

and groom _____ (have) a prosperous life together.
(9)

D Listen to the lecture on marriage. While you listen, fill in the missing words.

1. People who don't find the happiness they expect in a marriage _will be_ very unhappy.

2. Such a marriage probably _____.

3. In societies with more traditional values, you _____ a high tolerance for marriages that are arranged by parents and elders.

4. Couples in arranged marriages _____ more likely to stay together through difficult times.

5. They _____ the marriage because their personal needs aren't gratified.

E What expectations do people have about marriage? Write three statements about these expectations using *will*. You can write about the United States and/or any other culture or country you know well.

1. ___*Americans believe that marriage will bring them personal happiness.*___

2. _____

3. _____

4. _____

■ COMMUNICATE

F **PAIR WORK** Take turns. Imagine that you are getting married next month. Describe what is going to happen and when. Use *will, be going to,* the present progressive, and the simple present in your description. Include at least one negative statement.

I'm **getting** married next month. We'**re going to have** a big wedding. All of our family and friends **are going to be** there.

How exciting! Is it going to be a traditional wedding?

Sounds like it'll be wonderful.

The wedding **won't be** in a church, if that's what you mean. It'**ll be** on my favorite beach in Carmel. After the ceremony, we **fly** by helicopter over the ocean.

■ GRAMMAR IN CONTENT

Future Progressive with *Will Be* + *-ing* Verb

Affirmative Statements			Negative Statements		
Subject	***Will Be***	***-ing* Verb**	**Subject**	***Won't Be***	***-ing* Verb**
We They	will be	**staying** at a small hotel.	We They	won't be	**staying** for very long.

Yes/No Questions

Will	Subject	*Be* + *-ing* Verb	Short Affirmative Answers	Short Negative Answers
Will	you she	**be coming** with friends?	Yes, I **will**. Yes, she **will**.	No, I **won't**. No, she **won't**.

Future Progressive with *Be Going To Be* + *-ing* Verb

Affirmative Statements			Negative Statements		
Subject	***Be***	***Going To Be* + *-ing* Verb**	**Subject**	***Be***	***Not Going To Be* + *-ing* Verb**
I We He	am are is	**going to be having** a party.	I We He	am are is	**not going to be serving** alcohol.

Yes/No Questions

Be	Subject	*Going To Be* + *-ing* Verb	Short Affirmative Answers	Short Negative Answers
Are Is	you they he she	**going to be having** a traditional ceremony?	Yes, I **am**. Yes, they **are**. Yes, he **is**. Yes, she **is**.	No, I'm **not**. No, they **aren't**. No, he **isn't**. No, she **isn't**.

Notes:

1. Use ***will be* + *-ing* verb** and ***be going to be* + *-ing* verb** to:
   - tell about events that will be in progress in the near future (*The guests **will be arriving** soon*).
   - tell about future events that will last for a certain period of time (*They'll **be staying** with friends for the weekend*).
   - make polite questions about future plans (***Are** you **going to be having** a traditional wedding?*)
   - make excuses or apologies for something in the near future (***I'll be leaving** now; I'm sorry, but **I'm not going to be staying** for the reception*).
2. Adverbs such as *probably* occur after the first helping verb *(will, am, is, are)*, except in negative statements (*The newlyweds **will probably go** on a honeymoon; They **probably won't be staying** in town*).

A Marc is making reservations for his honeymoon. Fill in the blanks with the future progressive form of the verb in parentheses. Use *will* or *be* as indicated.

Receptionist:	Good afternoon, may I help you?
Marc:	Hello. My wife and I <u>will be spending</u> (1) (will spend) our honeymoon in Hawaii and I'd like to ask about your rates.
Receptionist:	Certainly. How many nights _____ (2) (will you stay)?
Marc:	We _____ (3) (going to arrive) on Friday, and we _____ (4) (will leave) on Monday.
Receptionist:	So you _____ (5) (will need) a room for three nights?
Marc:	Yes, and by the way, we _____ (6) (not going to arrive) until very late on Friday night.
Receptionist:	That won't be a problem. A receptionist _____ (7) (will probably work) at the front desk until midnight. If not, there will definitely be a security guard who can let you in.

B Transform these sentences into the future progressive. Follow the example.

1. The bride and groom will have a traditional wedding ceremony.
   _____ The bride and groom will be having a traditional wedding ceremony. _____

2. More than a hundred guests are going to attend.
   _____

3. The bride's parents will travel all the way from India.
   _____

4. They won't stay at a hotel.
   _____

5. They are probably going to stay with relatives.
   _____

C **PAIR WORK** Tell a partner about a celebration you will be attending in the near future. Describe the celebration using the future progressive. If you aren't planning on attending a celebration anytime soon, imagine one you might attend.

Connection | Putting It Together

GRAMMAR AND VOCABULARY Read the syllabus and answer the questions below on a separate piece of paper. Use complete sentences in your answers.

Syllabus
Sociology 214

Professor: Dr. S. P. Yi   Office: 305 Watson Hall
Office Hours: 3–5 Mon.   Class Meeting: 1–3, Mon. & Weds.
    2–4 Thurs.   Classroom: Hershey Hall, Room 313

This class is an introduction to the sociology of marriage and family. We will use statistical data to trace key changes in the American family over the last century. The class will cover the following topics:

Weeks 1–2: Introduction to Sociology
Weeks 3–4: Characteristics of the American Family
Weeks 5–6: History of the American Family
Weeks 7–8: Current Trends
Weeks 9–10: Projections
Week 11: Final Exam: Wednesday, 1–4

1. When is Dr. Yi going to be in her office?
2. What time is the class going to be meeting?
3. Where will class be held?
4. What kind of data will the class be using?
5. What is the class going to be studying in its fifth week?
6. When are they going to be studying current trends in the American family?
7. When will they be taking their final exam?

PROJECT In small groups, discuss different wedding customs around the world. When you are finished, summarize your discussion for the whole class.

 INTERNET Search the Internet for statistics pertaining to marriage and family in the United States or a country that interests you. Put your findings in the form of a graph. Show your graph to the class and explain the trends it represents.

PART 1
Present Perfect

PART 2
Past Perfect

PART 3
Future Perfect

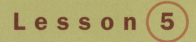
Lesson 5

Ecology: Climate Change

■ CONTENT VOCABULARY

Look at the diagram. What do you know about global climate change?

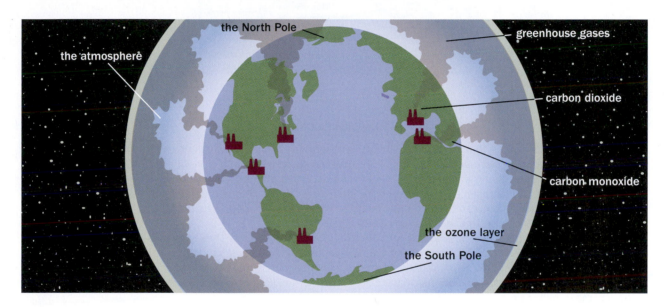

The world's cities have **emitted** dangerous **gases** into our atmosphere for more than a century. As a result, **average temperatures** around the world have risen by one degree Fahrenheit over the last 30 years, a phenomenon known as **global warming**, or **climate change**. Some scientists believe that the average global temperature will have increased by 4 degrees 100 years from now.

Read the caption and labels. Look up any words you don't know. Write each word, its definition, and a sentence that illustrates its use in your vocabulary journal.

■ THINK ABOUT IT

Discuss the following questions with a partner: In your opinion, what has caused global warming? What are its effects? Do you think there will have been any reversal of these trends by 2030? Why or why not?

■ GRAMMAR IN CONTENT

CD1,TR13

A Read and listen to the following article.

Global Climate Change

Some scientists believe that the earth's climate **has begun** to change. They claim that the earth's atmosphere is becoming warmer. Certain chemicals **have increased** in the atmosphere over the last century. Many scientists believe that the increase in these chemicals in the atmosphere **has caused** the changes in the earth's climate. It **has taken** a while to track the changes. With the help of satellites and instruments on the ocean floor, scientists **have learned** that ocean levels **have risen**, temperatures on the earth's surface **have increased,** and ice at the North and South poles **has started** to melt.

One team of scientists **has collected** data at the North Pole for five years. They **have measured** the changes in ice at the North Pole. In 2005, they noticed that conditions at the pole **had changed** significantly from the previous years. Previously, the team **had** always **camped** on a solid mass of ice. But when they arrived in 2005, they found that the ice mass **had shrunk** to the size of a soccer field. They were forced to conclude that much of the ice mass **had melted.**

Changes such as these **have prompted** some scientists to predict that dramatic shifts in the world's geography **will have taken** place by 2100. They say, for example, that ocean levels **will have risen** by several inches, and that the shape of some coastlines **will have changed.** Fierce storms **will have become** much more common.

In 1999, many of the world's leaders signed an international agreement called the Kyoto Protocols. The protocols established limitations on the pollution that each country can produce.

a climate: the type of weather that a place or region generally has

a coastline: the line between the ocean and land

to shrink: to make or become smaller

significantly: in a major way

B Reread the passage on page 38. (Circle) the 11 verbs in the present perfect in the reading. Check your answers with your partner. If you need help, use the chart below.

Present Perfect

Affirmative Statements

Subject	Have/Has	Participle
Greenhouse gases	have	increased since 1950.
Polar ice	has	started to melt.

Negative Statements

Subject	Haven't/Hasn't	Past Participle
Some politicians and businessmen	haven't	accepted these findings.
The local ecosystem	hasn't	recovered from last year's hurricane.

Yes/No Questions

Have/Has	Subject	Past Participle	Short Affirmative Answers	Short Negative Answers
Has	the class	studied the effects of global warming?	Yes, it has.	No, it hasn't.
Have	the students	expressed concern?	Yes, they have.	No, they haven't.

Wh- Questions

Question Word	Have/Has	Subject	Past Participle
What	has	the government	done about global warming?
Why	have	temperatures	increased?
How	have	people	begun to address the problem?

Notes:

- Use simple past to talk about a definite time in the past. Use present perfect to tell about an action or state that began in the past and is still continuing in the present, or to talk about an action or state that occurred at an indefinite time in the past. (*Global warming **has affected** every region of the earth.*)
- Use *for* + a length of time to show how long a present condition or action has been true (*Temperatures have risen **for the last 30 years.***)
- Use *since* + a point of time to show when a present condition started (*Scientists have studied global warming seriously **since the early 1990s.***)
- **Adverbs** are placed between **have** or **had** and the **past participle** (*The public **has slowly begun** to accept that global warming is happening.*) In a negative sentence, however, the **adverb** is placed before **have** or **had** (*The public **probably hasn't had** enough time to consider all the evidence.*)

C Fill in the blanks, using the words in parentheses. Arrange the words in the correct order. Follow the example.

The latest scientific report on global warming claims that human activity

_____*has probably caused*_____ (has/caused/probably) global warming. Due to toxic
(1)

emissions, a _____ (has/hole/appeared/recently) in the ozone
(2)

layer over the South Pole and the average temperature _____
(3)

(30 consecutive years/risen/has/for). Extreme weather _____
(4)

(negatively/has/affected) the seasonal migration of butterflies and birds. Bees and other

insects _____ (have/disappeared/also) in record numbers. Natural
(5)

weather cycles _____ (caused/haven't/probably) these changes.
(6)

_____ (have/what/concluded/scientists) based on all the evidence?
(7)

They've concluded that _____ (created/has/pollution) a greenhouse
(8)

effect.

D Fill in the blanks, using *since* or *for*.

A record number of icebergs have detached from the

Larsen Ice Shelf _____*since*_____ 2000. One iceberg has
(1)

broken into smaller pieces _____ it separated
(2)

from the ice shelf. The icebergs have circled Antarctica

_____ three years. Water levels have risen
(3)

_____ December. Penguins haven't returned
(4)

to their nesting grounds _____ a long time. The ice shelf hasn't gone back to its
(5)

original shape _____ it broke apart.
(6)

E **GROUP WORK** Take turns talking about climate change and its effects. What changes have you noticed in the last ten years or so? Use the present perfect during your discussion.

The weather **hasn't been** normal for a long time.

I've **noticed** that too. There **have been** a lot of storms in the summer.

Yeah, and it **hasn't snowed** much during the winter. That's a change.

PART TWO	Past Perfect

■ GRAMMAR IN CONTENT

A Reread the passage on page 38. Draw a box around the four verbs in the past perfect. Check your answers with your partner. If you need help, use the chart below.

Past Perfect

Affirmative Statements			Negative Statements		
Subject	*Had*	**Participle**	**Subject**	*Hadn't*	**Past Participle**
Weather patterns	had	**begun** to change before the 1990s.	World leaders	hadn't	**reached** any agreement on global warming by the mid-1990s.
Worldwide climates	had	**changed** significantly by the late 1990s.	The U.S. still	hadn't	**ratified** the Kyoto Protocols as of 2006.

Yes/No Questions

Had	**Subject**	**Past Participle**	**Short Affirmative Answers**	**Short Negative Answers**
Had	scientists	**given** any warnings before 1990?	Yes, they **had**.	No, they **hadn't**.
Had	the president	**agreed** to sign the protocol?	Yes, he **had**.	No, he **hadn't**.

Notes:

- The past perfect shows that an action began before a specific point in the past (*Most of the participants* ***had arrived*** *by the early afternoon.*)
- When comparing two events in the past, you can put the earlier event in the **past perfect**; put the more recent event in the **simple past** (*The ecologist Rachel Carson* ***had written*** *about the dangers of pollution long before other scientists* ***took*** *the issue seriously.*)
- Put *already, never,* and ***just*** between ***had*** and the **past participle** (*I* ***had never heard*** *of global warming until I took an ecology course.*)
- Use ***yet*** after *not* or at the end of the sentence in a negative statement (*I can't offer an opinion because I* ***haven't seen*** *the report* ***yet.***)
- Use ***still*** before ***had*** in a negative statement (*The professor* ***still hadn't arrived*** *by 3:30.*)

B **Look at this article from a college newspaper. It's about a debate on global warming and climate change. Fill in the blanks using the correct past perfect form of the verb in parentheses.**

Dr. Shaw and Dr. Patel held a debate on global warming in front of the Student Union yesterday. Dr. Shaw claimed that global warming _____had already begun_____ (already **(1)** begin) to affect the world. She noted that in the past century the average temperature

_____ (rise) by at least one degree, and that carbon dioxide levels
(2)

_____ (increase) more in the last year than in the previous 1,000
(3)

years. She maintained that computer models _____ (predict) these
(4)

changes based on weather patterns. Finally, she stated that changes in the atmosphere

_____ (occur) as a result of the changes caused by humans.
(5)

Dr. Patel challenged Dr. Shaw's claims. He stated that human activity

_____ (not bring about) the changes in temperature over
(6)

the last century; climate had. He also asserted that 90% of the carbon dioxide in the

atmosphere _____ (be) caused by volcanoes, and that humans
(7)

_____ (be) responsible for only about 3%. He also argued that
(8)

recent satellite data _____ (show) that most models of climate
(9)

change were inaccurate. Finally, he noted that there was no evidence that human activity

_____ (cause) any of the changes that scientists observed.
(10)

C **WRITE** Look at Exercise B again. Create a written summary of the two arguments presented during the debate between Dr. Shaw and Dr. Patel. Change the wording, but keep the past perfect tense.

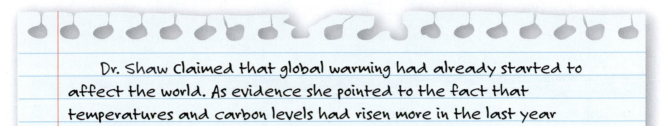

>   Dr. Shaw claimed that global warming had already started to
> affect the world. As evidence she pointed to the fact that
> temperatures and carbon levels had risen more in the last year

---

Future Perfect

■ GRAMMAR IN CONTENT

A Reread the passage on page 38. Draw a ~wavy line~ under the four verbs in the future perfect. Check your answers with your partner. If you need help, use the chart below and on the next page.

Future Perfect with *Will Have* and *Be Going To Have*					
Affirmative Statements			**Negative Statements**		
Subject	***Will Have/ Be Going To Have***	**Past Participle**	**Subject**	***Won't Have/Not Be Going To Have***	**Past Participle**
Global sea levels	**will have**	**risen** 7 inches by 2100.	Global warming trends	**won't have**	**stopped** by the end of this century.
Great Britain	**is going to have**	**cut** its carbon dioxide emissions in half by 2050.	Much of the world's coral	**isn't going to have**	**survived** by then.

Yes/No Questions

Will/ Be	Subject	Have/Going To Have + Past Participle	Short Affirmative Answers	Short Negative Answers
Will	some islands	**have disappeared** by then?	Yes, they **will** (have.)	No, they **won't** (have.)
Is	the ice	**going to have melted** before it's too late?	Yes, it **will** (have.)	No, it **won't** (have.)

Wh- Questions

Question Word	Will/Be	Subject	Have/Going To Have + Past Participle
What	will	the researchers	**have discovered** by the end of their project?
When	are	we	**going to have seen** the results of our efforts?
How	will	the animals	**have survived** without any food or water?

Note:

Use future perfect to tell about an action or event that will have been completed before some other time or event in the future: *By May the team* **will have reached** *the North Pole; This summer Dr. Shaw* **will have been** *at State University for 40 years; By 2100, the Atlantic Ocean* **is going to have flooded** *the Florida coast.*

B **Fill in the blanks with the correct future perfect form of the verb in parentheses. Then read the passage aloud with a partner.**

Some researchers believe that the changes caused by global warming will

not be particularly dramatic. However, most agree that by the year 2100, these

changes _____*will have affected*_____ (affect) Earth and life on it to some degree.
(1)

The most important prediction is that the average temperature at Earth's surface

_____ (increase) by 3–5 degrees Fahrenheit. This increase
(2)

in temperature _____ (melt) some of the ice at the North and
(3)

South poles. The melting ice _____ (cause) the ocean to rise
(4)

several inches, and the ocean _____ (flood) low areas of land
(5)

and _____ (cover) some small islands. Moreover, the warmer
(6)

temperatures in northern climates _____ (attract) mosquitoes and
(7)

other insects to new areas, resulting in more diseases. Thus, although climate change may

not have the kinds of effects that many fear, these scientists claim that by 2100 its effects

_____ (become) noticeable.
(8)

C Listen to the recording. Three students (Franz, Farah, and Lisa) are giving their opinions on the future effect of volcanoes on the world's climate. Answer the questions when you have finished listening.

1. According to Franz, what effect will volcanoes have had on the world's climate?

   _____

   _____

2. Does Farah agree? Why or why not?

   _____

   _____

3. What does Lisa predict will have happened by the year 2100?

   _____

   _____

4. What does she think will have happened by 2200?

   _____

   _____

■ **COMMUNICATE**

D **GROUP WORK** In a group, make your own predictions about future weather patterns and climate trends. Use the future perfect.

By 2100, I think there **will have been** a worldwide ecological disaster.

Oh, I don't think so. I think the world's climate **will have become** stable by then.

Maybe, but we'll really have to cut down on pollution.

GRAMMAR AND VOCABULARY Write a short essay about global warming, climate change, or another topic related to environmentalism and conservation. In your essay, be sure to use the present perfect, past perfect, or future perfect.

PROJECT Research one aspect of the ecology of your local area.

1. Choose a plant or animal that lives in your area; alternatively, you might choose to learn more about an entire habitat or ecosystem, such as the ocean, a marshland, forest, meadow, desert, mountain, or even a deserted plot in the middle of the city.

2. Investigate the plant, animal, ecosystem, or habitat you chose. You can learn about it by going to your local library, or you may want to study it personally. You can take pictures of it, for example, or you might bring a notebook outdoors for taking notes and/or drawing sketches. Find out if the plants and animals you chose to learn about are threatened or challenged by pollution or other human factors.

3. Tell the class what you learned, and share any pictures you created or found. Invite the class to ask questions, and answer them as best you can. If you are unable to answer a question, you can get the information later on and bring the information to the next class.

 INTERNET Search the Internet for "climate change" or "global warming." Find an article that summarizes what has happened to Earth's climate in the last fifty years. You may also find an article that predicts where these trends will be leading and what we can do to reverse them or slow them down. Take notes or print copies of the articles you find and share your findings with the class.

A Liza and Aaron work at Community Hospital. Complete their conversation with the correct verb or phrase in parentheses.

Liza: I'm so tired. I've been working for fourteen hours straight.

Aaron: That's a long time. When ___*do you get*___ (would you get/do
(1)
you get) a chance to rest?

Liza: I _____ (have got off/get off) at 10:00 tonight, and I
(2)
_____ ('m going to go/go) straight to bed.
(3)

Aaron: _____ (Did you go/Are you going to go) home to sleep?
(4)

Liza: Yes, I'm going to go home. There's nowhere quiet here at the hospital.

Aaron: You _____ ('re being/'re going to be) much too tired
(5)
to drive. I _____ ('ll be/'m going to be) glad to drive
(6)
you. I _____ (have been leaving/'m going to be
(7)
leaving) the hospital around 10:00.

Liza: Gee thanks. But how _____ (am I getting/am I going
(8)
to get) back to work tomorrow?

Aaron: I _____ ('ll ask/'m asking) my sister to follow us to
(9)
your house in your car. I'm sure she _____ (won't
(10)
mind/doesn't mind).

B Select the appropriate adverb or preposition from the words in parentheses.

I've been getting involved in the movement to save the environment lately. I _____
(1)
(ever/never) thought I'd be doing this. But I worked as a volunteer for the Save Our Earth

organization _____ (from/until) June _____ (from/until) September, and I
(2) (3)

got very interested in the movement. _____ (Now/Always) I'm working there part-
(4)

time. _____ (Usually/Never) I write up and print out fliers, but _____ (never/
(5) (6)

sometimes), I attend meetings. I'll probably stay with SOE _____ (before/until)
(7)

graduation. Then I'm thinking about going into environmental law.

C Complete the following dialog with the correct form/tense of the verb in parentheses.

Marcia: Hey, what *have you been doing* (1) (do) lately?

Amy: Well, I _____ (2) (work) on a new bridge.

Marcia: Oh, that's right. You _____ (3) (be) a civil engineer. How _____ (4) (like) the work?

Amy: It's OK, but there _____ (5) (be) a number of unexpected problems recently.

Marcia: Like what?

Amy: Well, just last week one of our trucks _____ (6) (fall) into the lake. It _____ (7) (take) two days just to get it out.

Marcia: You must be joking.

Amy: No, and I _____ (8) (not have) time to see my fiancé since then.

Marcia: You _____ (9) (be) engaged? I _____ (10) (not know) that. Who's the lucky man?

Amy: His name's Ray. We _____ (11) (know) each other for years. Since high school, in fact.

Marcia: Well, congratulations! I _____ (12) (expect) an invitation to the wedding!

LEARNER LOG Check (✔) Yes or *I Need More Practice.*

Lesson	I Can Use . . .	Yes	I Need More Practice
1	Present Tense, Past Tense, Future Tense		
2	Present Progressive, Past Progressive, Future Progressive		
3	Present Tense vs. Present Progressive, Past Tense vs. Past Progressive, Adverbs of Frequency		
4	Future, Future Progressive		
5	Present Perfect, Past Perfect, Future Perfect		

PART 1
Comparing the Present and Present Perfect

PART 2
Comparing the Past and Past Perfect

PART 3
Comparing the Future and Future Perfect

Lesson 6

Public Policy: Predicting and Planning for Earthquakes

■ CONTENT VOCABULARY

What do you know about earthquakes? Look at and talk about the photo.

Loma Preita Earthquake, San Francisco, 1989

Earthquakes happen all the time, in every part of the world. But, some places are more **geologically** active than others. There have been several very **destructive** earthquakes in California, for example. A major **quake** struck the San Francisco area in 1989. Before that, another quake had hit the city in 1906. The San Francisco Bay Area lies on several **fault lines**, and **seismologists predict** another major quake will have occurred there before the end of the 21st century.

Read the caption. Look up any words you don't know. Write each word, its definition, and a sentence that illustrates its use in your vocabulary journal.

■ THINK ABOUT IT

Write for five minutes on the following topic: Do earthquakes give any warning signs before they strike? How can people prepare for a coming quake?

■ GRAMMAR IN CONTENT

A Read and listen to the following.

CD1,TR15

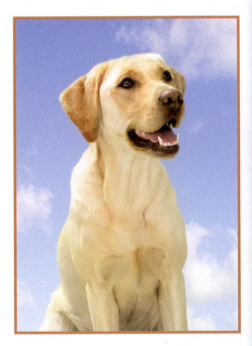

Can Animals Predict Earthquakes?

For thousands of years people **have argued** that animals can sense that an earthquake **is going to happen**. The first recorded earthquake **was** in the Greek city of Helice in 373 BCE. The quake **destroyed** the city. Historians **say** that before the earthquake **hit**, great numbers of snakes and rats **had** already **left** the city.

Since then, there **have been** numerous claims of unusual animal behavior prior to some major earthquakes. Some researchers **have identified** several kinds of unusual behaviors that **occur** prior to an earthquake: hibernating animals **will leave** their dens, even in the middle of a freezing winter, and bees **will leave** their nests. Earthworms **will come** out of the ground, and other wild animals **will leave** their homes. Some researchers **have examined** the number of reports of dogs and cats that **had run** away from home before major earthquakes. They **found** that owners **had reported** an unusually high number of missing pets just prior to several major earthquakes.

Most researchers **don't think** that animals can tell when an earthquake is coming. They **argue** that odd animal behavior **does not** always **precede** a major earthquake, and earthquakes **don't** always **follow** odd animal behavior. So animal behavior **is** not a reliable predictor of earthquakes. Perhaps in 50 years researchers **will have made** enough advances in seismology to be able to predict earthquakes. Perhaps animal behavior **will play** a part in that discovery. In either case, public officials should plan for such emergencies.

to sense: to feel strongly based on intuition

to tell: to determine, detect

odd: strange, unusual

to precede: to come before

reliable: regularly does what it should do

seismology: a science that deals with earthquakes and with artificially produced vibrations of the earth

B Reread the passage above. (Circle) all the verbs in present perfect. Underline all the verbs in simple present. If you need help, use the chart below.

Present vs. Present Perfect	
Simple Present	**Present Perfect**
Earthquakes **happen** all the time.	Five earthquakes **have happened** in the last ten years.
My dog **is** very faithful.	My dog **has saved** my life twice.
Odd animal behavior **doesn't** always **precede** an earthquake.	Seismologists **haven't yet discovered** how to predict earthquakes with any certainty or precision.

Notes:

- Use **simple present** to tell about repeated actions, habits, routines, and general facts (*Earthquakes happen all the time*). Use the **present perfect** to tell about things that happened at an indefinite time in the past (*Five earthquakes have happened in the last ten years*).
- The **present perfect** tells about past events that have some relevance to the present (*My dog has saved my life twice, and that's why I'm still alive today.*)
- Use *yet* with the **present perfect** to ask a question or make a negative statement (**Has** *the emergency crew* **arrived yet?** *I* **haven't seen** *them* **yet.**)
- In the present perfect, **adverbs** such as *already, hardly, even,* and *never* go between **have** and the **past participle** (*The city* **has already prepared** *for a major earthquake. In fact, it* **has even created** *an evacuation plan.*)
- In written reports, the **present perfect** often is used to frame a story or provide context (*People* **have** *always* **wondered** *whether animals can sense an earthquake before it happens.*)

C Fill in the blanks with the correct form of the verb in parentheses. Use present perfect in the first sentence of each paragraph to frame the story. Continue with simple present. Write the verbs in the blanks. Check your answers with your classmates.

Throughout recorded history there _____*have been*_____ (be) reports before
_____(1)_____

earthquakes of unusual behavior in animals, such as mice, pigs, chickens, goats, sharks,

and elephants. There _____(2)_____ (be) reports that pigeons seem to have

some difficulty navigating before an earthquake. What _____(3)_____

(animals sense) before an earthquake? That _____(4)_____ (be) a good

question.

Researchers in Japan, such as Dr. Motoji Ikeya, from Osaka University,

_____(5)_____ (study) the relationship between animal behavior

and earthquakes. Dr. Ikeya _____(6)_____ (believe) that animals

_____(7)_____ (sense) electromagnetic changes. These changes

_____(8)_____ (occur) close to a quake's epicenter. Other researchers

_____(9)_____ (think) that animals _____(10)_____

(respond) to sounds that humans cannot hear or measure. Others

_____(11)_____ (think) that animals _____(12)_____

(react) to electrical changes. Others _____(13)_____ (believe) the animals

_____(14)_____ (respond) to gas from the earth.

D Listen to the lecture. Fill in the blanks while you listen. Listen again to check your work.

CD1,TR16

People _have always had a personal interest_ in earthquakes, but the scientific study of
(1)

earthquakes _____. Scientists who _____
(2)   (3)

are called seismologists. Seismic waves _____. Rocks
(4)

breaking inside the earth and explosions _____. Scientists
(5)

_____. Seismologists _____ where
(6)   (7)

earthquakes _____ in the past. This _____
(8)   (9)

them where earthquakes will probably happen in the future.

E Read the lecture from Exercise D. Then answer the following questions.

1. What do seismologists study?

   _____

2. What causes seismic waves?

   _____

3. How do seismologists predict where earthquakes will happen in the future?

   _____

■ C O M M U N I C A T E

F **PAIR WORK** With a classmate, ask and answer questions about earthquakes. Use the
present and present perfect.

Have you ever **been** in an earthquake?

Yes, I've actually **been** in quite a few
earthquakes. Where I come from,
earthquakes **happen** all the time.

G **WRITE** Summarize what you learned about your classmate from Exercise F. Use the
present and present perfect as necessary.

Luis isn't afraid of earthquakes. He's used to them because
he's been through so many. In fact, Luis has been through three very
strong earthquakes in his life.

■ **GRAMMAR IN CONTENT**

A Reread the passage on page 50. What's the difference between the past and past perfect?

Past vs. Past Perfect	
Simple Past	**Past Perfect**
A series of powerful tsunami waves **swept** across the Indian Ocean on December 26, 2004.	An earthquake **had triggered** the tsunami.
The tsunami **killed** more than 300,000 people.	The biggest tsunami before that **had occurred** in 1998, in Papua New Guinea.

Notes:
- Use the **simple past** to tell about an action that happened at a specific point in the past (*Tourists and residents **ran** for their lives when they **saw** the tsunami.*)
- Use the **past perfect** to tell about an action that happened <u>before</u> another action or event in the **past** (*Some people **had managed** to escape <u>before</u> the tsunami **hit** the village.*)

B Listen to Larry's report on the Alaska Earthquake of 1964. Then, put the following events in the correct order, from 1 to 5.

CD1,TR17

_____   The magnitude of the earthquake was 8.4.

___*I*___   The Alaska earthquake occurred in 1964.

_____   The earthquake lasted 3–4 minutes.

_____   The quake caused a tsunami that carried a ship to the top of a mountain.

C Listen to the conversation. Write "T" for true and "F" for false.

CD1,TR18

___T___   Petra and her husband had just gone to bed before the quake hit.

_____   Petra and her husband had gone to bed early that night.

_____   There were boxes everywhere because Janet had just moved.

_____   Janet's husband hadn't been able to go to sleep.

_____   Petra couldn't turn on the lights because they had lost power.

_____   Janet's apartment was a mess because all the boxes had fallen.

_____   Petra's apartment was flooded because the water line had burst.

_____   Petra couldn't call the fire department because she had lost power.

■ **COMMUNICATE**

D **WRITE** Write a summary of Janet or Petra's story in Exercise C. Use the past and past perfect. Compare your summary with a classmate's version of the same story.

| PART THREE | Comparing the Future and Future Perfect |

■ **GRAMMAR IN CONTEXT**

A Reread the passage on page 50. What's the difference between the future and the future perfect?

Future vs. Future Perfect

Future	Future Perfect
What **will happen** in the next earthquake?	All communication systems **will have shut down**.
There **aren't going to be** any public services.	Many residents **will have left** the city.

Notes:
- Use the **future** to tell about an action that is definitely going to happen in the future (*There's no doubt that another earthquake **will hit** San Francisco in the future. The only question is when.*)
- Use the **future** to make predictions (*Most of the city's newer buildings **will withstand** an earthquake.*)
- The **future perfect** is sometimes used to tell about hypothetical situations, plans, or wishes for the future (*We hope the city **will have created** an emergency plan before the next earthquake.*)
- Adverbs such as *already* and *also* go between **will have** and the **past participle** (*By Thursday, I **will have stored** enough water and canned food to last a whole week. I **will have also decided** on an evacuation route.*)

B Change the following sentences from the future to the future perfect. Follow the example.

1. The city will evacuate all of its residents.

   The city will have evacuated all of its residents.

2. A tsunami will crash on the city's harbor.

   _____

3. School officials will move children to a shelter.

   _____

4. All traffic will come to a stop.

   _____

5. The Board of Health will create a supply of clean water.

   _____

C Fill in the blanks with the correct form of the verb in parentheses. Use either the future (with *will* or *be going to*) or the future perfect as appropriate.

Aziz: Next semester I _____*'m going to take*_____ (take) extra courses and
(1)

complete my program, so I _____ (graduate)
(2)

this summer. So by the fall of this year, I _____
(3)

(graduate) and, if I'm lucky, I _____ (already,
(4)

find) a good job with a great salary. If all goes well, in five years I

_____ (pay off) my student loan.
(5)

Won Ho: Oh, yeah? Who _____ (pay) you a great salary?
(6)

Aziz: Who knows? But somebody _____ (pay). By the
(7)

fall, I _____ (earn) a degree in geology with a
(8)

specialty in seismology. With my work this summer at the Alta Earthquake

Institute, I _____ (work) four summers as an
(9)

intern at a research center by then. I _____
(10)

(also, earn) some extra credits while I'm at Alta this summer. I

_____ (be) a great job candidate. Maybe the
(11)

Earthquake Research Project _____ (hear) about
(12)

me by the time I start looking for jobs. How about you?

Won Ho: I _____ (probably, fail) Dr. Morse's exam next
(13)

week, so I _____ (still, be) in school.
(14)

■ **COMMUNICATE**

D **GROUP WORK** Imagine you have the rest of the day to prepare for an earthquake or other emergency. What will you have done by the end of the day? Discuss your ideas in a group, using the future and future perfect.

If an earthquake comes, I'll be prepared, because I **will have put** aside canned food and batteries.

That's a good idea. I'll be prepared, too. My family and I **will have decided** on a meeting place.

I'm going to do the same thing.

GRAMMAR AND VOCABULARY Write a dialog using the words in the box below. Try to use at least four of the following six verb forms: *present, present perfect, past, past perfect, future,* and *future perfect.*

earthquake	emergency plan	fault line	predict	seismologist	tsunami

PROJECT In a group, draw up an evacuation route that you can follow in the aftermath of an earthquake or other disaster.

1. Get a map of your local region or area.
2. Find the safest, most direct route out of the area.
3. Draw a map of your evacuation route, and write directions that can be followed in the event of a disaster.
4. Share your evacuation plans with the class. Compare your plan with other groups' plans, and talk about the advantages and disadvantages of each.

 INTERNET Search the Internet using the terms "North America" and "earthquake" to find out about major earthquakes that have happened in Mexico, the United States, and Canada. Take notes and download images on one of these earthquakes. Make a short presentation to the class, sharing what you found out.

PART 1
Tense Sequencing in Discourse

PART 2
Simple Present as Background
Information in Discourse

Lesson (7)

English Composition: Writing Papers

■ CONTENT VOCABULARY

Look at the picture and read the description.

Enrique is in his first-year **composition** class. The teacher has explained how to organize an **essay** in English. Next he is going to discuss appropriate vocabulary and grammar forms for **academic writing** and **formal writing** in general. Enrique wrote formal papers in school in Ecuador. He knows that he needs to learn appropriate vocabulary, grammar, and **organization** to write academic papers in English.

Read the description below the picture. Look up any words you don't know. Write each word, its definition, and a sentence that illustrates its use in your vocabulary journal.

■ THINK ABOUT IT

Discuss the following questions with your partner: Have you ever taken a course in academic writing in English? If so, what did the course focus on? How is academic writing different from the language you use when writing an e-mail to a friend, for example?

■ GRAMMAR IN CONTENT

A Read and listen to the following.

CD1,TR19

Enrique's University Writing Experience

This semester Enrique is taking ESOL 102. He likes to write, but he doesn't have much experience with writing in English. His professor, Dr. Williams, is helpful and friendly. Enrique is learning how to write a composition that is appropriate for university-level assignments. He started the class three weeks ago. Since then he has written three compositions. On the first one he got a C, and on the second, a B-. He hasn't received the third one back from his professor yet.

Before Enrique began ESOL 102, he had the choice of taking either mainstream English composition classes or those designed for speakers of other languages. Many students face this difficult decision. He had just registered for a mainstream class when Jun, a friend from high school, called. Jun advised Enrique to enroll in an ESOL class. He said that he had taken the ESOL course at his college last year and had learned a lot. Enrique dropped his mainstream class and added the ESOL composition class.

In four years, Enrique will graduate from the university. As soon as he gets his degree, he's going to start work at an engineering firm. Engineers write lots of reports. If Enrique is going to succeed, he will need to write well. Over the next four years, he is going to work hard on his writing skills. By Enrique's junior year, he will have taken three writing courses, and by the time he graduates, he will have written a paper for practically every class he has taken. When he finally begins work as an engineer, he'll probably have learned to write better in English than in Spanish.

to drop: to unenroll from a class at a university

to enroll: to join officially

ESOL: English for Speakers of Other Languages

mainstream: the type of classes taken by most students (in this case, native speakers of English)

practically: virtually, just about, almost

to register: to add one's name to an official list

B Look back at the reading on page 58. What is the focus time for each paragraph? Circle past, present, or future.

1. Paragraph 1   Past   Present   Future

2. Paragraph 2   Past   Present   Future

3. Paragraph 3   Past   Present   Future

Tense Sequencing in the Present			
Focus Time	**Before**	**After**	**Example**
Simple Present	Present Perfect Simple Past	Future	Linda **is studying** in the library. (focus time) She **has been studying** there for hours. (before focus time) She **will study** for a few more hours. (after focus time)

Tense Sequencing in the Past			
Focus Time	**Before**	**After**	**Example**
Simple Past	Past Perfect	Simple Past	Sami **graduated** while he was on crutches. (focus time) He **had broken** his leg a month before. (before focus time) After the graduation, he **celebrated** with his friends. (after focus time)

Tense Sequencing in the Future			
Focus Time	**Before**	**After**	**Example**
Future	Future Perfect	Future	Camilo **will graduate** in the spring. (focus time) By spring, he **will have finished** all of his required courses. (before focus time) After he graduates, he **will begin** his new job. (after focus time)

Notes:
- When a time has been established in a piece of discourse (focus time), this time is usually maintained as described above unless the speaker/writer uses an explicit time expression that changes the focus time.
- Use the correct sequence of tenses for the focus time of the piece of discourse. (INCORRECT: ~~John wrote a novel. Before that he has written many short stories.~~ CORRECT: *John* **wrote** *a novel. Before that he* **had written** *many short stories.*)

C Circle the correct form of the word to complete the paragraph.

Right now, Enrique ((is worrying) / worried) about his class. His instructor
(1)
(assigns / has assigned) a new composition. Enrique's last composition (isn't / wasn't) good
(2)   (3)
enough. He only (gets / got) a D. Yesterday he (had gone / went) to the writing center on
(4)   (5)
campus. They really (help / helped) him. This evening he (writes / will write) a first draft,
(6)   (7)
and then he (is taking / will take) it to the writing center again.
(8)

D Read the following passage. Use the correct form of the verb in parentheses to complete
the paragraphs.

Ten years ago Jack Edelman _____established_____ (establish) Valley State
(1)
University's first writing center. He _____ (hire) four tutors and
(2)
_____ (train) them to work with students on their grammar, vocabulary,
(3)
and organization. For a while, very few students _____ (go) to the center
(4)
for help. After a few years, however, Jack _____ (notice) that instructors
(5)
_____ (begin) to send their students to the center for help with their
(6)
writing. In fact, last year more than 250 students _____ (visit) the center.
(7)

Next year, Jack _____ (move) the writing center into a new
(8)
building. The new building _____ (have) state-of-the-art facilities. By
(9)
the time the center moves it _____ (employ) four more tutors. Jack
(10)
_____ (retire) after the move.
(11)

■ **C O M M U N I C A T E**

E **PAIR WORK** How do you write an essay? Tell a partner about the steps you took the first
time you wrote an essay. Then tell him/her about the steps you usually take. Then tell your
partner what steps you will take when you write your next composition.

A Look at the passage on page 58. There are two examples of the present tense being used for background information in paragraphs two and three. <u>Underline</u> them.

Simple Present as Background Information in Discourse

I **went** to the writing center yesterday. (focus time) It **is** the best place to get advice about compositions. (background information) I **had gotten** a bad grade—again! (before time)

Notes:
- Sometimes the focus time is not maintained in a piece of discourse.
- Use the present tense to give general, background comments when the focus time is the past.

B Read the following monolog. Indicate in which blank each of the five sentences below fits into the monolog.

_____ It really works!

___*1*___ He teaches English Composition.

_____ He is such a great professor.

_____ I can't believe he's that old!

_____ A thesis statement gives the writer's main point.

I took English 102 my first year here. I had Dr. Dixon. _____ I'll never forget
                                                                                      (1)
our first class. I learned that all compositions in English begin with an introduction. He

told us to find the thesis statement in the first paragraph of an essay in our books and

underline it. _____ Well, then Dr. Dixon told us something I will never forget. He
              (2)
said that if we are having trouble writing an introduction, we should try something he had

learned in college in the 1960s. _____ Anyway, he told us to begin writing in the
                                 (3)
middle of the composition and when we had finished, to go back and write the introduction.

_____ Dr. Dixon really taught me how to write. _____
(4)   **(5)**

■ **COMMUNICATE**

C **PAIR WORK** With a partner, discuss the reasons for the time frame changes in Exercise B.

GRAMMAR AND VOCABULARY Imagine that you are in Enrique's college composition class. Here is your next assignment.

ESOL 102
College Composition

Write a composition about how you learned English. Write about when and how you learned English and learned to write in English. What did you experience? Who helped you? What was easy? Difficult? Fun? Frustrating? Why did you do it? This part of your essay should have two or three other paragraphs. The focus time will be past. Then write two or three paragraphs about what you are doing now to improve your English. The focus time is present. Finally, write two or three paragraphs about your plans to improve your English and set some goals for the future. The focus time will be future. Make sure that each paragraph has a topic sentence.

PART 1
Present Perfect Progressive

PART 2
Past Perfect Progressive

PART 3
Future Perfect Progressive

Lesson 8

Linguistics: The History and Globalization of English

◼ CONTENT VOCABULARY

Look at the map. It shows many of the countries where English is currently spoken. Do you know how English came to be spoken in these places?

People around the world speak many different **varieties** and **dialects** of English, a language that has **evolved** over the last 1,600 years. Other **languages** have been disappearing at an alarming rate as English continues to spread its influence across the globe. **Linguists** predict that the number of English speakers may double in the near future.

Read the caption. Look up any words you don't know. Write each word, its definition, and a sentence that illustrates its use in your vocabulary journal.

◼ THINK ABOUT IT

In a group, discuss the following questions: How has English spread around the world? What changes does it go through as it spreads from one part of the world to another? After the discussion, record your own thoughts and conclusions in your writing journal.

■ **GRAMMAR IN CONTENT**

CD1,TR20

A **Read and listen to the following article about English.**

The First Printing Press.

Johann Gutenberg assembled the first printing press in 1440. Its use rapidly spread throughout Europe and the rest of the world.

Today, more than 80% of the world's population has a cell phone subscription. Some countries have more cell phones than people.

The History and Future of English

In CE 449, Germanic tribes invaded the island we now call England. The inhabitants of England at that time, known as Celts, **had been depending on** the Romans for hundreds of years to defend them. The Romans couldn't stop the Germanic invaders, however, and many of the Celts were forced out of England.

The Germanic invaders established a permanent settlement in England. They **had been living** there for four hundred years when Norsemen from Scandinavia invaded England and settled in the region, along with the Germanic tribes. The two language groups combined to form an early variety of English. The two languages **had been combining** and **influencing** each other for more than two hundred years when England was invaded for a third time by the Normans of France. Like the Norsemen before them, the Normans had a huge influence on the development of English.

Since then, English **has been continuing** to absorb the influences of other languages and cultures. At the same time, English **has been spreading** its own influence throughout the world. The printing press and other forms of communication technology have played a major role in the spread of English. These forms of technology will continue to shape the way English is written and spoken around the world.

Fifty years from now, people **will have been using** cell phones, computers, and other electronic devices to communicate for several generations. Much of that communication will be conducted in a common language, most likely English. By that time, a majority of the world's population **will have been speaking** English as a first or second language since childhood.

a settlement: a newly established community
to absorb: to take in

B Reread the passage. (Circle) all the verbs in the present perfect progressive. Compare your answers with a partner. If you need help, use the chart below.

Present Perfect Progressive

Affirmative Statements

Subject	*Have Been*	*-ing* Verb
I You We They	have been	studying the history of English.
He She	has been	

Negative Statements

Subject	*Have Not Been*	*-ing* Verb
I You We They	have not been (haven't been)	studying other subjects.
He She	has not been (hasn't been)	

Yes/No Questions

Have	Subject	*Been + -ing* Verb
Have	you we they	been studying the history of English?
Has	he she	

Short Affirmative Answers	Short Negative Answers
Yes, I **have**. Yes, we **have**. Yes, they **have**.	No, I **haven't**. No, we **haven't**. No, they **haven't**.
Yes, he **has**. Yes, she **has**.	No, he **hasn't**. No, she **hasn't**.

Wh- Questions

Question Word	*Have*	Subject	*Been*	*-ing* Verb
What	have	you		**studying** this semester?
When	have	the students	been	**getting** together to study?
Where	has	he		**finding** his information?

Notes:
- Use the **present perfect progressive** to tell about an action that started in the past and is still in progress (*I started my paper last week and I've been working on it every day since.*)
- Use the **present perfect progressive** to show that an action has some relevance to the present (*People have been using cell phones since the late 1990s.*) In this sentence, the fact that people are *still* using cell phones has emphasis.
- When two verbs have the same subject, the helping verbs *have* and *been* are not repeated (*English has been growing and evolving for over 1,500 years.*)

C Read the dialog and fill in the blanks, using the present perfect progressive form of the verb in parentheses. Use contractions whenever possible.

Pascal: How long ___*have you been studying*___ (study) English?
(1)

Chen: I _____ (study) it for about five years now.
(2)

Pascal: How _____ (learn) it?
(3)

Chen: I _____ (take) classes at a local community college
(4)
with my friend.

Pascal: I _____ (think) about taking an English class, too.
(5)
My sister _____ (try) to persuade me to enroll at
(6)
Bunker Hill College.

Chen: That's the school my friend and I _____ (attend).
(7)
They _____ (offer) an advanced course for several
(8)
years now.

Pascal: Is it any good?

Chen: Yes, it is. The instructor _____ (teach) us about the
(9)
globalization of English. It's very interesting.

D Listen to the lecture and then answer each of the following questions in complete sentences, using the present perfect progressive.

1. How long has English been spreading throughout the world?

   _____

2. How long have Cameroonians been speaking pidgin English?

   _____

3. What has the government of Canada been doing to integrate its territories and provinces?

   _____

4. Why have some people in Quebec been demanding their independence?

   _____

E **GROUP WORK** In a group, share your secrets for learning English. Use the present perfect progressive during your discussion.

I've **been watching** soap operas and other TV shows. I've **been learning** a lot of slang and idioms that way.

I know what you mean. I've **been watching** movies on DVD. The English subtitles **have been helping me** a lot.

My brother **has been teaching** me English in his spare time. He's **been working** in the U.S. for ten years and he's fluent in English.

PART TWO	Past Perfect Progressive

■ GRAMMAR IN CONTENT

A Reread the passage on page 64. <u>Underline</u> all of the verbs in the past perfect progressive. If you need help, use the chart below.

Past Perfect Progressive

Affirmative Statements			Negative Statements		
Subject	*Had Been*	*-ing* Verb	**Subject**	*Had Not Been*	*-ing* Verb
I You He She We They	had been	preparing a report.	I You He She We They	had not been (hadn't been)	intending to publish the results.

Yes/No Questions				
Had	**Subject**	*Been + -ing* Verb	**Short Affirmative Answers**	**Short Negative Answers**
Had	you he she we they	been taking good notes?	Yes, I **had.** Yes, he **had.** Yes, she **had.** Yes, we **had.** Yes, they **had.**	No, I **hadn't.** No, he **hadn't.** No, she **hadn't.** No, we **hadn't.** No, they **hadn't.**

Wh- Questions				
Question Word	***Had***	**Subject**	***Been***	***-ing* Verb**
What		you		**planning** to do?
When	**had**	Javier and Eco	**been**	**doing** their research?
How		they		**finding** enough time to do all the work?

Notes:

- Use the **past perfect progressive** to tell about a **continuous action in the past** happening *before* another action of shorter duration (*He finally published his book in May. He **had been working** on it **for five years.***)
- Use the **past perfect progressive** to tell about an action that was in progress *up until* a specific time in the past (*Professor Kahn **had been writing** a book **until** his death in 2005.*) The progressive emphasizes the continuing activity, not the end result.
- Non-action verbs aren't usually used in the progressive.
  Incorrect: ~~I had been understanding the lecture until the end.~~
  Correct: *I understood the lecture until the end.*
- When two verbs have the same subject, the helping verbs *had* and *been* are not repeated (*Scholars **had been reading** and **writing** in Latin until the Middle Ages.*)
- Adverbs such as *already, probably,* and *definitely* go between *had* and *been* (*The students **had probably been wondering** when they would get their grades.*)

B **Work with a partner. Take turns reading the following and using the correct past perfect progressive form of the verb in parentheses. When you both have had a chance to read, write the correct answer in each blank.**

Latin used to be the language of scholarship in European universities. By the end of the Middle Ages, the educated elite, that is, the leaders and professionals in the highest levels of society, _____ (write) in Latin for many years. They
(1)
_____ (learn) it in school and _____ (use)
(2) **(3)**
it for scholarly debate. They _____ (study) Latin grammar as one
(4)
of the core classes in the university. When English became the language for scholarship and intellectual life in English-speaking countries, Latin became frozen in time. Unlike English, Latin didn't change over time because no one _____ (learn) it as a
(5)
first language.

C Listen to the lecture on the history of scholarly writing in English. Then write an answer to each of the questions, using complete sentences in the past perfect progressive.

CD1,TR22

1. In what language had scholars been writing up until the end of the Middle Ages?

   <u>They had been writing exclusively in Latin up until</u>
   <u>the end of the Middle Ages.</u>

2. What language had scholars been using to translate the Bible?

   _____

3. For how long had playwrights been creating historical plays by the time Shakespeare began writing?

   _____

4. How was English spoken in the United Kingdom before the invention of the printing press?

   _____

5. By the 1900s, how long had Oxford University been offering courses in English and other subjects?

   _____

■ **COMMUNICATE**

D **WRITE** Use your answers to Exercise C to write a short letter to a friend summarizing the history of scholarly English. Use the past perfect progressive where appropriate.

   Up until the end of the Middle Ages, most scholars had been writing exclusively in Latin. They had used Latin to translate the Bible, for example, and other texts of a religious and historical nature.

▪ GRAMMAR IN CONTENT

A Reread the passage on page 64. Put a wavy line under all verbs in the future perfect progressive. Check your answers with a partner. If you need help, use the chart below.

Future Perfect Progressive

Affirmative Statements

Subject	Will Have Been	-ing Verb
I You He She We They	will have been	working on the thesis for a month.

Negative Statements

Subject	Will Not Have Been	-ing Verb
I You He She We They	will not have been (won't have been)	studying for the exams.

Yes/No Questions

Will	Subject	Have Been + -ing Verb	Short Affirmative Answers	Short Negative Answers
Will	you he she we they	have been attending all the classes?	Yes, I will have. Yes, he will have. Yes, she will have. Yes, we will have. Yes, they will have.	No, I will not have. No, he won't have. No, she will not have. No, we won't have. No, they will not have.

Wh- Questions

Question Word	Will	Subject	Have Been	-ing Verb
What How long	will	you the class	have been	doing all year? waiting by the time the teacher arrives?

Notes:
- The **future perfect progressive** describes an action that will be in progress at a certain point **in the future**.
- The action in the **future perfect progressive** may start sometime **in the future** or it may have **already started**. Compare:
  *I enrolled in City College last year. By this time next year, I **will have been studying** here for two full years.* (The action has already started.)
  *I'm going to enroll in City College next month. By this time next year, I **will have been studying** there for one full year.* (The action has not yet started.)
- Use the **future perfect** or the **future perfect progressive** with the **simple present** to show the relationships between two future events. The event that will happen first uses the **perfect**. The event that will happen second uses the **simple present** (*By the time the teacher **arrives**, we **will have been waiting** for almost an hour.*)

B Write sentences using the future perfect form of each verb. Follow the example.

1. attend   _I will have been attending this class for four months by the end of June._

2. come   _____

3. do   _____

4. make   _____

5. plan   _____

6. speak   _____

7. teach   _____

8. write   _____

C Look at the following pictures. Then answer the questions below, using the future perfect progressive.

1. Ivor is going to visit his uncle in Russia. He got to the airport on time for his 1:00 P.M. flight, but the plane is very late. How long will he have been waiting by 7:00 P.M.? _____

_____

2. Tae is studying for a test in Dr. Simpson's History of English class. He arrived at the library at 6:00 P.M., and it's almost 10:00 P.M., which is the closing time for the library. How long will he have been studying by the time the library closes? _____

_____

3. Dr. Simpson is working on her book. She started it in January of 2005. How long will she have been working on it by the end of this year? _____

_____

4. Stan started to work out at the gym on March 15. Since then, he hasn't missed a day. How long will he have been following his exercise program by the end of the year? _____

_____

D PAIR WORK With a partner, talk about your goals for the coming year. Tell what you will have achieved and how long you will have been doing it.

By the end of the year, **I will have been studying** English for about five years. I **will have been working** on my degree for two years.

I'm returning to my home country soon. By that time, I **will have been living** with my host family for about six months.

Connection   Putting It Together

GRAMMAR AND VOCABULARY Using the words in the box, write a paragraph using each of the three tenses you have learned in this lesson: *the present perfect progressive, the past perfect progressive,* and *the future perfect progressive.*

dialect	evolve	globalization	language	linguist	spread

PROJECT In small groups, create a small glossary of English slang and idioms.

1. Ask several English-speaking friends and classmates from other classes to explain a few idioms or examples of slang. Take notes on each expression and its meaning.

2. Organize your list in alphabetical order to make a glossary.

3. Share the glossary with your class, comparing and contrasting the terms you discovered with the terms that other groups discovered.

4. To practice using the expressions, write a short skit or dialog that features at least six idiomatic expressions, and then perform the skit for the class.

INTERNET On the Internet, search some aspect of English that interests you, such as its history, grammar, or the globalization of English. Take notes and orally summarize what you learned for your classmates.

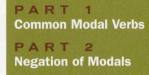
Health Sciences: Influenza and Other Infectious Diseases

■ CONTENT VOCABULARY

Look at the the picture. What do you think is wrong with the patient? What is the nurse doing?

The **flu** is caused by the **influenza virus**. It is usually very **contagious**. Symptoms of **infection** by the virus include a **fever** with a cough, tight chest, and shortness of breath. There is no **cure** for influenza. One way you can avoid it is by getting a **vaccination**.

Read the description below the picture. Look up any words you don't know. Write each word, its definition, and a sentence that illustrates its use in your vocabulary journal.

■ THINK ABOUT IT

In your writing journal, write about the last time you were sick. Did you have the flu? What were your symptoms?

■ GRAMMAR IN CONTENT

A Read and listen to the following article about the influenza virus and its symptoms.

CD1, TR23

Influenza: Warning Signs and Precautions

Everyone is home with a fever or back at school with a cough. It **must** be flu season. If it follows its normal pattern, the number of cases **should** peak between January and March. A flu shot **should** reduce the possibility of a serious infection. However, last year's flu shot **may not** be effective against this year's strain of the flu.

Researchers always make predictions about the upcoming flu season. This year's season **could** be mild, but many researchers think that it **may not** be. In fact, it **might be** much worse than usual. If it is, it **will** hit the very young and the elderly very hard. It **could** even affect many healthy young adults. In a bad year in the United States, the flu **will** kill up to 40,000 people. Flu patients who recover from the flu itself **may not** survive the pneumonia that often follows a serious case of the flu.

Flu symptoms **may** include fever, headache, and an aching body. You **may** also have a sore throat and a cough. Flu spreads from one person to another through coughing, but after the first few days, you **won't** be contagious. Your symptoms **will** last from one to two weeks. You **should** be able to return to work, although you **may** be weak and tired for several weeks.

The best thing you **can** do to avoid the flu is to get vaccinated. Your local clinic or health department **will** most likely provide vaccinations at the beginning of the flu season. The vaccination contains a trace of the virus. Once your body detects the virus, you **will** develop an immunity to it.

pneumonia: a serious viral or bacterial disease of the lungs

to recover: to get better

to survive: to live through something

to detect: to sense

an immunity: the ability to resist a particular disease

B Reread the passage. (Circle) all the modal verbs in the reading. Check your answers with a partner. If you need help, use the chart below.

Common Modal Verbs and Phrasal Modal Verbs	
Possibility and Probability	**Sample Sentences**
can could may might should	A few cases of the flu **can** easily turn into an epidemic. An exposure to the virus **could** place you at risk. You **may** develop symptoms overnight. The symptoms **might** last for two or more weeks. You **should** avoid getting the flu if you get a vaccine.
Necessity and Obligation	**Sample Sentences**
must have to have got to should be supposed to	All students **must** get a vaccination prior to registration. You **have to** pay a fee of ten dollars to get the vaccination. My doctor said I**'ve got to** take lots of vitamin C. You **should** rest for at least 8 hours after getting a vaccination. A vaccine **is supposed to** protect most people from infection.
Prediction and Intent	**Sample Sentences**
will be going to	The flu season **will** last until at least the end of May. The clinic **is going to** offer free vaccinations on Wednesday afternoon.
Suggestions and Polite Requests	**Sample Sentences**
may ought to should could would	**May** I help you? You **ought to** get a vaccination. You **should** wash your hands frequently during the flu season. **Could** you please call a doctor for me? **Would** you give me a ride to the hospital?

Notes:
- **Modals** are always followed by the **simple form of the verb** (not by an infinitive or a gerund).
  Correct: A flu-like virus **might be** the cause of his fever.
  Incorrect: A flu-like virus ~~might being~~ the cause of his fever.
- *Could, may, might, should, ought to,* and *must* can be used to make inferences and draw conclusions (*Everybody in the office had the flu last week, and now Carla has a fever and a sore throat. She* **must** *have the flu, too.*)
- Questions are formed by placing the **subject** between the **modal** and the **verb** (*Should I see a doctor?*)
- **Phrasal modals** *(be going to, have to, have got to, be supposed to)* behave differently from **true modals**. For example, they change form to show tense, person, and number.

C Choose the correct modal in parentheses to complete the dialog.

Dr. Weber: This year's flu _____could_____ (should/could) become very serious.
(1)

It _____ (might/will) even turn into a serious epidemic.
(2)

If it does, it _____ (could/must) kill thousands of people
(3)

across the country.

Mara: I thought a vaccine _____ (be supposed to/ought to)
(4)

protect people against influenza.

Dr. Weber: Well, an influenza virus is always changing, so it _____
(5)

(can/must) mutate, or change, into a new form of the virus.

Mara: How serious _____ (can/would) a flu epidemic get?
(6)

Dr. Weber: It can be quite serious. The flu epidemic of 1918, for example, killed

500,000 people. I think that _____ (must/should) be the
(7)

largest number of people killed by any contagious disease in U.S. history.

Sophia: But we'd be OK, right? Only young children and older adults are at risk.

Dr. Weber: Not really. The problem is that a deadly form _____ (has
(8)

got to/could) also kill many healthy young adults. But don't worry. If

you get your vaccination early in the season, you _____
(9)

(should/have got to) avoid getting the flu.

D Complete the paragraph using an appropriate modal in each blank.

We tend to think that vaccines _____are supposed to_____ give us infallible protection
(1)

against a virus. We believe that modern medicine _____ protect against
(2)

preventable diseases. This isn't always the case. A virus _____ easily
(3)

spread, especially in a small city or town. These infections don't usually spread to the

larger cities, however. Even when they are very contagious and _____
(4)

spread, they don't. For a virus to spread, people in the infected area _____
(5)

have contact with other population centers. The area also _____ have
(6)

a population of more than 250,000 people, or the virus quickly dies out. However, with

increased travel between population centers, this situation _____ change.
(7)

E **GROUP WORK** How does a contagious disease spread? What can people do to prevent the spread of a virus? Discuss your ideas using modals.

OK, we know that germs **can** spread when an infected person coughs, right? The germs are released into the air.

Yeah, and they **can** also stay on surfaces, like the handrail on a bus.

Right. That's why you **should** wash your hands after riding the bus, especially in the winter.

PART TWO	Negation of Modals

■ GRAMMAR IN CONTENT

A Look at the chart and study the negative modal forms.

Negation of Modals

Modal	Negative	Contraction
be going to	am not/is not/are not going to	isn't/aren't going to
be supposed to	am not/is not/are not supposed to	isn't/aren't supposed to
can	can not/cannot	can't
could	could not	couldn't
have to	do/does not have to	don't/doesn't have to
may	may not	mayn't (no longer used)
might	might not	mightn't (rarely used)
must	must not	mustn't
ought to	ought not to	oughtn't
should	should not	shouldn't
will	will not	won't
would	would not	wouldn't

Notes:

- Use *can't* and *couldn't* when you are 100% certain that something is untrue (*I have a cough, but I don't have a fever. So it **can't** be the flu.*)
- Use *must not* when you are less certain (*Jared seems tired. He **must not** be well.*)
- Use *shouldn't* when you can't make a prediction or statement with certainty (*The injection **shouldn't** hurt unless you're tense.*)
- Use *may not* and *might not* when you are uncertain (*The doctor **might not** be able to do anything for me.*)

B Mara has just gone to the university health center. She is describing her symptoms to the nurse. Complete the dialog, using the contracted negative form of the modal and verb in parentheses.

Mara: I have a fever and my body hurts, but it _____*can't be*_____ (can be) the
(1)

flu—it's summer.

Nurse: You're right. It _____ (should be) the flu, but occasionally we
(2)

come across cases in summer. Who have you been in contact with?

Mara: Mainly my roommate. She just got back from Australia. But she

_____ (could be) the source, could she?
(3)

Nurse: It's possible. It's winter in Australia now. Maybe she caught the flu there.

She _____ (may know) that she has the flu—and she
(4)

_____ (might have) a serious case.
(5)

Mara: She has been complaining that she aches all over. She _____
(6)

(may be) over it yet.

Nurse: Tell her to stay in bed and rest. She _____ (should be)
(7)

contagious any more.

Mara: I'll do that. Thanks. I guess that means I probably have the flu, too.

C Sophia is traveling to China this summer on a school trip. Listen to her discussion with Mara and then answer the questions in complete sentences.

CD1, TR24

1. How much does Sophia think the shots will cost?

_____

2. Is Sophia afraid to get the shot? Why not?

_____

3. What does Mara think about getting a flu shot before going to China?

_____

4. What does Sophia say about the availability of the vaccine?

_____

D There are six modal errors in Mara's e-mail to her friend Sandi. One has been corrected. Correct the five errors that remain.

Hey Sandi,

This summer I'm going to visit Lina in Morocco. Tomorrow I'm going to get my shots. Lina's told me that I shouldn't ~~to~~ need a flu shot, and I ought not getting a typhoid shot because I had one before my trip to Chengdu last year. A booster should being enough. The Internet also mentioned hepatitis, but Lina says it shouldn't a problem in Morocco, and the consulate said that diseases ought not be a problem if I stay in Morocco. I've concluded that big cities must to have fewer health problems than small towns in the countryside.

Talk to you later,
Mara

■ COMMUNICATE

E **PAIR WORK** Imagine that one of you is a nurse and that the other is a patient. The patient describes symptoms that he or she is having (see the list of symptoms below). The nurse draws conclusions and makes suggestions based on the symptoms. The nurse can ask further questions to exclude certain possibilities.

I've had a cough for three days. But I don't have a fever.

Well, then it **can't be** the flu. Do you feel tired?

Yes, I've been sleeping much more than usual.

Then it **could** just be a cold. But we **should** do some tests.

Symptoms

- achy joints
- cough
- dry mouth
- fatigue
- fever
- headache
- loss of appetite
- sore throat
- swollen glands

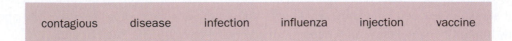

GRAMMAR AND VOCABULARY Using the words in the box, write a paragraph with at least three affirmative sentences and two negative sentences. Use modals and phrasal modals that you studied in this lesson.

contagious	disease	infection	influenza	injection	vaccine

PROJECT Working in small groups, find out about vaccination programs in your city and/or county.

1. Look in your local phone book or on the Internet for the phone numbers of a campus health clinic or hospital.

2. Call the clinic or visit their website to find out what vaccination programs they offer. Ask who the vaccinations are recommended for, how much they cost, and when they are offered.

3. Tell the class what you found out.

 INTERNET Search for information on the flu epidemics, such as the great influenza epidemic of 1918 in the U.S. Look for maps and timelines. Prepare a presentation for the class, explaining how the epidemic developed.

PART 1
Negative Statements

PART 2
Negative Statements with *Either* and *Neither*

Lesson 10

Mathematics: Game Theory

■ CONTENT VOCABULARY

Look at the picture and read the caption. What is meant by a "hypothetical problem"? Do you know any other games that involve hypothetical problems?

The Prisoner's Dilemma is a **hypothetical** problem about two people that are arrested and detained as suspects in a crime. It is based on the **mathematical calculations** of two mathematicians from the Rand Corporation who were studying game **theory** in 1950. Although the problem is more than 50 years old, the **implications** of The Prisoner's Dilemma are still discussed today.

Look up any words in the caption you don't know. Write each word, its definition, and a sentence that illustrates its use in your vocabulary journal.

■ THINK ABOUT IT

Sometimes we are faced with a dilemma that has several possible solutions. There are pros and cons to each side, and the "right" choice is not obvious. Write for five minutes about a difficult choice you have had to make.

■ GRAMMAR IN CONTENT

A Read and listen to the following article.

CD1, TR25

The Prisoner's Dilemma

In this game, you and a partner imagine that you have committed a serious crime and the police have arrested you. The police **didn't** find **any** evidence to convict you of the crime, but they found **some** evidence of a lesser crime. The police **haven't** interrogated **either** one of you yet, but they are planning to do so soon. You and your partner will have **no** opportunity to speak to each other before the interrogation. After the interrogation is over, you will **not** be able to change your statement. There will be **no** chance of making or withdrawing a confession.

You are faced with a problem that requires a rational solution. You **can't** let your emotions tell you what to do. Should you confess or should you remain silent? There is **no** right answer, and the problem **isn't** easy to solve because there are several possible courses of action.

Possibility 1: When you are interrogated, you **don't** confess to the crime and your partner **doesn't either.** In this case there **won't** be **any** evidence to convict you or your partner of the serious crime, so you will both go to prison for six months for the lesser crime.

Possibility 2: You confess to the serious crime, but your partner **doesn't.** In this case, you **won't** have to spend any time in prison because you will have helped the police. Your partner, however, will be sentenced to three years because of your evidence.

Possibility 3: You **don't** confess, but your partner does. You will be sentenced to three years because of your partner's evidence, and your partner will spend **no** time in prison.

Possibility 4: You both confess. A judge can convict you and sentence you both to three years in prison on the basis of your confession. But in exchange for your cooperation, the judge will be lenient. He **won't** sentence you to prison for the full term. Instead, you'll both be sentenced to two years.

---

to confess: to admit something, especially guilt for doing something bad

to convict: to find someone guilty of a crime in a court of law

evidence: words or objects that support the truth of something

to interrogate: to ask questions, often in a strong or aggressive way; questioning by the police

to sentence: to give a punishment, usually prison time

B **Reread the passage. Look at the negative constructions and study the chart below.**

Negative Statements with *Not*	Notes
I'm not guilty.	The negative *not* comes after the verb *to be* or the first auxiliary verb.
The judge **did not give** the defendants the maximum sentence. They **might not have been given** such a lenient sentence if they hadn't had such a good attorney.	*Not* comes between an **auxiliary verb** and a **main verb**. It comes after the first auxiliary verb if there are two or more auxiliaries.
The prisoner claims he **hasn't** committed a crime. He insists he **isn't** guilty.	*Not* can contract with the auxiliary verb or the verb *to be*.
He **doesn't** have **any** good excuses for his behavior.	If there is no auxiliary verb or the verb *to be,* add the correct form of *do.* (Use the same tense, person, and number as the main verb, and change the main verb to the base form.) *Any* is used to make negative statements with **count** and **noncount nouns**.
We **don't** have **much time** to make up our minds.	*Much* is used only with **noncount nouns**.
The prisoner **won't ever** be released from prison.	Use *ever* in questions and negative statements. You can use *never* in negative statements too, but only with verbs in the affirmative. **Correct:** *You'll never* know the answer. **Correct:** *You won't ever* know the answer. **Incorrect:** *You won't never* know the answer.

Negative Statements with *No*	Notes
The judge gave **no reason** for his decision.	*No* can be used to modify the **object** of a verb.
There is **no logical argument** in favor of a confession.	*No* can also be used to modify the subject of a sentence. The **main verb** must be in the affirmative.
No judge would agree to that.	*No* can be used to modify a **noun phrase**.

C **Fill in the blanks, using the negative form of the verbs in parentheses.**

The Prisoner's Dilemma was worked out by two Rand Corporation scientists

in 1950. At first _____*it was not*_____ (was) a dilemma story. It was a
(1)

mathematical problem. Later, another scientist articulated the problem in terms of a

dilemma, or story, so that it _____ (would be) so difficult to
(2)

explain to people who _____ (were) mathematicians. The story
(3)

_____ (is) about law and legal processes. It proposes a situation in
(4)

which there _____ (is going to be) an easy or obvious choice.
(5)

It _____ (does say) what to do or what
(6)

_____ (to do), but it nevertheless presents a challenge to basic
(7)

game theory. One of the fundamental questions in game theory is whether there is always

a rational move to make in any given game. Game theory assumes that the participants

_____ (are) irrational and that there is always a rational move to
(8)

make if the opponents' interests are in opposition.

D Complete the dialog, using the correct word in parentheses. Discuss your choices.

Lin: Have you _____ (ever/not ever) heard of game theory?
(1)

Charles: No. Why?

Lin: I'm taking some math classes this quarter, and one of them is game theory.

_____ (It's not/It's no) as easy as you might think.
(2)

Charles: That sounds interesting. I'm not taking _____ (some/any)
(3)

classes now, because I'm taking the semester off. Who do you have for game

theory?

Lin: His name is Jones. Have you _____ (ever/not ever) had him?
(4)

Charles: I've _____ (never/not ever) heard of him. Is he a good
(5)

instructor?

Lin: Yes, I really like how he teaches. He never gives us _____
(6)

(any/no) boring assignments. This week, for example, he asked us to design

our own game.

■ **COMMUNICATE**

E **GROUP WORK** Create a chart summarizing all of the possibilities in The Prisoner's
Dilemma. (Reread the passage on page 82 if necessary.) Draw your group's chart on the
board. Explain it to the class.

	Prisoner B Stays Silent	Prisoner B Confesses
Prisoner A Stays Silent	Each prisoner serves six months.	
Prisoner A Confesses		

■ **GRAMMAR IN CONTENT**

A Reread the passage on page 82. <u>Underline</u> a combined negative sentence. If you need help, use the chart below.

Negative Statements with *Either*	Negative Statements with *Neither*
The prisoner said, "I don't want to be released from prison, but I don't want to be executed, either."	The prisoner wanted **neither** freedom nor death.
The prisoner won't confess. His partner won't confess **either**.	The prisoner won't confess and **neither** will his partner.
A police officer cannot judge a suspect. He can't convict a suspect **either**.	A police officer can **neither** judge **nor** convict a suspect.
Erin doesn't think the suspect is guilty. Zora doesn't think he's guilty **either**.	**Erin:** I don't believe the suspect is guilty. **Zora:** Neither do I.

Notes:
- *Either* can be used to show a choice between two possibilities (*There are two pieces left. You can have either one.*)
- *Either* is used with *or* to state two possibilities or choices (*We can either stay or go.*)
- *Either* shows similarity or agreement between two negative statements. The verbs in both sentences are in the negative. *Either* comes at the end of the second sentence (*I'm not convinced and the jury isn't either.*)
- Like *either,* the negative *neither* also shows similarity or agreement between two negative statements. The verb in the first sentence is in the negative; the verb in the second sentence is in the simple (affirmative) form, with *neither* coming first, followed by the verb and then the subject (*I'm not convinced and neither is the jury.*)
- If two verbs in the same sentence are in the simple (affirmative) form, use *neither* before the first verb and *nor* before the second verb. *Neither* and *nor* can also be used with other parts of speech (*The answer is neither right nor wrong.*)
- *Neither* is combined with an **auxiliary** to show agreement with a previous statement (*Teri doesn't understand chess. Neither does Samuel.*)
- *Neither* can be used to refer back to two previously mentioned nouns (*Both players did their best, but neither scored a point.*) Here, *neither* refers to "both players."

B Fill in each blank with *either, neither,* or *nor,* as appropriate.

The game of chess is ___*neither*___ easy ___*nor*___ simple. The pieces are divided
                 (1)   **(2)**

into two matching sets. The players can use _____ color. A player can _____
                           (3)   **(4)**

move to an empty space or capture an opponent's piece. A pawn can move _____
                                                  (5)

backwards _____ sideways. After their first move, pawns cannot move more than
        (6)

one square at a time. _____ can the king. When the king can _____ advance
                   (7)   **(8)**

_____ retreat, he is in checkmate and the game is over.
  (9)

C **PAIR WORK** Play The Prisoner's Dilemma with a partner. Each person writes down his or her choice in secret. Both players then reveal their written answers to each other at the same time. Play 10 times. Keep track of how much time each person has to spend in prison. Report the results of your game to the class.

Connection | Putting It Together

GRAMMAR AND VOCABULARY Do you have a favorite game of chance or skill? Write the rules and directions for the game, using as many negative constructions as you can. Give any necessary background information, and then write a detailed set of instructions for playing the game. Share your work with classmates in a small group.

The Game of Mahjong

The game of Mahjong originated in China thousands of years ago, but these days it isn't just played in China. People around the world are crazy about it.

To play this fascinating game, you need a Mahjong board and tiles. The first player turns up two tiles. If the tiles match, the player keeps the tiles and takes another turn. If the tiles don't match, the player doesn't get to keep the tiles.

Play continues in this way until the players have matched all the tiles. The game stops if neither player can match any more tiles. The player with the most tiles is the winner.

So you see, you don't need to travel to China to play Mahjong. You don't even need to have a partner, nor do you really need a board. You can simply play by yourself on your home computer, if you have the right software.

 INTERNET Search an online encyclopedia for the subject "game theory." You can learn the basic theories that game designers use when creating games. Consulting these guidelines will help you in doing the project.

PROJECT In a group, design your own game. Decide on the following elements: What is the goal of the game? What are the rules? How does a player win, or how does the game end? Present your idea to the class, and play one or two rounds of the game with other groups.

A Complete the following dialog with the correct form/tense of the verb in parentheses, or choose from the words or phrases in parentheses.

Rachel: I _____ (cough) continuously for a couple
(1)

of weeks now. I _____ (not sleep), and I
(2)

_____ (not go) to work since Monday.
(3)

Nurse: For how long exactly _____ (have) you _____
(4)   (5)

(have) this cough?

Rachel: It _____ (begin) a few weeks ago at work. By
(6)

tomorrow evening _____ (cough) nonstop for
(7)

exactly three weeks. I _____ (not ever, have) a
(8)

cough like this before. My throat _____ (be) dry and
(9)

my ribs _____ (hurt) for the last few days.
(10)

Nurse: _____ (do) you _____ (have) any other
(11)   (12)

symptoms before the cough _____ (start)?
(13)

Rachel: Well, I _____ (not feel) very well for a couple of
(14)

days before the cough _____ (begin).
(15)

Nurse: _____ (do) you _____ (have) a fever during
(16)   (17)

the last three weeks?

Rachel: I _____ (not think) so.
(18)

Nurse: It could be an allergy. _____ (have) you
(19)

_____ (be) around any new or different plants
(20)

during the last few weeks?

Rachel: Now that you mention it, I _____
(21)

(receive) some beautiful flowers from a friend the day before I

_____ (start) coughing. That might be the cause.
(22)

B Select the modal or phrasal modal from the words in parentheses.

Louis: I went to the library to print out my paper, but it's closed.

Marv: It _____ (can't/isn't going to) be closed. Today's a
(1)

Thursday, and the library stays open until 10:00 on Thursdays.

Louis: Well, it is. They _____ (may/are going to) be having
(2)

a problem with power. I noticed that there were no lights on.

Marv: Or they _____ (might/should) have closed because of
(3)

a fire drill. It _____ (should/can) be open now.
(4)

Louis: Well, it isn't. So what _____ (should/would) I do?
(5)

Marv: Dr. Black _____ (is going to/might) accept the paper
(6)

late if you e-mail her and let her know what's happening.

C Fill in each blank with the correct negative form of the verbs *be, do, could,* or *have.* Use contractions whenever possible.

Mehmet: When I tried to register for the History of English class, there

_____ any room left, so I _____ get in.
(1) (2)

Arturo: I _____ either. My problem was that I _____
(3) (4)

remember to register in time.

Mehmet: Yeah, I _____ either. And I _____
(5) (6)

been able to register in three other classes I need to graduate. There

_____ an advisor in the English Department who could help
(7)

me. I _____ want to put off graduation, but I may have to.
(8)

LEARNER LOG Check (✔) *Yes* or *I Need More Practice.*

Lesson	I Can Use . . .	Yes	I Need More Practice
6	Present and Present Perfect, Past and Past Perfect, Future and Future Perfect		
7	Tense Sequencing in Discourse, Simple Present as Background Information		
8	Present Perfect Progressive, Past Perfect Progressive, Future Perfect Progressive		
9	Common Modal Verbs, Negation of Modals		
10	Negative Statements, Negative Statements with *Either* and *Neither*		

American Literature: Crime Novels

■ CONTENT VOCABULARY

Look at the picture. It shows the cover of a novel. What kind of novel is this? What would you expect it to be about?

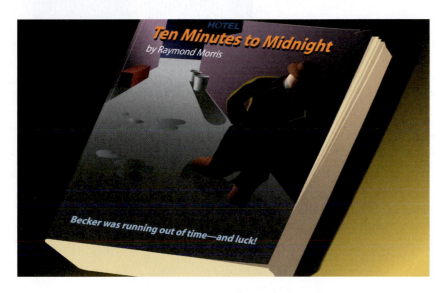

Ten Minutes to Midnight is a kind of **novel** that was very popular in the 1950s. Full of action and **suspense**, **crime novels** and **detective stories** such as these were part of a broader **genre** called "**pulp fiction**," which included romances, westerns, and other kinds of novels. They were called "pulp fiction" because they were printed on cheap paper that was made of wood pulp. For many years they weren't taken seriously, but pulp fiction and crime novels are studied today for their unique **literary** qualities.

Read the caption. Look up any words you don't know. Write each word, its definition, and a sentence that illustrates its use in your vocabulary journal.

■ THINK ABOUT IT

Discuss these questions with a partner: What are the elements of a good detective story? Why do people find crime novels so interesting? What kind of literature do you like to read? Summarize your discussion in your journal.

■ GRAMMAR IN CONTENT

A Read and listen to this excerpt from a crime novel.

CD1, TR26

Ten Minutes to Midnight

Chapter 2

Suddenly I felt something cold and hard in my back.

"Drop it!" he growled. "Come on, Becker, you heard me!"

I dropped my gun. It clattered onto the ground. The man behind me **kicked** it **away**, his gun still in my back.

"That's a good boy. Now **put** your hands **up** and **turn around**. Slowly. Don't make any sudden moves."

My eyes were getting accustomed to the dark and I could just **make out** the scarred and ugly face of Eugene Petrocelli, a well-known crime boss.

"Mr. Petrocelli!" I said pleasantly. "It's a little late, isn't it? Shouldn't you be home **pulling** the wings **off** flies?"

"**Shut up**, wise guy," Petrocelli snapped, "or I'll rearrange your face! **Check him out**, Lefty! See if he's got a gun."

One of Petrocelli's men **stepped out of** the shadows. He hesitated.

"Go on! **Hurry up!**" Petrocelli ordered.

Petrocelli's assistant **patted** me **down**. His breath smelled like hot air blowing over a garbage dump.

"Hey, Petrocelli!" I said. "I hate to **point** it **out**, but your assistant here needs a breath mint."

"Shut up and **sit down**!" Petrocelli ordered. Before I could comply, his assistant punched me in the stomach. I bent over and he gave me a karate chop on the back of the neck. I **went down** like a sack of potatoes, and the lights **went out**. When I **came to**, a tall, slender blond I had never seen before was standing over me. I started to **sit up**, but my head began to swim and I **lay down** again. "It's about time you **woke up**," she said.

to clatter: to make a loud, rattling sound	**lights went out:** became unconscious
to punch: to hit or strike, usually with a fist	**to come to:** to regain consciousness
a karate chop: a quick strike with the side of an open hand; used in martial arts	**it's about time you woke up:** you slept for a long time

B Reread the passage. <u>Underline</u> all the separable phrasal verbs. (Circle) all the particles. If you need help, use the chart below.

Separable Phrasal Verbs	
Paired Verb and Particle	**Separated Verb and Particle**
Becker could barely **make out** Petrocelli's face.	Becker could barely **make** it **out**.
The cops **patted down** the suspect.	The cops **patted** the suspect **down**.
I had to **point out** an unpleasant fact.	I had to **point** it **out**.

Notes:

- Phrasal verbs combine a verb and a particle. They can be transitive (followed by an object that receives the action) or intransitive (no object). If a noun or pronoun can come between the verb and particle, the verb is "separable." All separable phrasal verbs are transitive.
- When the **verb** and the **particle** are together, the emphasis is on the <u>direct object</u> that follows the phrasal verb. Compare: *Becker **turned on** <u>the lights</u>.* (The emphasis is on the lights, as opposed to some other machine or appliance, such as the TV.) *Becker **turned** <u>the lights</u> **on**.* (Here the emphasis is on the act of turning the lights on.)
- If the direct object is a pronoun, and the phrasal verb is separable, the particle must come after the pronoun (***Turn** them **on**, please.*) NOT: ~~Turn on them please.~~
- See the list of phrasal verbs in Appendix 1.

C **Fill in the blanks, using the correct form of one of the verbs from the box. Put particles after pronouns, as in the sample answer.**

find out	make up	beat up	take on	pass up	~~kick off~~	turn down

In early detective novels, the hero was almost always male. In many cases, he might have been a police officer at some point in his life. The department _____ *kicked* _____ (1) him _____ *off* _____ (2) the force, but we never _____ (3) why. Everyone tells stories about his past—they probably _____ (4) them _____ (5) because they are never accurate. Now he's a private eye. He has friends and enemies on both sides of the law—both sides _____ (6) him _____ (7) at least once in the novel or film, and he'll _____ (8) either side. Even when he is in danger, he continues to joke. He never _____ (9) the chance to make a clever remark. He is never at a loss for words. He seldom _____ (10) a job, especially if it involves a beautiful woman.

D Fill in the blanks, using the correct phrase in parentheses. Sometimes more than one choice may be correct.

The hero in a crime novel has many contradictions. All the female characters find him attractive, especially women in trouble. He never _passes up the chance_ (1) (passes up the chance/passes the chance up) to _____ (2) (help out them/help them out), but he is also a cynic. He distrusts everyone. He has a very unhealthy lifestyle, yet somehow he is quite physically fit and fearless. He will _____ (3) (take on five men/take five men on) at once if he has to, and _____ (4) (take out all of them/take all of them out). He is smart, yet he is vulnerable to a beautiful woman in trouble. When she wants to hire him, he should _____ (5) (turn her down/turn down her), but he never does. He seems to _____ (6) (turn his emotions off/turn off his emotions), but he never _____ (7) (shuts them down/shuts down them) completely. He feels deeply and is very loyal.

■ COMMUNICATE

E **PAIR WORK** How many phrasal verbs can you make with the verbs and particles listed below? Work with a partner, creating as many phrasal verbs as you can. Talk about the meaning of each phrasal verb you discover.

> **Verbs:** *back, burn, call, draw, fall, hand, mark, pass, pull, put, stand, take, turn*
> **Particles:** *after, around, away, back, behind, down, in, off, on, out, over, through, up*

PART TWO	Inseparable Phrasal Verbs

■ GRAMMAR IN CONTENT

A Reread the passage on page 90. Put a wavy line under all the inseparable phrasal verbs in the passage.

Inseparable Phrasal Verbs		
Verb + Particle	**Meaning**	**Sample Sentences**
call on	to ask a student a question	*The professor **called on** a reluctant student.*
come across	to find something by accident	*Becker **came across** an important clue.*
eat out	to eat in a restaurant	*Harold and his wife **ate out** every Friday night.*

Verb + Particle	Meaning	Sample Sentences
get over	to forget or heal from a painful memory	Charlotte never **got over** Martin's betrayal.
look into	to investigate	Maxwell **looked into** the suspect's alibi.
stand up	to rise on one's legs	The defendant slowly **stood up** on his shaky legs.

Verb + Particle + Preposition	Meaning	Sample Sentences
face up to	to acknowledge reality	It's time to **face up to** the facts.
find out about	to seek and then find information	Did you ever **find out about** the missing money?
get along with	to enjoy another person's company	They **got along with** each other very well.
watch out for	to be cautious	You'd better **watch out for** pickpockets on the train.

Notes:
- The phrasal verbs on the previous page are inseparable. That means the verb and particle always appear together. Some verbs—such as those in the second half of the chart—also have a preposition. Prepositions are never separated from the particle.
- Phrasal verbs are more common in conversation and creative writing than in academic writing. See Appendix 1 for a comparative list of phrasal verbs and their more formal, academic equivalents.

B Fill in the blanks, using a phrasal verb instead of the more formal, academic term in parentheses. See Appendix 1 for a list of phrasal verbs.

An important character in many crime novels is the *femme fatale,* or "deadly woman." She is usually very attractive and somewhat mysterious. There may be other female characters, but they don't ___*measure up to*___ (meet the
(1)
standards of) the *femme fatale.* The plot becomes more complicated as soon as she

_____ (appears). She _____ (gives the
(2)   (3)
impression of being) vulnerable, and the hero wants to _____
(4)
(protect) her. But the *femme fatale* isn't nearly as helpless as she appears. She is

dangerous and eventually _____ (retaliates against) the
(5)
hero. He finally _____ (becomes aware of) her tricks and
(6)
_____ (no longer believes in) her lies. But by the time he
(7)
_____ (acknowledges) the facts, it's too late. The hero knows
(8)
that he has to _____ (forget about) his deadly attraction and
(9)
_____ (make personal progress).
(10)

C **WRITE** Try your own hand at being a novelist. Write the first paragraph or two of a crime novel, using at least five inseparable phrasal verbs. When you are finished, read your work aloud to the class.

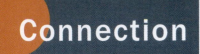

Connection | **Putting It Together**

GRAMMAR AND VOCABULARY Write a paragraph of at least five sentences with the following words, phrases, and phrasal verbs. Use two words or phrases in each sentence.

act like	check out	crack down	crime	detective
face up to	find out	hero	novel	suspense

PROJECT Work with a group of three or four students. Use the lists of phrasal verbs in your vocabulary notebook to make up a skit or dialog about a criminal investigation. Practice reading the skit and then perform it for your classmates.

 INTERNET Many detective novels and crime stories have been made into films. *Film noir* is a distinct genre of crime movies noted for its dark, shadowy look and other stylistic traits. You can learn more about this genre by doing an Internet search for "film noir." Take notes on one of the movies you find and summarize it for the class. You might even want to rent it.

PART 1
Core Determiners: Articles,
Demonstratives, Possessives,
and Quantifiers

PART 2
Pre-Determiners and
Post-Determiners

Lesson 12

Science: The Human Brain

■ CONTENT VOCABULARY

Look at the diagram of the human brain. What do you know about each part of the brain and its function?

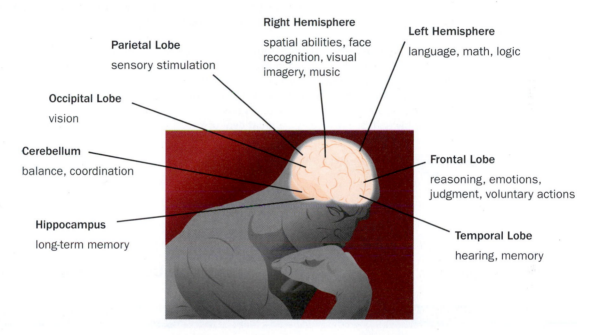

Right Hemisphere
spatial abilities, face recognition, visual imagery, music

Left Hemisphere
language, math, logic

Parietal Lobe
sensory stimulation

Occipital Lobe
vision

Cerebellum
balance, coordination

Hippocampus
long-term memory

Frontal Lobe
reasoning, emotions, judgment, voluntary actions

Temporal Lobe
hearing, memory

The **human brain** is divided into two halves, or **hemispheres**. Each hemisphere is **dominant** for certain behaviors. Other regions, or **lobes**, specialize in other functions.

Read the labels and the caption. Look up any words you don't know. Write each word, its definition, and a sentence that illustrates its use in your vocabulary journal.

■ THINK ABOUT IT

Do you know how the various parts of the brain interact? What happens if one of these regions is damaged in an accident? Discuss these ideas with a partner, and then summarize the discussion in your journal.

■ GRAMMAR IN CONTENT

A Read and listen to the following passage.

CD1, TR27

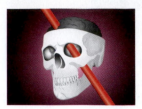

In 1848, **an** extraordinary event happened that changed **an** ordinary man's life forever. **The** man's name was Phineas Gage. He was **a** railroad construction supervisor. As **a** result of **an** accidental explosion, **a** 3'7" (1.09 meter) steel rod went straight through **his** head. **The** force of **the** explosion shot **the** rod through Gage's head and 30 feet beyond. Amazingly, **the** accident didn't kill Gage. There was **some** blood, but not **much** pain. In fact, he was conscious. **Several** men from **his** construction crew loaded Gage into a wagon and took him to **the** nearest town. However, **the** doctor was not there, so one of Gage's men had to ride to **the next** town to find help. While Gage was waiting, he told the story of **his** terrible ordeal to his landlord. When the doctor arrived, **many** people from **the** town gathered around the doctor and Gage to watch. Gage remained cheerful and alert while **the** doctor treated **his** injury.

After **some** time, Gage regained **enough** strength to return to work, but **the** accident had resulted in **an** unexpected side effect: **his** personality had changed in **two** ways. He had become indecisive and he had become rude. Because of **his** inability to make decisions, Gage was no longer able to supervise **other** men, and because of **his second** problem—**his** offensive behavior—**many of his** former workers became uncomfortable around him. **Such a** man had **no** place as a supervisor, and so he lost **his** job.

Although **this** story is terribly sad, science gained **a great deal of** knowledge about **the** brain from **Gage's** unfortunate experience.

offensive: rude

an injury: bodily damage

to treat: to give medical attention to

B Reread the passage. <u>Underline</u> all of the core determiners. Use the chart below for help.

Core Determiners: Articles, Demonstratives, Possessives, and Quantifiers		
Articles	**Sample Sentences**	**Notes**
a, an, the	**An** accident victim was admitted to **the** hospital. **A** surgeon gave **the** patient **an** anesthetic. **The** anesthetic took effect almost immediately. **The** body cannot function without **the** brain. It provides **the** automatic impulses that make **life** possible.	Use the indefinite articles *a* and *an* when referring to a noun for the first time. Use the definite article *the* to specify a person, place, or thing that has already been mentioned or is known to <u>both</u> the speaker and listener. Use *the* when referring to something unique and singular (*the sun, the moon, the North Pole,* etc.). Use *the* when referring to parts of the body (*the brain, the heart, the liver,* etc.). Don't use an article when referring to abstract nouns (*life, death, love,* etc.).

Demonstratives

| this, that, these, those | **Doctor:** Hand me **that** scalpel.
Nurse: **This** one?
Doctor: No, the other one. And give me **those** clamps, too.

Many experts believe that the brain continues to grow throughout life, and recent research supports **this** claim. One project studied adult learners. It showed that the brains of **these** learners continued to grow, even though they were in their 30s. | *This, that, these,* and *those* are demonstratives. They either modify nouns as determiners or function as pronouns that replace nouns. They show how close the noun is in relation to the speaker (*this/these* = close; *that/those* = far). Demonstrative determiners can refer to previously established topics. |

Possessives

| my, your, its, his, her, our, their | **My** son has a developmental disability. **His** brain was injured in an accident. As a result, **its** capacity to process language was impaired. | Possessive determiners modify nouns. They show possession (*her car*), source (*their ideas*), and relationships (*our teacher, his brother*). |

Quantifiers

| each, every, no, any, some, enough | **Some** people with head trauma can remember events from childhood but they have **no** short-term memory. And yet **some** cases are the exact opposite. You can't make **any** generalizations, because **every** case is different. | *Each, every, either,* and *neither* are used with count nouns.
These quantifiers can be used with plural count <u>and</u> noncount nouns: *no, any, some, enough.* |

C Fill in each blank with either a definite or indefinite article.

Phineas Gage was _____*a*_____ **(1)** railroad worker who had _____ **(2)** terrible accident. One day, as a result of _____ **(3)** explosion at work, _____ **(4)** steel rod flew through his head, leaving _____ **(5)** small hole. After some time, _____ **(6)** hole healed, but Gage's personality had changed as a result of _____ **(7)** accident, and _____ **(8)** railroad company dismissed him. Gage then went around _____ **(9)** country talking about his accident. He took _____ **(10)** rod with him and showed it whenever he made _____ **(11)** speech about his experience. In fact, when Gage died, _____ **(12)** rod was buried with him.

D Complete each pair of sentences below. Use *this* or *these* plus a noun or noun phrase to refer to the underscored noun phrase in the first sentence. Follow the example.

1. The brain is separated into <u>two halves</u>. _These two halves_ are each called hemispheres.

2. Skin contact creates <u>electrical signals</u> that flow through the nervous system.

   _____ are processed in the parietal lobe.

3. <u>The left hemisphere</u> controls the right side of the body. Nerves connect the right side

   of the body to _____.

4. The frontal lobe is the center of <u>abstract thought processes</u>.

   _____ include reasoning and judgment.

5. The temporal lobe and hippocampus have <u>related functions</u>.

   _____ include short- and long-term memory.

6. <u>The cerebellum</u> is an important region of the brain. _____

   coordinates balance and muscular control.

7. <u>The occipital lobe</u> processes visual stimuli. The ability to make sense of visual stimuli

   can be impaired as a result of damage to _____.

E Fill in the blanks, using either a possessive determiner or a quantifier.

1. _____Some_____ bodily functions are regulated unconsciously by the brain.

2. _____ region of the brain works in coordination with every other region.

3. My sister has a problem with _____ speech because of a birth defect.

4. Almost _____ computer scientist has been comparing the brain with computers.

5. _____ interest has been focused on comparing the brain with computers.

6. The human brain is connected to the spinal cord at _____ base.

■ COMMUNICATE

F **GROUP WORK** Play a memory game with your classmates. Take turns telling what you bought on an imaginary shopping trip. The first person tells about something that starts with the letter *A*. Each successive item must start with the next letter of the alphabet, and every player has to name all the previous items. Don't forget to use the determiners *a*, *an*, and *some*, as needed.

I went on a shopping trip and I bought **an** <u>apple</u>.

I went on a shopping trip and I bought **an** <u>apple</u> and **some** <u>bananas</u>.

■ **GRAMMAR IN CONTENT**

A Reread the passage on page 96. Put a <u>wavy line</u> under all of the pre- and post-determiners. Draw an arrow from the pre-determiner and the post-determiner to the core determiner.

Pre-Determiners	Core Determiners	Post-Determiners
Quantifiers: *all, both, half*	**Articles:** *a, an, the*	**Cardinal Numbers:** *one, two, three,* etc.
Multipliers: *double, twice, three times,* etc.	**Possessives:** *my, your, his, her, its, our, their*	**Ordinal Numbers:** *first, second, third,* etc.
Intensifiers: *such (a), what (a)*	**Demonstratives:** *this, that, these, those*	**General Ordinals:** *next, last, another,* etc.
	Quantifiers: *some, any, no, each, every, either, neither, enough*	**Quantifiers:** *many, much, few, a little, several, more, less, most, least*
		Phrasal Quantifiers: *a great deal of, a good number of,* etc.

Notes:

• Determiners are combined in the following sequence: **pre-determiner, core determiner, post-determiner.** It's not necessary, however, to use one of each in all instances. Various combinations are possible, as long as the basic sequence is followed; for example: ***double the*** expense (**pre, core**); ***these next two*** weeks (**core, post, post**); ***several more*** days (**post, post**).

• In general, there can only be one pre-determiner and one core determiner, although there can be more than one post-determiner. There usually aren't more than three determiners in a row.

B Look at each of the following phrases. Rewrite each phrase, putting each word in the appropriate column. Follow the example.

	Pre-Determiner	Core Determiner	Post-Determiner	Noun
1. the next two weeks	_____	*the*	*next two*	*weeks*
2. the last time	_____	_____	_____	_____
3. a great deal of money	_____	_____	_____	_____
4. each half of the brain	_____	_____	_____	_____
5. a few men	_____	_____	_____	_____
6. twice the power	_____	_____	_____	_____

C **GROUP WORK** With several classmates, create a sentence about the brain that includes a string of determiners. Separate the sentence into words and phrases, and write each word or phrase on a separate index card. Shuffle the cards. Then, exchange your set of cards with another group. See if you can unscramble their sentence, and check to see if they correctly unscrambled yours.

| Each | half of | the brain | is called | a hemisphere. |

Connection | Putting It Together

GRAMMAR AND VOCABULARY Write a paragraph about the brain. Include as many determiners as possible.

PROJECT Are you "right-brained" or "left-brained"? The terms *right brained* and *left brained* are popularly used to describe the dominance of one hemisphere over the other. "Right-brained" people are thought to be intuitive, creative, and emotional. "Left-brained" people are supposed to be analytical, logical, and less emotional. Talk with a classmate about your favorite subjects, your favorite activities, your preferences, and your abilities. Try to determine whether each of you is "right-brained" or "left-brained." Tell the class what you learned about each other.

 INTERNET Search the Internet for diagrams of the human brain. Use the diagrams as a model for drawing and labeling your own diagram. Include the lobes and regions you learned about in this lesson, as well as other parts, such as the corpus callosum and the pineal gland.

PART 1
Adjectives Preceding Nouns
PART 2
Predicative Adjectives
PART 3
Adjective Sequences

Lesson (13)

Fashion and Apparel: Design

■ CONTENT VOCABULARY

Look at the picture below. What kind of event is this? What is happening in the picture?

It's that time of year again. The **fashion industry** is ready to show us their latest **creations,** and the **critics** are preparing to deliver their judgments.

Here come the **models.** The first ones down the **runway** are **showcasing** the season's latest **designs.** Soheila is wearing a **sporty beige cotton** jacket with a **classic navy** skirt. Maggie is modeling a **sophisticated wool pants** suit. Pedro has on a **tan linen** jacket with **white** slacks. This evening's show promises to be an exciting event full of surprises.

Read the caption. Look up any words you don't know. Write each word, its definition, and a sentence that illustrates its use in your vocabulary journal.

■ THINK ABOUT IT

What style of clothing do you prefer? What do you wear for everyday occasions? What do you wear for formal occasions? In your writing journal, draw, label, and describe the clothing you prefer for casual situations. Then draw, label, and describe what you would wear for a formal event.

■ **GRAMMAR IN CONTENT**

A Read and listen to the following article.

CD1, TR28

Sweet River College News

Fashion Show Success

Sweet River College just held its annual fashion show in which **senior design** students display some of the outfits they designed in their advanced design class. The school always invites many **important fashion** critics and buyers from **famous American** fashion houses to the event. Buyers have discovered some **talented young** designers at this show. Critics enjoy the possibility of seeing **fresh new** creations.

This year was especially **exciting**. Three of the students worked as a **creative** team to design **classic** clothes for **professional** women. **Young professional** women want to look **attractive**, but they need to appear **serious**, too. They have a **large** budget for clothes, so this **smart light-weight** clothing is popular with buyers.

The team designed three outfits for the show. Sergio worked on a **long red wool** dress with a **soft round** collar. He complemented it with a **gold** necklace and **matching** earrings. Another team member, Rosaleen, designed a **navy linen** suit with a **full** skirt and a **short square** jacket with **large round silver** buttons. Rosaleen paired it with a **light silk turtleneck** blouse. The third member of the team, Jin, created a **simple white cotton** dress with **tiny green diagonal** stripes and a **wide green leather** belt.

Reviews of the show were very **positive**. One critic noted, "Sergio Vargas's **chic red** dress is **perfect** for the **busy professional** woman who wants to appear **elegant** without effort." Another critic described Rosaleen as a **gifted new** face on the **fashion** scene. All three students have received invitations for interviews with **established fashion** houses.

classic: timeless
an outfit: a set of clothing

smart: fashionable and neat
a turtleneck: a pullover or sweater with a high, close-fitting neck that rolls over in layers

B Reread the passage. (Circle) all the adjectives preceding nouns. Compare your answers with a partner. If you need help, use the chart below.

Adjectives Preceding Nouns	Notes
The **tall** model is wearing a cotton suit.	Adjectives come after determiners (*a, the, this, these,* etc.)—if there is one—and before nouns.

Participial Adjectives	
The industry's top designers put on an **exciting** show. The public was **excited,** and the critics were **interested** too.	The *-ing* and *-ed* forms of a verb are known as participles. Many participles can be used as adjectives. Participial adjectives can come before a noun and/or after the verb *be* or other linking verbs (see Part Two). Subjects "send" *-ing* adjectives and "receive" *-ed* and *-en* adjectives.

Nouns Modifying Nouns	
fashion house = a house of fashion **design** student = a student of design **jacket** collar = a collar of a jacket **business** partner = a partner in business	Some nouns may act like adjectives. When combined with another noun, they modify or describe the second noun.

Hyphenated Adjectives	
long-legged model = model with long legs **blue-eyed** boy = boy with blue eyes **8-meter-long** runway = runway that is 8 meters long **three-year-old** model = model that is three years old	Hyphenated adjectives can be used to shorten descriptive phrases, especially phrases that describe length, weight, distance, and age. Nouns that serve as modifiers usually appear in singular form. **Correct:** *three-year-old boy* **Incorrect:** ~~three years old boy~~

C Read the conversation and (circle) the correct form of the adjective in parentheses.

Ros: I thought the first part was awfully (bored, (boring)).
(1)

Mai: Oh, you're always (bored, boring).
(2)

Ros: I know, but this show was really (excited, exciting).
(3)

Mai: Yeah, I got pretty (excited, exciting) about it, too.
(4)

Ros: And Sonia's fashions usually aren't very good, but this year I was

(surprised, surprising). They were awesome.
(5)

Mai: Yeah, that was (surprised, surprising).
(6)

Ros: All in all it was a good show, but it ran too late. I was (tired, tiring) by the end.
(7)

Mai: I agree—it was a great show, but a (tired, tiring) evening.
(8)

D Rosaleen and Mai are looking at photos from last year's fashion show. Rephrase the words in parentheses to make a noun-noun combination. Follow the example.

Ros: Last year our show was held in _____a hotel ballroom_____ (the
       (1)

       ballroom of a hotel). The _____ (photographer
       (2)

       of fashion) missed the first few models. He was waiting outside until

       _____ (manager of the hotel) pointed out that the
       (3)

       _____ (show of fashions) was beginning.
       (4)

Mai: Did he miss any of the designs?

Ros: He missed two of my favorite _____ (designs by a
       (5)

       student). One was a long _____ (skirt with pleats) and
       (6)

       matching top. That was worn by the _____ (girl with
       (7)

       pink cheeks) over on the left.

Mai: Oh, yeah, the _____ (one with dark eyes).
       (8)

E Listen to the description of the Sweet River College fashion show. Then answer each of the questions using the adjectives in the box.

CD1, TR29

| long-legged | diagonal | striped | excited | gold |
| exciting | matching | wool | casual | young |

1. What does Naomi look like?

   _____Naomi is a long-legged model._____

2. What was Naomi wearing at the fashion show?

   _____

3. What did her accessories include?

   _____

4. What was Belle wearing?

   _____

5. Who particularly liked Belle's T-shirt?

   _____

6. How does the report describe the show?

   _____

F Rewrite the following sentences so that all the adjectives precede a noun. (Circle) the adjectives in your revised sentences. You may have to change the order of the sentences. Look ahead to the chart for adjective sequences on page 108 as needed.

1. Monica, who is wearing a dress, is waiting at the station for Sergio. Monica's dress is short and pink and cotton.

   Monica, who is wearing a (short pink cotton) *dress, is waiting for Sergio at the station.*

2. Sergio is wearing his business suit. The suit is wool and it's new.

   _____

3. They have bought a train ticket to New York. The train ticket cost fifty dollars.

   _____

4. The trip to New York is exhausting. The trip is twelve hours long.

   _____

5. They want to see some museums in New York. The buildings are famous all over the world.

   _____

G Read the questions below. Then listen to what Sergio's career counselor tells him about each of three local fashion designers. Take notes. Answer the questions in complete sentences.

CD1, TR30

1. What kinds of clothes is Sonia Wright famous for?

   _____

2. What kinds of clothes does Fifi LaRouche specialize in?

   _____

3. What kinds of clothes does Tommy Lester's organization produce?

   _____

4. What kinds of working conditions do the designers offer?

   _____

■ **COMMUNICATE**

H **PAIR WORK** Take turns describing what someone in your classroom is wearing. Guess who is being described.

I'm thinking of someone who is wearing a blue blouse and a gray skirt.

Hmm. That must be Tina, right?

■ GRAMMAR IN CONTENT

A Reread the passage on page 102. <u>Underline</u> all the predicative adjectives. Compare your answers with a partner. If you need help, use the chart below.

Predicative Adjectives		
Subject	**Linking Verb**	**Adjective**
The show	was	**heart-stopping.**
Coco Chanel	remained	**influential** throughout her career.
Her outfit	looks	**expensive.**
My favorite pair of jeans	is	**old** and **faded.**

Notes:
- Predicative adjectives describe the subject.
- When two or more **predicative adjectives** occur together, they are usually separated by a conjunction such as *and* or *but* (*The dress is* **simple**, *but* **elegant.**)
- Adjectives that begin with an *a*-prefix (such as *asleep, awake, alive, alone, aware*) appear only as predicative adjectives (never as adjectives preceding a noun).
  Correct: *The photographer who was* **asleep** *woke up at the end of the show.*
  Incorrect: ~~The asleep photographer woke up at the end of the show.~~
- Adjectives that are modified by a prepositional phrase appear only as predicative adjectives (never as adjectives preceding a noun); for example: *good at design; interested in jewelry; driven by ambition.*
- Certain adjectives (*same, main, principal, future, only*) can only precede a noun; they never occur as predicative adjectives.
  Correct: *the* **same** *show*   **Incorrect:** ~~the show was same~~

B Fill in each blank with an appropriate adjective from the list below.

comfortable	~~influential~~	elegant
prominent	popular	successful

The clothing designer Coco Chanel

Coco Chanel

Coco Chanel was a designer from France who became extremely

_____*influential*_____ throughout the fashion world. She opened a small shop
          (1)

in Paris in 1910, and soon became highly _____. The clothes she
                                              (2)

designed were _____ yet _____ to wear.
                  (3)   **(4)**

Although Chanel died in 1971, her fashion house is still _____ on (5)

the fashion scene. And her designs have remained _____ over the (6)

years.

C Use the most appropriate phrase from the list to fill in each blank. Be sure to use the correct form of the verb.

feel optimistic	turn red
be upset	~~seem bored~~
seem interested	be aglow
look sophisticated and chic	

After the show Maria began to worry because some of the critics

_____ *seemed bored* _____ while her clothes were being modeled. On the other hand,
(1)

Sergio _____ because the critics _____ in (2) (3)

his designs, and they complimented him after the show. He _____ (4)

with pride when they told him how much they liked his outfits, but Maria's face

_____ with embarrassment. Sergio noticed that Maria (5)

_____. He told her not to worry. One of the critics had told him that (6)

Maria's clothes _____. (7)

■ **COMMUNICATE**

D **WRITE** Write a paragraph describing how you look and what you're like. What impression do you think your appearance gives? What are you really like underneath the appearance? Use a variety of predicate adjectives in your description.

> I am tall and slim, so a lot of people think I'm athletic and self-confident. Actually, I am very shy, and I don't like sports very much either.

■ GRAMMAR IN CONTENT

A Reread the passage on page 102. Put a wavy line under all the adjectives of measurement, size, and length. Compare your answers with a partner. If you need help, use the chart below.

> **Adjective Sequences**
>
> Adjectives preceding a noun usually follow this sequence:
> 1. **quality:** beautiful, classic
> 2. **measurement, size, length:** large, long
> 3. **age:** old, modern
> 4. **shape:** round, triangular
> 5. **condition:** chipped, perfect
> 6. **color:** beige, navy
> 7. **origin, material:** French, cotton, wool
> 8. **noun modifier:** fashion (as in fashion show)
> Examples:
> the **beautiful long beige** coat (quality, length, color)
> a pair of **traditional navy wool** slacks (age, color, material)

B Fill in the blanks, putting the adjectives in parentheses in the correct order.

Sergio is visiting New York for a job interview with a major fashion house. He is

carrying a ___*heavy black leather*___ (leather/heavy/black) folder that is full of his
(1)

latest designs. The interview is in a _____ (brick/tall) building
(2)

close to his hotel, but it's on a _____ (dirty/long) street. The
(3)

_____ (cotton/trendy/blue) shirt that he bought especially for
(4)

the interview no longer looks so chic, but it's too late to change. He walks through a

_____ (modern/red) door, and the receptionist greets him warmly.
(5)

She shows him into the interview room. He shakes hands with the three interviewers,

sits down at a _____ (polished/large/wooden) table, and opens his
(6)

folder. The interview has begun.

C Look at the following pictures of models in a show. Write a description of each model in the space provided. Use complete sentences and a variety of adjectives in your description.

Naomi

_____

_____

_____

_____

_____

Kika

_____

_____

_____

_____

_____

Reiko

_____

_____

_____

_____

_____

Sasha

_____

_____

_____

_____

_____

D **GROUP WORK** Imagine that you are putting on a fashion show. In a group, take turns playing models and commentators. Have one student walk down a "runway" while a "commentator" describes what the "model" is wearing. Make sure you use a variety of adjectives.

Here comes our **first** model of the evening. Miguel is wearing a **nice** outfit with slacks and **dress** shoes.

And he's wearing a **brown striped** jacket.

His belt is also **brown**. He has **excellent** taste and a **good** eye for combining colors.

Connection | Putting It Together

GRAMMAR AND VOCABULARY Clothing designers begin by drawing a sketch of their creations. Try your own hand at designing an outfit. First, draw a sketch of it. Then, write a short paragraph describing it in detail, using as many adjectives as you can. When you are finished, share your work with a small group of classmates.

PROJECT Some popular T-shirts feature iconic images and simple slogans such as "Have a Nice Day." Compete with your classmates to see who can create the best T-shirt design and slogan.

1. Form teams. With your teammates, brainstorm a list of clever logos, and decide on the best one.

2. Design a logo or image to go with your design. Make sure your slogan has at least one adjective in it.

3. Create a "prototype" for your T-shirt. You can dye or stencil a white cotton T-shirt, or you can simply display your design on poster board.

 INTERNET Search for a famous designer on the Internet. Find some examples of his or her designs, and show them to your classmates. Explain what makes these designs interesting to you. Some designers you might search for include Michael Kors, Betsey Johnson, Ralph Lauren, or Kenzo.

PART 1
Subject and Object Pronouns and Possessive Forms

PART 2
Reflexive and Reciprocal Pronouns

PART 3
Indefinite Pronouns

Lesson (14)

Zoology: Animal Communication

■ CONTENT VOCABULARY

Look at the pictures. How do animals communicate with each other?

Gorillas and other **primates communicate** with **gestures** and **facial expressions**.

Birds attract **mates** by singing.

Ants and other insects touch one another and communicate through **scent**.

Honeybees use **bodily movements** to give each other directions. Their language is mostly a mystery to **zoologists**.

Read the caption below each picture. Look up any words you don't know. Write each word, its definition, and a sentence that illustrates its use in your vocabulary journal.

■ THINK ABOUT IT

Do you know the similarities and differences between human language and animal communication? Do you think people and animals can communicate with each other? Record your thoughts in your writing journal.

■ GRAMMAR IN CONTENT

CD1,TR31

A Read and listen to the following conversation. Diane and her friend Leon are talking to each other in the student union.

The Debate Over Animal Communication

Diane: Do **you** think animals are intelligent enough to communicate with **each other?**

Leon: Sure. I've heard that bees give directions, so to speak, by dancing. And when **they** come back to **their** hive, they know which one is **theirs.** That shows **they** are highly intelligent.

Diane: OK. But do **they** *talk* to **each other?** Do **they** communicate **their** desires and opinions?

Leon: Language may not serve the same function for **them** that **it** does for **us.** I rather doubt that bees gossip about **one another** or that **they** talk to **themselves** like **we** do.

Diane: What's the difference?

Leon: Animals don't have language, because **they** can't talk about abstract concepts like time. **They** only communicate about concrete things.

Diane: What do **you** mean?

Leon: For example, vervet monkeys have different calls to alert **each other** to the presence of a predator. One call might be for "snake." When one of **them** makes that sound, **everyone** looks down trying to find the snake. But **they** don't have a way to talk about snakes that aren't in the immediate environment. **They** can't say "**I** saw a really big snake yesterday over by the lake." **They** have a communication system, but **it** doesn't meet the criteria for being a language.

Diane: I'm not so sure about that. In **my** communication class **we** read about an African gray parrot named Alex. **He** can say where **he** wants to go and even what **he** wants to eat. **He**'s learned dozens of words. **It** makes **you** wonder what else animals are capable of learning.

a hive: a structure made by bees

to gossip: to talk informally about other people and local events

abstract concepts: general ideas that don't refer to specific things, people, or events

concrete: specific

a predator: an animal that kills other animals for food

immediate: nearby, close to

criteria: factors on which you judge or decide something

B Reread the passage on page 112. Look at the pronouns in boldface and then study the chart below.

Personal Pronouns			
Subject Pronoun	**Object Pronoun**	**Possessive Determiner**	**Possessive Pronoun**
I	me	my	mine
you	you	your	yours
he	him	his	his
she	her	her	hers
it	it	its	———
we	us	our	ours
they	them	their	theirs
who	whom	whose	whose

Notes:

• Pronouns take the place of nouns and noun phrases. They belong to one of three cases: subjective, objective, or possessive. The forms *my, your,* etc. are not pronouns. They are classified as determiners.

• A pronoun refers to a noun and all the words that modify it; for example:
  A: *I saw a cute little black and white dog.*
  B: *Bill saw a cute little black and white dog, it too.*

• *It* can refer to a clause or a whole topic; for example:
  Bill: *Dr. White said we were supposed to summarize our field notes for the class tomorrow.*
  Mac: *This is the first I've heard about it.*

• Usually pronouns refer back to a noun or noun phrase:

  Lawrence has been interested in communication since he was in high school.

• To vary sentence structure and emphasis, pronouns can also refer forward:

  Although he is just a parrot, Alex can say exactly what he wants to eat.

• *You, they,* and *we* can be used as "impersonal pronouns" when they refer to people in general or nobody in particular (*They say that pets communicate with their owners, but we really can't be sure. You either believe it or you don't.*)

• If the gender of an animal is known, use the gender specific pronoun. Otherwise, use *it*.
  (*My sister's dog likes carrots. He eats them all the time.*
  A chimpanzee glared at me through the bars. It looked angry.)

C Complete each sentence, using the correct determiner.

1. Wolves bare _____*their*_____ teeth to signify aggression.

2. A rattlesnake uses _____ rattle to warn potential predators.

3. In many bird species, a male sings to attract _____ mate.

4. Sometimes I talk to my cat. Do you ever talk to _____?

5. Most mammals raise their young and teach _____ how to survive.

6. A chimp _____ offspring is lost will call it back.

7. All the workers in a beehive serve the queen bee and bring _____ food.

D **Read the following transcript of a lecture. Fill in each blank using a correct personal pronoun. In some cases, more than one answer may be correct.**

Biologists tell _____us_____ that _____ (2) have lots of evidence that animals
(1)

communicate with each other. The question that _____ want answered is this:
(3)

Is there some way _____ can communicate with _____? A good
(4)   (5)

way to answer this question is by studying other primates. _____ have more
(6)

genes in common with _____ than any other animal. Some researchers have
(7)

tried teaching sign language to primates. _____ thought that _____
(8)   (9)

would be easier for _____ to learn than a spoken language because non-
(10)

human primates don't have the vocal equipment to make human speech sounds. One

popular primate subject is Koko, a female lowland gorilla. _____ has been
(11)

learning sign language from Dr. Penny Patterson since 1970. Dr. Patterson reports that

_____ and Koko communicate with each other every day. Koko talks about all
(12)

sorts of things. _____ even tells jokes and lies. _____ had a pet cat that
(13)   (14)

_____ named "All Ball." The cat was completely _____.
(15)   (16)

_____ took care of _____ and loved _____. Sadly,
(17)   (18)   (19)

_____ was hit by a car. Koko was terribly upset for months after _____
(20)   (21)

died. _____ says that certain things still remind _____ of All Ball
(22)   (23)

and make _____ sad. Dr. Patterson also taught sign language to another
(24)

gorilla, Michael. _____ didn't learn as quickly as Koko, but _____ did
(25)   (26)

learn. _____ and Koko talked to each other using sign language. Dr. Patterson
(27)

thinks _____ have language. The work with Koko is very controversial, but
(28)

_____ is also very interesting.
(29)

E Listen to the lecture. Then, (circle) the word that correctly completes each sentence.

1. Dr. Pepperberg is (male / female).

2. (Primates / Parrots) can make human speech sounds.

3. Alex is (male / female).

4. (Alex / The research team) can count objects and tell about their size, shape, and color.

5. (Dr. Pepperberg / Alex) speaks clearly.

F Listen to another short lecture, then write the answers to the questions in complete sentences. Use pronouns as appropriate.

1. How many different kinds of warning calls do vervet monkeys have?

_____

2. How do other monkeys respond to these calls?

_____

3. How does a crow's caw work?

_____

4. Why do bees "dance"?

_____

■ **COMMUNICATE**

G **GROUP WORK** Do you believe that animals can communicate with each other? Why or why not? Share your ideas, reasons, and examples in a group discussion. Use pronouns as appropriate.

Certain animals have an ability to communicate. **They** may not use words, but **they** can still communicate. Communication and language are the same thing.

I disagree. I think language is a complex system of signs. **It's** more complicated than communicating basic needs and wants.

Have you ever listened to birds? **Their** songs have a lot of variation and complexity. **It** could be a form of language **we** don't understand.

PART TWO	Reflexive and Reciprocal Pronouns

GRAMMAR IN CONTENT

A **Reread the passage on page 112. Look at the reflexive and reciprocal pronouns and then study the chart below.**

Reflexive Pronouns	
Subject	**Reflexive Pronoun**
Sometimes **I** talk to	**myself** when I'm alone.
Did **you** teach	**yourself** sign language?
The zookeeper let	**himself** into the animal's cage.
Koko looked at	**herself** in the mirror.
The tiger groomed	**itself** by the river.
We handled	**ourselves** well in a difficult situation.
You and Mariah should protect	**yourselves** with safety equipment.
Mr. Barrios and his team kept	**themselves** at a safe distance from the gorilla.

Reciprocal Pronouns	
Subject	**Reciprocal Pronoun**
The cubs played with	**each other** while their mother was gone.
The gorillas eyed	**one another** with curiosity.

Notes:

- Use reflexive pronouns when the subject and object are the same.
- Reflexive pronouns can also be used to show emphasis (*I have never thought about that* ***myself.***)
- Reflexives with or without *by* are used to mean "without help" (*The chimp opened the cage (by)* ***itself.***)
- To refer to two individuals, use *each other.* To refer to individuals within a group, use *one another.*

B **Write a paragraph that goes with each of the pictures.**

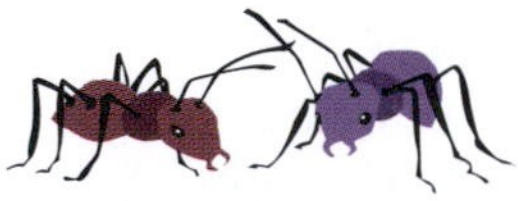

1. ______________________________

____

____

____

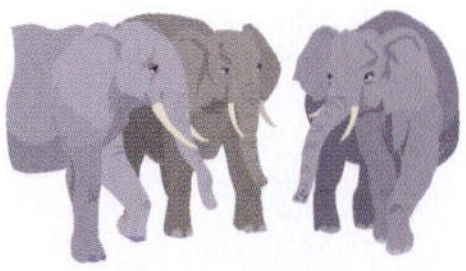

2. ______________________________

____

____

3. _____

_____

_____

_____

4. _____

_____

_____

_____

C The following passage is a joke. It plays on the word "ruff," which is an English word for the sound that dogs make. Use the correct reflexive or reciprocal pronoun to complete each sentence. Practice telling the joke with a partner.

A man walked into a coffeehouse with his dog on a leash. All of the guests were talking and laughing with ___*one another*___ . When they saw the man, they stopped talking. The
(1)

man seated _____ at a table with the dog next to him and began to look at the
(2)

menu. A server walked up, excused _____ , and said, "I'm sorry sir, but no dogs are
(3)

allowed." The dog and the man looked at _____ for a moment, and then the man
(4)

said, "I don't think you understand. This isn't just any dog. This is a talking dog. If he can

talk, can he stay?"

"I don't believe you," said the server. "But if he can really talk, he can stay."

"OK," said the man. He turned to the dog and said, "What's on top of a house?"

The dog promptly barked, "Roof! Roof!"

All the customers began looking at _____ and laughed. The server and the
(5)

man looked at _____ ."Very funny, mister. Get that dog out of here."
(6)

As the man and dog left, the man shook his head and said to the dog, "You should be

ashamed of _____ ."
(7)

The dog stopped and looked at the man. "Why? What's the matter?" asked the dog.

"Should I have said 'chimney'?"

D **PAIR WORK** Practice telling the joke you read in Exercise C. If you know another joke that involves the use of reciprocal or reflexive pronouns, tell that one too.

PART THREE	Indefinite Pronouns

■ GRAMMAR IN CONTENT

A Reread the passage on page 112. Work with a partner. Put a <u>double line</u> under all the indefinite pronouns. If you need help, use the chart below.

Indefinite Pronouns				
Affix	*Some-*	*Any-*	*No-*	*Every-*
-body	somebody	anybody	nobody	everybody
-one	someone	anyone	no one	everyone
-thing	something	anything	nothing	everything

Notes:
- Indefinite pronouns are written as single words, except for *no one*.
- Indefinite pronouns don't refer to a specific person or thing (*Nobody* really knows how bees communicate; The chimp communicated *something* by raising its eyebrows.)
- Indefinite pronouns are singular in agreement, although many are followed by the plural forms *they* and *their* in casual speech (*Everyone learns* how to say *their* first words by the time *they* are eighteen months old.)
- Indefinite pronouns with *any* are used in questions and negative statements. Pronouns with *some* and *any* can both be used in questions but with slightly different meanings (Does *anybody* here know how to use sign language?) The speaker has no expectation either way. (Does *somebody* here know how to use sign language?) The speaker thinks or hopes that somebody in the room knows sign language.

B Rewrite the sentences, changing them into negative, affirmative, or interrogative statements as indicated.

1. **Negative:** Nobody knows how birds learn to sing.

   Question: _____

2. **Question:** Did the professor say anything about the assignment?

   Negative: _____

3. **Affirmative:** Everybody agreed on the conclusions drawn by the research report.

   Negative: _____

4. **Affirmative:** The chimp seemed to say something with its hands.

   Question: _____

5. **Negative:** The counselor didn't leave a message on his door for anybody.

   Affirmative: _____

6. **Affirmative:** Zoologists have discovered something new about animal communication.

   Negative: _____

C Read the following passage and fill in each blank using the appropriate indefinite pronoun.

In cartoons, animals speak to each other, but _____*nobody*_____ seems surprised by
                                                    (1)

that. Judging by TV shows, _____ seems to accept the idea that animals can
                              (2)

communicate. During the 1960s, a very popular TV show was *Mr. Ed.* The star was Mr. Ed, a

talking horse. He had long and humorous conversations with his owner, Wilbur. He drove a

truck, played baseball, and involved Wilbur in funny situations. _____ other than
                                                                      (3)

Wilbur ever heard him speak, however. Whenever _____ else came around, Mr.
                                                   (4)

Ed would be silent. He wouldn't speak in front of _____ or to anyone other than
                                                      (5)

Wilbur. Before Mr. Ed, _____ loved Francis the talking mule. Francis was the
                          (6)

star of a series of movies during the 1950s. Francis was a military mule, and like Mr. Ed,

would only speak to his human friend, Peter. _____ else (other than the audience,
                                                (7)

of course) ever heard him speak. Based on the success of these and other, similar shows, it

appears that _____ loves the spectacle of a talking animal.
                (8)

■ **C O M M U N I C A T E**

D **WRITE** What kinds of ideas do people have about animal communication? Write a short
essay noting your observations. Make generalizations using *everybody* and *nobody.* Use
other indefinite pronouns as appropriate.

Animal Communication

    Nobody really believes that animals are as intelligent as people.
Everybody agrees that only humans are capable of language.

GRAMMAR AND VOCABULARY Make sentences of your own with the words and pronouns given. Follow the example.

1. gorillas/each other: _Gorillas communicate with each other using facial expressions._

2. zoologists/anything: _____

3. bees/one another: _____

4. tiger/itself: _____

5. researchers/something: _____

6. animals/their: _____

7. monkeys/themselves: _____

8. ant/its: _____

9. scientists/their: _____

10. pets/them: _____

PROJECT Several websites are dedicated to the research that has been done with Koko the gorilla. Visit http://www.koko.org/world/talk_aol.html or search for "Koko." Find and read a transcript of a conversation with Koko, and then have a debate with your classmates. Does Koko have the ability to communicate with sign language, or is she merely imitating signs? What other implications does this research raise? Share your ideas in a group discussion.

 INTERNET What other animal communication systems interest you? Find information on the Internet about another animal communication system. Report on what you find to your class or a small group.

PART 1
Using *This, That, These, Those,*
and *It* for Discourse Reference

PART 2
Discourse Reference with *Such*

Lesson 15

Sociolinguistics: Conversational Styles

■ CONTENT VOCABULARY

Look at the pictures and read the captions. Each person is essentially saying the same thing. How does their way of saying it change in each situation?

Want coffee?

Casual

Would you like some coffee?

Polite

May I offer you some coffee or tea while you wait?

Formal

Sociolinguistics is a **branch** of **linguistics**. It **analyzes** how **social norms** and expectations **influence** the use of language in different **contexts**. Incomplete sentences that include **slang** and **ungrammatical** expressions are commonly used in **casual** situations. This isn't acceptable in formal situations, however. Such situations require a **register** that is marked by complete sentences and signs of **courtesy**.

Read the text. Look up any words you don't know. Write each word, its definition, and a sentence that illustrates its use in your vocabulary journal.

■ THINK ABOUT IT

In your journal, write about the following questions: How do people show courtesy and respect when they speak in a formal situation? How does that way of talking differ from the way that friends or family members might talk to each other?

■ GRAMMAR IN CONTENT

A Read and listen to the following passage.

CD2,TR1

High Involvement and High Considerateness Styles

Sociolinguists have found that people can be very evasive when they engage in conversation. When people talk, they often have certain strategic goals in mind. All of **this** is usually unconscious, and for **that** reason, people may give "mixed messages." That is, they may not say exactly what they mean, and there are good reasons for **this**. If a listener perceives that the speaker has made a rude remark, the speaker can say she never intended **such a thing**, as long as her comment is sufficiently ambiguous. Similarly, if I ask you for a favor and you don't want to do **it**, neither of us will be embarrassed by your refusal if I give you a built-in "escape route." **Such** tactics have important social advantages. They allow conversational partners to establish rapport and to save face if necessary.

According to the linguist Deborah Tannen, individual conversational styles range between "high involvement" and "high considerateness." A high considerateness

Deborah Tannen

style is characterized by signs of distance and deference. A few **such** signs include a slower rate of speech and longer pauses. **This** gives listeners ample opportunities to participate in the conversation.

A high involvement style has a different goal and employs very different linguistic devices. **It** is distinguished by a faster rate of speech and more frequent overlap. Reactions to **this** type of delivery will vary, depending on the context. In some parts of the United States, **such** behavior is expected, especially in certain situations. **It** gives an impression of involvement—it shows that the speaker is interested in the topic and his or her conversational partner. However, **such** a conversational style can also be seen as intrusive. In general, high involvement is seen as being appropriate for casual situations, while high considerateness is more typical of a formal context.

evasive: tending to hide one's motives; refusing to commit to any particular point of view

strategic: with a certain goal in mind

ambiguous: having more than one possible interpretation or meaning

to range: to vary

rapport: intimacy; friendliness

to save face: to retain one's self-respect; to lessen embarrassment

a tactic: a way or method of doing something

B Reread the passage on page 122. Find all the instances of *this, that, these, those,* and *it*. Draw a line from these pronouns to the phrases or sentences that they refer to. If you need help, use the chart below.

Using *This, That, These, Those,* and *It* for Discourse Reference	
Sample Sentences	**Notes**
In a casual conversation, two Americans might interrupt each other or speak at the same time. **This** conversational style can be confusing for nonnative speakers, however. **It** can easily be mistaken for rudeness.	The demonstrative pronouns and determiners *this* and *that,* along with the pronoun *it,* can all refer to a statement or topic that has already been mentioned. *This* is usually used to refer to a previous statement made by the <u>same</u> speaker. It implies a strong connection between the present statement and the previous statement. To avoid repetition, *it* can be used in subsequent sentences. In the sample sentences, *this* and *it* refer to the first statement.
To be fluent in another language, you must be able to interpret nonverbal signs and body language as well as the spoken words. **That's** why it often takes many years to become truly bilingual.	*This* and *that* are often used interchangeably for discourse reference, with some exceptions (see below). In this example, it would also be acceptable to say: *This is why it often takes many years to become truly bilingual.*
Jay: I'm studying the sociolinguistics of language use at home—how parents and children talk to each other. Wilmar: **That's** interesting. I'd like to hear more about it.	Use *that* to refer to the totality of <u>another</u> person's statement. Here, Wilmar uses *that* in reference to Jay's entire statement. In this situation, it would be unnatural to say ~~This is interesting.~~ or ~~It's interesting.~~
Child: I don't want to share my toys! Mother: Don't say **that.** Be nice and share like everybody else.	Using *that* conveys distance between the speaker and the statement that is being referred to. ~~Don't say it.~~ and ~~Don't say this.~~ would not be appropriate responses to the child's statement, even though they are grammatically well-formed sentences.
Student: Our group wants to study language use in public schools. We were thinking about videotaping classrooms and then analyzing the interactions between teachers and students. Professor: **Those** are good ideas. Why don't you write **them** up in a proposal?	Use the **plural demonstratives** *these* and *those* to refer to multiple statements by another speaker.

Note:
Sometimes it is difficult to determine whether *this* or *that* should be selected in a particular situation; the speaker's or writer's attitude toward the referent at the moment determines which is used.

C Look at the short dialogs. Complete the sentences using *this, that,* or *it*. Follow the example.

1. **Caller:** I'd like to make a call to Vermont.

   Operator: I didn't quite hear _____*that*_____. Did you say Vermont or Belmont?

2. **Javier:** I've heard it's impossible to become truly bilingual.

   Sharon: Oh, really? I wouldn't agree with _____ claim.

3. **Professor:** Social language is very different from academic language.

   Student: How would you describe _____?

   Professor: _____ is a good question. Let's listen to a taped conversation

   and discuss _____ further.

4. **Waiter:** Our special tonight is fresh trout, and the soup of the day is gazpacho.

   Customer: Could you please repeat _____? I didn't hear what you said.

5. **Employer:** You've been late every day for the last month. _____ is

   turning into a problem.

   Employee: Don't worry. _____ won't happen again.

6. **Wife:** The kids are going to spend the weekend with their friends.

   Husband: Why didn't you tell me _____ before?

D Read the passage. On a separate piece of paper, write 5 sentences telling what the pronouns *it* and *that* refer to. Follow the example.

Japanese Communication Style

I went shopping in a department store one time when I was in Japan. **It** was an
(1)
interesting experience. At one point, I gave the clerk a credit card to pay for my purchase.
Unfortunately, my credit card wasn't valid in Japan, and the sales clerk couldn't process the
charges. After a moment he came back and said, "**It** is difficult." At first, I wasn't sure how
(2)
I should interpret **that.** I thought **it** might mean that I needed to wait. Finally, my friend
(3)   (4)
Hiroshi explained that the clerk was telling me in a very discreet way that my credit card
had been rejected. **It** made me realize that I had misunderstood what the clerk said.
(5)

1. <u>It</u> refers to the experience that the student had when he went shopping in Japan.

E **PAIR WORK** With a partner, talk about your favorite activity or a topic that interests you. Elaborate and comment using *that, those,* and *it,* as appropriate.

I love to cook dishes from around the world. **That's** why I'm taking a class in French cuisine.

That sounds interesting. Is **it** fun?

PART TWO	Discourse Reference with *Such*

■ GRAMMAR IN CONTENT

A Reread the passage on page 122. Find all the instances of *such* and study the chart below.

Discourse Reference with *Such*

Sample Sentences	Notes
Mr. Dubois said that nobody can be truly bilingual. **Such** a statement is ridiculous.	Like the determiners *this, that,* and *it,* the determiner *such* can serve as a discourse referent. It refers to the previous and all similar statements.
In her book, Deborah Tannen identifies several different conversational styles. She describes **one such** style as "high involvement."	*Such* is used to give examples and to show similarity. It may come after words like *one, many,* and *several.*
A: When I was a teenager, my parents and I often had very heated discussions about politics. B: I've never had **such a discussion/such discussions** with my parents.	*Such* can be used with singular and plural count nouns. Use *a* or *an* with singular count nouns. Do not use *a* or *an* with plural count nouns.
Harold and Mabel have been together for fifty years. **Such** devotion is rare these days.	When using *such* with noncount nouns, don't include *a* or *an.*
Did you see how the waiter acted? I've never seen **such** rudeness. Incorrect: ~~I've never seen *such kind* of rudeness.~~	Do not combine *such* with *kind, type,* or other similar modifiers.
My boss said that I had been given detailed instructions telling me what to do, but I never received **any such** information. My boss thinks I complained about him to the company president, but I've never made **any such** complaints.	In negative statements such as those shown, *any such* can be used with both count and noncount nouns.

B Look at the beginning of Karen's paper below. Complete her paragraph with the correct form of the phrase in parentheses and *such*. Remember, you will need to determine whether the noun is singular, plural, or noncount.

Karen Lang
Ling 320

High Involvement Style

Deborah Tannen discusses several characteristics of high

involvement style. One is the use of questions in rapid succession.

Such questions (questions) are intended to demonstrate interest in
        (1)

the speaker's topic. But _____ (demonstration)
                                        (2)

isn't always appreciated. For example, a high involvement listener

may produce four or five _____ (questions)
                                        (3)

during one turn by a speaker. In _____ (cases),
                                                (4)

the questioner often overlaps the speaker, that is, starts to speak

before the other speaker is finished. If the speaker is a person with

a high considerateness style, that speaker may be confused by

_____ (enthusiasm). And in fact,
        (5)

_____ (speaker) often stops talking in an
        (6)

attempt to stop the overlap. _____ (response)
                                                (7)

is very confusing to the high involvement questioner.

C Look at the following sentences from Marti's paper. The instructor wants her to elaborate on each idea with an additional sentence. Help Marti by using *such* and the correct noun form.

1. Many people dislike having to answer a series of rapid questions.

   They think such questions are rude.

2. These people prefer conversations in which everyone takes a turn.

   _____

3. One interviewee said she usually prefers to talk about a favorite sport or hobby.

   _____

4. Another said he felt uncomfortable in conversations about people's personal lives.

   _____

5. Most people agreed they didn't like people to shift the topic abruptly.

   _____

6. My roommate enjoys some silence in a conversation. It gives her time to think.

   _____

■ **COMMUNICATE**

D **WRITE** Think about the conversational style that you use when talking to friends. List at least three characteristics. Then elaborate on each characteristic using *such*. See the example below.

<u>My Conversational Style</u>

I like long, thoughtful conversations with lots of time to think and reflect. Some people are uncomfortable with lots of pauses in a conversation. They think that conversations with such gaps are awkward or even boring, but I don't. In fact, I find such conversations quite interesting. They give me time to think about what I want to say and what the other person has said.

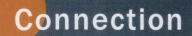

GRAMMAR AND VOCABULARY For this activity, find a DVD of a movie or TV show that has lots of dialog. Watch it with your classmates, paying attention to the conversational style. What kind of speech style do the characters use? Would you characterize their way of talking as casual, polite, or formal? What does this reveal about the characters? Pay attention to the use of silence as well. Are there gaps or pauses in the dialog? Such gaps in a conversation can serve many purposes. For example, silence can be used to create suspense, to show intimacy between characters, or to convey a character's disapproval, among other things. What purposes do such gaps serve in the film you have viewed?

PROJECT In a group, write a dialog between two or more characters. The dialog can be based on a video that you have viewed, or it can be an original creation. Use what you have learned about discourse reference and conversational styles. Read the dialog aloud for your classmates, and invite them to share what they noticed about the conversational style of your dialog.

 INTERNET Find a video site on the Internet (such as youtube.com or metacafe.com). Locate two short videos of people having a conversation or giving a speech. Be sure to choose subject matter that will not offend your classmates. Compare the two videos. What differences do you notice in the way the people speak? How do you explain the differences? Share your videos and thoughts with a classmate or group of classmates.

A Choose the correct phrasal verb from the box. On the blank space, combine the correct form of the verb with the object in parentheses. Place the object between the verb and the particle if possible.

check out	find out	make up	take on	turn down
~~come across~~	look into	pass up	take down	

I _____ *came across an ad* _____ (an ad) last week for an intern to work with animal
 (1)

language. It really looked interesting. I wanted to know about the researchers, so I

_____ (them) on the Internet. I _____ (the
 (2)   (3)

information) and gave it to my dad. He's going to _____ (the job) and
 (4)

let me know if it's really a good opportunity for me. According to the job description, the

researchers want to _____ (more about animal communication)—
 (5)

whether animals have a grammar and whether they _____ (new
 (6)

words).

It seems like such a great opportunity. If it's really as good as it sounds, I'd hate to

_____ (it). I already have a summer job, and I don't know if I want
 (7)

to _____ (any new work). But if I apply and they offer me the job, I
 (8)

won't _____ (it).
 (9)

B Complete the text below with the correct determiner or pronoun.

Some pet owners think that _____ *their* _____ animals can communicate with them.
 (1)

For instance, _____ brother Stan has _____ dog named Ralph who
 (2)   (3)

communicates with _____ by barking in different ways. Stan has told all
 (4)

_____ friends about Ralph, but when _____ visit _____
 (5)   (6)   (7)

house, _____ dog just sits there. Stan claims _____ dog is shy and will
 (8)   (9)

only communicate with _____.
 (10)

Then there's _____ friend Janet. _____ has _____ parrot
 (11)   (12)   (13)

named Artie who can tell when Janet is sad or happy. When _____ is sad, Artie
 (14)

sings to _____(15)_____; when _____(16)_____ is happy, they sing with _____(17)_____.

Unfortunately, Artie also swears. Janet says _____(18)_____ didn't know about

_____(19)_____ bad language when she got _____(20)_____.

Stories _____(21)_____ as _____(22)_____ show how strongly people *believe*

_____(23)_____ can communicate with _____(24)_____ pets. _____(25)_____ is

why _____(26)_____ is pointless to argue with _____(27)_____. You either believe

_____(28)_____ or you don't.

C **Circle** the correct word or phrase from the two choices in each set of parentheses.

The spring fashion show takes place every year in April. This year a

((young French) / French young) designer is coming out with a (daring new / new daring)
    (1)   (2)

line. No one knows what to expect, but we have heard that he'll be showing

(leather short / short leather) skirts and (silk long / long silk) blouses with
        (3)   (4)

(large round / round large) silver buttons and a (leather narrow / narrow leather) belt.
      (5)   (6)

The (belted / belt) blouses should be (really popular / popular really) with the crowd. The
     (7)   (8)

(enthusiastic design / design enthusiastic) students who are attending will be driving six
    (9)

hours the day before to see the show. The (six-hour / six-hours) drive is worth it because
                                    (10)

they will be present to see a(n) (young exciting / exciting young) designer enter the
                              (11)

(New York dazzling / dazzling New York) fashion world.
    (12)

LEARNER LOG Check (✔) Yes or *I Need More Practice*.

Lesson	I Can Use . . .	Yes	I Need More Practice
11	Separable Phrasal Verbs, Inseparable Phrasal Verbs		
12	Core Determiners, Pre-Determiners, and Post-Determiners		
13	Adjectives Preceding Nouns, Predicative Adjectives, and Adjective Sequences		
14	Subject and Object Pronouns and Possessive Forms; Reflexive and Reciprocal Pronouns; Indefinite Pronouns		
15	Using *This, That, These, Those,* and *It* for Discourse Reference; Discourse Reference with *Such*		

PART 1
Intensifiers with Adjectives,
Adverbs, and Nouns

PART 2
Too and *Enough* with Infinitive
Phrases

PART 3
So . . . that

Lesson 16

Political Science:
Elections

■ CONTENT VOCABULARY

Look at the pictures. They show two political ads. One is in favor of Al Farmer, a political candidate. The other one is opposed to him. What techniques do political ads such as these use to persuade voters?

Would you trust a crook? Then don't trust Al Farmer!

Al Farmer: A Leader for Our Times

Political ads can be very **influential**. Ads in favor of a particular **candidate** use positive images that inspire confidence. Sometimes candidates **sponsor** negative **campaigns** criticizing their **opponents**. Negative ads are often very effective, but they can also be quite **controversial**.

Read the text. Look up any words you don't know. Write each word, its definition, and a sentence that illustrates its use in your vocabulary journal.

■ THINK ABOUT IT

Have you ever seen a political advertisement? Describe the ad. Was it positive or negative? Did it influence your opinion? Why or why not? In your writing journal, describe the ad and its effect on you. If you haven't seen such an ad, write about one of the ads above.

PART ONE | Intensifiers with Adjectives, Adverbs, and Nouns

■ **GRAMMAR IN CONTENT**

A Read and listen to this lecture from a course in political science.

The Role of Media in Elections

The media play a **very** important role in elections. Some people believe that television in particular has **too** much influence on the results of elections. In fact, television can be **so** influential **that** it has a strong effect on the public's perception of the candidates. However, an advertisement on TV costs **too** much money for most candidates to buy without help. In fact, only a few candidates are wealthy **enough** to fund their own campaigns without the aid of volunteers and donations.

Even when they have **enough** money to ensure adequate exposure, politicians have to develop ads that are effective **enough** to make an impression on voters. Positive campaign commercials, those ads that praise the candidate himself and talk about his achievements, can be **quite** effective. However, negative commercials, which may attack the opposing candidate for being **too** soft on crime or **too** close to big business, are often even more effective. Some of these negative ads, such as U.S. President Lyndon B. Johnson's *Daisy Girl* commercial in 1964, are **so** effective **that** people remember them for years afterwards.

Negative ads are effective because the public is usually **very** interested in a candidate's character. Often the attacked candidate does not have **enough** time or money to respond effectively to attacks. It may be **very** difficult to refute negative claims successfully. Sometimes negative ads contain **too** many factual errors for the candidate to address without appearing defensive. In the meantime, volunteers in an attacked candidate's campaign often become **so** discouraged **that** they quit.

Daisy Girl **commercial:** an infamous television ad in the 1964 presidential campaign. See the Internet activity on page 140.

B Reread the passage. Find all the instances of *very, quite, too,* and *enough* and study the chart below.

Intensifiers with Adjectives, Adverbs, and Nouns	
Sample Sentences	**Notes**
We're **very** pleased with the results. There isn't **very** much time before the election. Susan Rodgers's campaign has **very** few volunteers.	*Very/Quite* • mean "extremely." • modify an adjective or adverb. *Very* can also modify much/little and many/few. • precede the adjective or adverb that they modify. • are often substituted in casual conversation with *awfully, really,* and *pretty* when modifying an adjective or adverb.
They won't hire her for the campaign because she's **too** young. Art is spending **too** much money on the campaign. There are **too** few volunteers at the voting booths. There are **too** many candidates running for office.	*Too* • modifies an adjective, adverb, much/little, and many/few. • precedes the adjective or adverb that it modifies. • means "excessively" (a negative sense is conveyed).
Jack Wright isn't trustworthy **enough** for my vote. Voters don't have **enough** confidence in Jack Wright.	*Enough* • modifies an adjective, adverb, or noun. • means "sufficient" or "sufficiently." • follows the adjective or adverb that it modifies. • usually precedes the noun that it modifies.

C Read the following passage and complete the text with *very/quite, enough,* or *too.*

Campaigns can be ____*quite*____ costly, so many politicians rely on positive news
(1)

coverage to get their pictures on TV. Politicians are _____ aware that every
(2)

time they make a speech, some short part of that speech may appear on the nightly news.

They know that their speech must be short _____ for a short media segment.
(3)

If the speech is _____ long or _____ substantial, a reporter may
(4)   (5)

find something to criticize in it. So the speech must have _____ substance,
(6)

but not _____ many facts or new ideas, and it should have language that is
(7)

catchy _____ for a TV news audience. The candidate must also look tough
(8)

_____, but not _____ aggressive. A politician without a positive image
(9)   (10)

in the media has _____ little chance of success.
(11)

D In the following dialog, Scott and Abdul are discussing the local election campaign. Read the dialog and fill in each blank with an adjective or noun from the box and an intensifier.

catchy	~~negative~~	time
hours	simple	wordy
interest	substance	

Scott: Have you seen the campaign ads against Susan Rodgers? They're

_____*awfully negative*_____.
(1)

Abdul: Yeah, I don't like them. I think they're _____.
(2)

Scott: But you know, even without the negative ads, I don't have

_____ in Rodgers's campaign. Her speeches don't
(3)

seem to have a point, and they're _____.
(4)

Abdul: I know what you mean. Actually, I like Al Farmer. His speeches are

_____. On the other hand, they seem to have
(5)

_____.
(6)

Scott: You know, the *Times* has reported some of Farmer's positions, and they're

pretty thought-provoking. I guess they weren't _____
(7)

for a 30-second TV news segment.

Abdul: That's interesting. Obviously, I'm spending _____
(8)

in front of the TV and not _____ reading the
(9)

newspaper.

■ **COMMUNICATE**

E **PAIR WORK** What qualities make a good leader? Discuss these qualities with your partner. Use *very, quite, too,* and *enough* as appropriate.

I think that a leader should be **very** self-confident.

Yes, but not **too** self-confident. Leaders who are **too** self-confident don't have **enough** humility.

A Reread the passage on page 132. Underline all the examples of *too* or *enough* followed by an infinitive. Check your answers with a partner's. If you need help, use the chart below.

Too and *Enough* with Infinitive Phrases	
Too + Adjective/Adverb + Infinitive Phrase	**Adjective + enough + Infinitive Phrase**
I'm **too** young to vote. That's **too** far for Scott to drive in one day.	You're old **enough** to understand the issues. He's distinctive **enough** for Abdul to recognize.
Too + much/little + Noncount Noun + Infinitive Phrase	**Enough + Noun Phrase + Infinitive Phrase**
That's **too** much money to pay for one ad. There is **too** little time for us to finish that assignment.	There is still **enough** time to organize discussion groups. The campaign has **enough** money for Scott to hire a secretary.
Too + many/few + Plural Noun + Infinitive Phrase	**Note**
We have **too** many bills to pay. There are **too** few pamphlets to hand out at the meeting tonight.	*For* can be used to show who the comment pertains to. Put the phrase with *for* before the infinitive phrase: *The election results will be too close **for the experts to predict.***

B Read the following text aloud with a partner. Take turns reading. Use *enough* or *too* to complete the text. Discuss your choices.

Scott is a candidate for president of the Sweet River College student body. He

is worried because he doesn't have _____ *enough* _____ money to pay for
(1)

campaign ads. Ads in the school newspaper are _____ expensive
(2)

for him to afford. He feels _____ discouraged to continue, but
(3)

it's _____ late for him to withdraw. One of Scott's volunteers,
(4)

Abdul, reminds Scott that he has _____ volunteers to organize
(5)

some open meetings with students to discuss the issues. These meetings are inexpensive

_____ for Scott to afford, and they can be very effective. Scott
(6)

realizes that although he has _____ little money for ads, there
(7)

is just _____ time for his volunteers to organize three evening
(8)

meetings on topics of interest to the students.

C In the conversation below, Abdul is talking to Scott about Scott's campaign. Complete the dialog, putting the words in parentheses in the correct order. Add infinitive *to* whenever appropriate. Follow the example.

Scott: We haven't had <u>*enough time to organize the open meeting tonight.*</u>
(1)
(enough/time/organize the open meeting tonight).

Abdul: It's _____ (enough/early/for us/set everything
(2)
up by 8:00). You're _____ (enough/
(3)
charismatic/attract a lot of students). I'm just concerned that there won't be

_____ (enough/chairs/seat all the interested
(4)
students).

Scott: Do you really think there will be _____ (too/many
(5)
students/fit in this room)?

Abdul: It's been _____ (too/busy around here/for us/
(6)
worry about that kind of problem). But the room is actually pretty big.

Scott: It is? Will I need a microphone? I may be _____
(7)
(too/far away/for students in the back/hear).

Abdul: We have one just in case, but your voice is _____
(8)
(enough/strong/for everyone/hear).

Scott: You seem to have a good grasp of this process. Are you interested in running
for office some day?

Abdul: I'm just a freshman now. I'm _____ (too/young/
(9)
run for office now), but I want to get _____
(10)
(enough/experience/run for office in my junior year).

D **PAIR WORK** What is something that you are too short to do? Too tall? Too lazy? Not energetic enough? Take turns talking about these limitations.

> This year I'm **too** busy to play on the tennis team.

> Oh, do you play tennis? I love to play, but I'm probably not good **enough** to make the team.

PART THREE   *So . . . that*

A Reread the passage on page 132. Put a wavy line under all the instances of *so . . . that*. Check your answers with a partner. If you need help, use the chart below.

So . . . that
***So* + Adjective/Adverb + *that* + Sentence**
Scott's voice is **so** strong **that** you can hear it in the back of the room.   The other candidate speaks **so** softly **that** you can barely hear her.
***So* + *much/little* + Noncount Noun + *that* + Sentence**
The student body president has **so** much influence **that** he or she can affect school policy.   There was **so** little time **that** the volunteers couldn't decorate the room with all of Scott's posters.
***So many/few* + Plural Noun + *that* + Sentence**
Scott had **so** many volunteers **that** he didn't need to pay anyone to help him.   There were **so** few seats **that** many of the volunteers had to stand.
Note: The conjunction **that** can be omitted in these constructions in informal contexts; for example: *His voice was so strong ~~that~~ you could hear it from the back of the room.*

B Take turns reading the passage below aloud with a partner using *so* and *that*. Watch your word order. Explain your choices to your partner. After you have both had a chance to read, write each answer in the space provided.

Scott is running for school council. His opponent's campaign has become

_____*so negative that*_____ (negative) Scott feels he needs to respond. But there is
        (1)

_____ (little time before the election) he isn't sure how to go
        (2)

about it. He is already _____ (overscheduled) he can't take on any
        (3)

more personal appearances. He has already given _____ (many
        (4)

speeches) his throat is sore, and he's shaken _____ (many hands)
        (5)

his right hand is in constant pain. Abdul has suggested using the Internet. He says that

designing a web page is _____ (simple) he can do it in an hour.
        (6)

A mass e-mailing can reach _____ (many students) Scott can give
        (7)

his response to the negative ads and then take a day to relax.

C Look at the pictures. Complete the sentence that goes with each picture, using *that*. Follow the example.

1. Scott is so tired from his campaign _____*that he fell asleep in class.*_____

2. The lecture hall was so crowded _____

_____

3. Mario has spoken for so long _____

_____

4. Cynthia has spent so much money on her campaign _____

_____

5. Abdul has missed so many classes _____

_____

6. Marisa became so nervous _____

_____

■ COMMUNICATE

D **WRITE** Have you ever been so tired you fell asleep, even though you needed to stay awake? Write a paragraph telling what happened. Use *so . . . that* at least once.

> When I moved from St. Louis to San Antonio, I had to drive for two days straight. I was fine for the first 12 hours, but then I started to get very sleepy. As I crossed the border into Texas, I was so tired that I fell asleep at the wheel. It was only for about a minute, but it scared me. I was so scared that I decided to pull over and sleep in my car.

GRAMMAR AND VOCABULARY Think about an election that is coming up, or an election that recently happened. Who were the candidates? What were their campaigns about? Write a paragraph describing the candidates and their promises. Use *very, quite, too, enough,* and *so . . . that.*

PROJECT Conduct an election for class president. In groups of four, create a campaign for one of your group members. What is the main theme of your campaign? What kinds of promises will you make to the voters? Brainstorm an ad campaign and present it to the class. Summarize your strategies and present your campaign's main slogan. Have the class discuss the benefits and disadvantages of the various campaign strategies.

 INTERNET In 1964, Lyndon B. Johnson ran for president of the United States. His campaign featured one of the most controversial ads in U.S. political history. You can learn more about it (and probably even find a sample video clip) by searching for "Daisy Girl campaign" on the Internet. Write a paragraph describing this ad's techniques and why you think it was so controversial.

Geography: Topography and Cartography

■ CONTENT VOCABULARY

Look at the pictures. Talk about these careers and occupations with your classmates.

Zhonghai is a **cartographer.** He creates maps for the U.S. government.

Professor Worley has taken her graduate students to a **geological site.** They are studying **land formations.**

Sarita is a **developer.** She is submitting a proposal for **urban development** to the **city planner.**

Geography is an **interdisciplinary** social science that studies the location and movement of physical and **natural phenomena** on the planet. **Geographers** come from a variety of **disciplines** such as **climatology, anthropology,** and **computer science.** They spend time in the field and at the computer. They study **landforms, politics, economics, history,** and **ecology.** They work in **city planning, disaster management, cartography, demographics,** and for governmental agencies, as well as private firms and nonprofit environmental groups.

Read the description below each picture and then read the paragraph. Look up any words or phrases you don't know. Write each word, its definition, and a sentence that illustrates its use in your vocabulary journal.

■ THINK ABOUT IT

Write about these questions in your journal: What do you know about geography? What would you like to know? Revisit your writing journal when you have finished this lesson and revise your entry, or make additional comments, depending on what you have learned.

■ GRAMMAR IN CONTENT

CD2,TR3

A Read and listen to the following conversation, which was recorded during an introductory geography course.

Geography 135

Professor Reidel: **There** are a number of things that geographers study, but basically they study the location of physical formations, whether natural or made by humans; why those things are there; and how and why they move. Let's start with "where things are," or location. We can locate everything on Earth with longitude and latitude. But **there** is more to location than this, isn't **there**? Who can tell me why? Shanti?

Shanti: Well, **there**'s altitude. **It** would make a difference. I mean, in the mountains, it's cold. In the desert, it's hot, relatively speaking, although the desert can be quite cold at night. **There**'s even a desert in Alaska.

Professor Reidel: Yes, **there**'s a part of Alaska that's near the Arctic, and it has a lot of desertlike features. Shanti makes a good point: Any extreme temperature makes survival for humans more difficult and sometimes impossible. What else? Andrew?

Andrew: I was thinking about water. **It**'s more important than food. If **it**'s 50 miles to the closest water source, people will live differently than if **it**'s 50 feet away.

Professor Reidel: How?

Andrew: Well, if **it**'s hot and dry and **there**'s no water in an area, crops won't grow and animals can't live there, so **there** won't be a source of food. People can't live where they can't get food, water, and shelter. They have to be able to get the things they need.

Professor Reidel: Excellent. That's another aspect of location: relative location. Geographers ask: Where is something located relative to things people want or need for survival? It's getting late, so I'll put the homework up on the board, and then you can go. Make sure you e-mail me your assignments before 11:00 P.M. See you next time.

altitude: distance above sea level

extreme: drastic or severe

latitude: imaginary lines of measurement of Earth's surface running parallel to the equator

longitude: imaginary lines of measurement of Earth's surface running from the North Pole to the South Pole

B Reread the dialog. Look at each instance of *it*. If *it* refers to something, draw a line with an arrow back to what it refers to. If *it* is non-referring, identify which of the four occasions below is being used. If you need help, use the chart below.

Non-Referring *It*	
Sample Sentences	**Notes**
Boston is three hours ahead of San Francisco. Right now **it's** 3:00 P.M. in Boston, which means that **it** is noon in San Francisco. **It's** more than three thousand miles from coast to coast. **It's** hot and dry in parts of Arizona all year long.	The non-referring *it* is used to tell time, measure distance, and describe the weather (including temperature) or general environment.
What**'s it** like in Chicago? When **does it start** to snow?	When you make a question with non-referring *it,* make sure that the verb comes before *it.* With verbs other than *be,* you need to also use the auxiliary verb *do* if there is no modal or other auxiliary verb.

C Look at the map of the Trans-Canada Highway and then provide the missing questions and answers, as appropriate. Follow the examples.

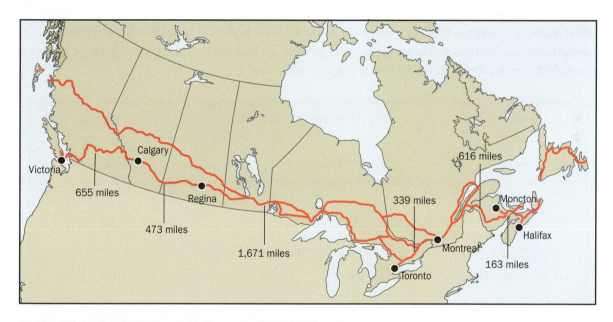

1. **Q:** How far is it from Calgary to Regina?

   A: _____ It's 473 miles. _____

2. **Q:** _____

   A: It's 339 miles.

3. **Q:** _____

   A: It's 1,671 miles.

4. **Q:** How far is it from Moncton to Montreal?

   A: _____

5. **Q:** _____

   A: It's 655 miles.

6. **Q:** How far is it from Halifax to Moncton?

   A: _____

CD2,TR4

D Listen to the weather report and then write about the weather in each city. Use the non-referring *it* in your descriptions. Follow the example.

1. **Los Angeles, CA:** _____ *It's 85 degrees and sunny.* _____

2. **San Diego, CA:** _____

3. **San Francisco, CA:** _____

4. **Eugene, OR:** _____

5. **Seattle, WA:** _____

■ **COMMUNICATE**

E **PAIR WORK** Imagine that you work for a TV station and that you are the station's meteorologist. With a partner, take turns giving an international weather report based on the chart below. Don't forget to use the non-referring *it*.

City	Forecast Conditions	High °F/°C
Cairo, Egypt	Partly cloudy	62°F, 16°C
Tokyo, Japan	Cloudy	43°F, 6°C
Rio de Janeiro, Brazil	Sunny	81°F, 27°C
Aspen, USA	Mostly sunny with cloudy periods and a chance of snow flurries	21°F, −6°C
Honolulu, USA	Sunny with morning rain	78°F, 26°C
London, UK	Rainy	48°F, 9°C

■ GRAMMAR IN CONTENT

A Reread the passage on page 142. Look at every instance of *there*. If it is referring *there*, draw a line and arrow back to what it refers to. If it is non-referring *there*, put a number above it to show which of the four uses it illustrates: 1) introducing; 2) claiming existence; 3) listing; 4) giving location. If you need help, use the chart below.

Non-Referring *There*	
Sample Sentences	**Notes**
There are several different routes we could take. Which do you prefer? (introduces a topic)	Non-referring *there* is used to: · introduce a topic. · claim or assert the existence of a person, place, or thing. · present a list. · give a location.
There's a device called a GPS system that gives directions while you drive. (asserts existence)	
There are four states along the border with Mexico: California, Arizona, New Mexico, and Texas. (presents a list)	
Two miles down the road **there's** a yucca tree by a gate. That's where you turn. (gives a location)	
There's hardly any more gas in the tank.	The non-referring *there* is combined with the appropriate form of the verb *be*. Use *is* and *was* for singular and noncount nouns. Use *are* and *were* for plural count nouns.
There's a gas station at the next exit.	
There are more stations farther down the road.	
There haven't been any signs for the last 30 miles.	
Judging by the steam coming out of the rocks, **there must be** thermal activity underground.	Use the appropriate tense or time frame of *be* with *there*. Modals and auxiliaries come after *there*.
Are there any sources of water nearby?	Invert *there* and *be* when forming questions. Put **modals** and **auxiliaries** before *there* if they are present.
Haven't there been land surveys in this area recently?	
Could there be another way of measuring the distance?	

Note:
In spoken English, *there's* is often used with plural as well as singular nouns.
Informal: There's some good places to stop on Highway 1.
Formal: There are some good places to collect soil samples near the highway.

B Read the lecture below. As you read, look at the boxed answer choices. Over each boxed example, write *S* if the term is appropriate in *spoken* English; *W* if it is appropriate in academic *written* English; and *N* if it is *not* appropriate in either context. In some cases, there is more than one possible answer. Follow the example.

S W   S   N

There is / There's / There are a new database management system, called GIS.
(1)

GIS stands for Geographic Information Systems. There is / There's / There are many
(2)

things that GIS can do, but one of the most interesting things is its ability to make

a sort of layered map instead of a static map. There is / There's / There are different
(3)

information about one specific location in each layer. Take our own campus as an example.

In our GIS lab, there is / there's / there are numerous databases with information
(4)

about the campus. There is / There's / There are one that gives all the road networks.
(5)

There is / There's / There are at least two that tell us the kinds of buildings that can be
(6)

built in different areas. There is / There's / There are others that give soil composition and
(7)

earthquake fault lines. There is / There's / There are a database that lists all the buildings
(8)

currently standing and their locations. There is / There's / There are another that lists the
(9)

locations of aesthetic landmarks such as the Duck Pond or the Rose Garden. Of course

there is / there's / there are databases that list underground structures, such as sewer and
(10)

water pipes and electrical and telephone cables, etc. So, a GIS map of campus is a layered

map that has different information about each layer of the campus.

Why is this important? Well, let's say you're the president of the university and you

want to build a new student union on campus. There is / There's / There are many things
(11)

you have to take into consideration. You might want the student union to be close to

roadways so that students can drive to it easily. You would also want it close to something

aesthetically pleasing, such as the Rose Garden or the Duck Pond. You can only build in

areas zoned for student recreation, and of course you don't want to build on an earthquake

fault line. You can't build where there is / there's / there are buildings already, and you want
(12)

to have access to water lines, power lines, and telephone and computer cables. You can ask

the GIS to find you a site on campus that meets all these requirements, and it will provide

you with all the relevant sites almost instantly.

C Write up Virginia's class notes from Geography 135 in complete sentences to make a paragraph. Use *there* + *be* in the first three and the last two sentences. Provide transitional sentences for variety, and make sure that *be* is conjugated correctly.

> ✓ maps throughout the history of humankind
> ✓ maps on animal skins and on cave walls
> ✓ always one basic problem for cartographers—
>   taking something that isn't flat (Earth)
>   and translating it into something that is
>   flat (cave wall, animal skins, papyrus, paper)
> ✓ Recently, much of that problem has been solved
>   by computers.
> ✓ still another problem: even computer-generated
>   maps are static
> ✓ new computer technology called GIS that solves
>   the problem of static maps

The History of Cartography

There have been maps throughout the history of humankind. In fact, we have even discovered some maps that date back to prehistory. There are maps on animal skins, for example, and maps on cave walls.

■ COMMUNICATE

D **PAIR WORK** With a partner, take turns asking and telling about your favorite natural place. Describe it in detail, telling your partner about its landforms and other natural resources. Remember to use the non-referring *there* in your questions as well as in your statements.

There's a beautiful place in southern Florida called the Everglades. It is full of wetlands and marshes.

Oh, **there are** lots of animals, and some of them are dangerous.

What kinds of animals **are there**?

I heard about that. Lately **there have been** lots of problems with the alligators. **There isn't enough water** for them, and so they wander into the residential areas.

GRAMMAR AND VOCABULARY Work with a partner. Do not look at your partner's paper.

1. Imagine you're a geography student. Sketch a scene from your most recent field trip so that your partner cannot see it. (Maybe you went to the desert, to the mountains, to the seashore, or any other place you can think of.) On the left-hand margin of your paper, write the date of the entry, the time of day, the distance to the closest big city, and the weather conditions. Note how far it is to water and transportation.
2. Describe the scene to your partner while he or she draws it. Begin by giving the information from your margin.
3. Trade places.
4. Compare the two drawings you both made for your scene and for your partner's. Are they the same? Were there differences? Why?

PROJECT Make a map of the area or region in which you live. Use a printed map or a map on the Internet as a model. Customize your map to show the landmarks, places, features, and resources that are important to you. Use symbols or icons to represent the different places on your map. When you are finished, show your map to your classmates, and explain why these places are important to you.

INTERNET With your classmates, decide on a place that you would all like to drive to if you had the time. Then form groups. With your group members, plan your route using a map-making tool or travel planner on the Internet (such as mapquest.com or maps.google.com). Share your itinerary with the class. Does it differ in any way from the route the other groups chose? Discuss the differences with the class.

PART 1
Coordinate Conjunctions

PART 2
Conjunctive Adverbs

PART 3
More Conjunctive Adverbs

Lesson 18

Paleontology: The Extinction of the Dinosaurs

■ CONTENT VOCABULARY

Look at the picture. What does it show?

Paleontologists study **fossils** to learn about the history of life on Earth. One event that paleontologists have studied closely is the **extinction** of **dinosaurs** about 65 million years ago. Although the reasons aren't known with certainty, it is **hypothesized** that dinosaurs became **extinct** due to a worldwide **cataclysmic** event. One such **theory** holds that a massive **meteor** crashed into Earth, causing **disastrous** changes in the world's **climate**.

Read the caption. Look up any words you don't know. Write each word, its definition, and a sentence that illustrates its use in your vocabulary journal.

■ THINK ABOUT IT

In your writing journal, write about the following questions: Have you heard any theories that explain the extinction of the dinosaurs? What are those theories? Which ones do you believe? What would you like to know about this period of Earth's history?

■ GRAMMAR IN CONTENT

CD2, TR5

A **Read and listen to the following passage.**

Extinction of the Dinosaurs

According to paleontologists, life on Earth changed dramatically 65 million years ago. This period, known as the end of the Cretaceous period, is of great interest for a number of reasons. For one thing, a number of species became extinct quite suddenly at the end of the Cretaceous period. These species did not become extinct because they were ill-adapted to their environments. **On the contrary**, many of them, such as the dinosaurs, had been well established for millions of years. **Nevertheless**, they all disappeared quite suddenly. **Furthermore**, there is evidence of dramatic changes in the Earth's environment at that time. The effects of these changes are well known, **but** it has been difficult for scientists to determine the causes.

The extinction of the dinosaurs is not the first mass extinction in the fossil record. **In fact**, there are records of other mass extinctions throughout the history of the Earth. This particular extinction is not unique, **yet** it is the most famous and possibly the most controversial. There are a number of hypotheses about what happened. The most popular one claims that an enormous meteor, about 6 miles in diameter, hit the Earth and created a gigantic crater more than 100 miles across. The impact of the meteor sprayed liquid rock and other particles into the atmosphere, **and** these particles blocked sunlight from the Earth's surface, **so** most plants and animals died. **In addition**, the crashing meteor started extremely hot fires that covered the Earth. If this "single meteor" hypothesis is true, it could explain why so many species disappeared; **on the other hand**, many species experienced heavy losses, **yet** they managed to survive. **Thus**, a number of questions still remain.

a crater: a large hole in the ground

contrary: different from; opposite

a hypothesis: a working theory

an impact: a shock, jolt, or collision

a meteor: a body of matter from outer space

a species: a grouping of very closely related living things

B Reread the passage. Find all the coordinate conjunctions in the reading and then study the chart below.

Coordinate Conjunctions	
Sample Sentences	**Notes**
A team of paleontologists has discovered dinosaur fossils in the Caribbean. The fossils indicate there was a worldwide disaster 65 million years ago. ↓ A team of paleontologists has discovered dinosaur fossils in the Caribbean, **and** the fossils indicate there was a worldwide disaster 65 million years ago. An asteroid hit the Earth **and** it caused a huge cloud of ash to rise into the sky.	Coordinate conjunctions can be used to connect two independent clauses (complete thoughts that can stand alone as sentences). Put a comma at the end of the first clause. Use **and** to combine two related clauses that the writer/speaker believes to be true. A comma is not used if there is no change of subject in the second clause and the subject is not repeated.
Some scientists accept the theory that the Earth was hit by a meteor, **but** many geologists suggest that dinosaurs became extinct due to a volcanic explosion.	Use **but** to contrast two ideas that are related yet different.
A meteor may burn up while it is traveling through the atmosphere, **or** it may hit the ground with the force of a bomb.	Use **or** to contrast two possibilities or choices.
The evidence is compelling, **yet** many scientists are still skeptical.	**Yet** means "at the same time," "however," or "in spite of." It is used to show that something is true even though it seems to contradict something else. It is often interchangeable with **but**.
The whole region became uninhabitable, **so** many animals were forced to migrate.	**So** means the same as "therefore," but is less formal. It is used to show the result of a particular action, event, or condition.

C Read the passage. Complete each sentence with *and*, *but*, *or*, *so*, or *yet*.

Paleontologists have used fossils to learn about the history of life on Earth, _____*but*_____ the picture **(1)** they have created is incomplete. Many biological remains have disintegrated, _____ there **(2)** are many gaps in the record. Another problem has to do with the way that fossils are dated. Radiocarbon analysis is relatively accurate _____ can only be used for artifacts that are **(3)** 500,000 years old or less. Another method called paleomagnetism can date artifacts that are millions of years old, _____ it has a wide margin of error. These kinds of issues **(4)** make the evidence inconclusive, _____ paleontologists are forced to draw certain **(5)** inferences. To establish a definitive chronology of life on Earth, we will need more fossil evidence, _____ our methods for dating materials will have to improve. **(6)**

D On a separate sheet of paper, combine each of the pairs of sentences into one. Use coordinate conjunctions, and change the order of the sentences if necessary. Make any other necessary changes in punctuation, pronoun use, and so on. Follow the example.

1. A meteor is a celestial body that enters a planet's atmosphere. An asteroid is a ball of ice and rock moving through space.

   A meteor is a celestial body that enters a planet's atmosphere, and an asteroid is a ball of ice and rock moving through space.

2. A meteor is visible as a streak of light. A meteor begins to burn as it enters a planet's atmosphere.

3. Very few meteors actually hit the Earth's surface. Meteors enter the Earth's atmosphere all the time.

4. There are many meteoric craters on the Earth. It takes a trained eye to find meteoric craters because they are so old.

5. The impact of a very large meteor can destroy everything in its vicinity. The impact of a very large meteor can also raise a large amount of dust.

6. Dinosaurs may have become extinct due to a meteoric impact. A massive volcanic explosion may have caused the extinction of the dinosaurs.

E Look at the passage below and complete the sentences by adding a clause that begins with *and*, *but*, *or*, *so*, or *yet*. There is more than one way of completing each sentence.

Dr. Feder spotted something on the shore of a lake, *but he couldn't determine what it was*.
(1)

He thought it might be a human bone, _____.
(2)

He wasn't certain, so he brought the bone to a lab for analysis,

_____. The lab claimed that the fossil was a
(3)

million years old, _____. Dr. Feder realized he had
(4)

made a major discovery, _____. The newspapers
(5)

called his discovery "Feder's Fossil," _____.
(6)

He always thought of it as the bone by the lake.

■ COMMUNICATE

F **WRITE** Read the following essay, and then write a short essay of one or two paragraphs expressing another possible reason for the extinction of the dinosaurs. Don't worry if you're not knowledgeable on the subject—just use your imagination, and use as many coordinate conjunctions in your essay as possible.

Dinosaur Extinction: A Down-to-Earth Explanation

Dinosaurs didn't become extinct because a meteor hit the Earth or because a volcano erupted. People are attracted to those ideas because they are so sensational, but the explanation, in my opinion, is a lot less glamorous. It could simply be that the dinosaurs failed to adapt to a changing environment. The world's climate has gone through many changes, so a species has to adapt if it's going to survive. As climate and vegetation patterns change, animals must move into new habitats and find new sources of food. Dinosaurs ruled the planet for eons, yet ultimately they weren't able to adapt. They gradually disappeared, leaving nothing behind but their footprints and bones.

You know, a major meteor could hit the Earth again, **and** it might even happen in our lifetime.

Well, that may be true, **but** I think we'll be ready for it.

PART TWO	Conjunctive Adverbs

■ GRAMMAR IN CONTENT

A Reread the passage on page 150. <u>Underline</u> the following conjunctive adverbs: *furthermore, in addition, nevertheless, thus.* Put parentheses around the sentences that they connect. If you need help, use the chart below.

Conjunctive Adverbs	
Sample Sentences	**Notes**
Tyrannosaurus rex was one of the largest dinosaurs; it was **also** one of the most fearsome.	Conjunctive adverbs can come at the beginning of a sentence or after the subject. If the two sentences are closely related, use a semicolon instead of a period to connect them. Use *also* to add new information in a second sentence about the same subject.
Satellites identified the outline of a large crater in Yucatan; **in addition/furthermore**, scientists found large amounts of iridium at the location.	The conjunctive adverbs *in addition* and *furthermore* add new information or connect a chain of thoughts. They are followed by a comma.
Paleontologists have discovered many dinosaur fossils in the last hundred years; **however**, these fossils only represent a small percentage of the different dinosaur species that have walked the Earth.	Use *however* to contrast ideas or information: *These fossils, however, only represent a small percentage of the different dinosaur species.*
Most fossils are incomplete; **nevertheless**, paleontologists are often able to make certain inferences about an animal's appearance and behavior on the basis of a partial skeleton.	The adverb *nevertheless* shows that the second sentence or statement is unexpected. It indicates that something is true *in spite of* something else also being true.
The single-meteor theory has been challenged, and many people have begun to question its validity; **therefore**, the question of what caused the extinction of the dinosaurs is again open to debate.	*Therefore* shows a result or inference; it is often used to introduce a summary or conclusion after several reasons or causes have been presented.
Dust from the meteor blocked the sun and cut off light from plants, causing them to die. **Thus,** plant-eating animals had little to eat, and they too died.	*Thus* is also used to introduce a result or inference.

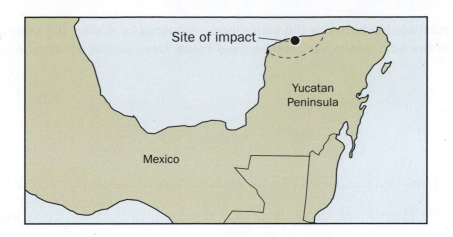

Site of impact

Yucatan
Peninsula

Mexico

CD2, TR6

B **Fill in each blank with a conjunctive adverb. To check your answers, listen to the recorded lecture.**

One of the problems with the claim that an enormous meteor hit the Earth 65 million years ago is the lack of physical evidence. Such a gigantic meteor would have left a huge crater where it struck the Earth. _____*Thus*_____, it should not be surprising that

(1)

scientists began an intense search for evidence of an enormous crater about 140 miles in diameter. They believed that the crater might be hard to locate because it would look very different after 65 million years; _____, the presence of a certain

(2)

metal, iridium, which is associated with meteors, could be used to narrow down promising locations. Eventually, a planetary scientist named Hildebrand identified a possible location in Yucatan, Mexico. Evidence that this was where the meteor had hit was supported by satellite maps, which indicated the outline of a circular crater 100 miles in diameter;

_____, physical evidence indicated that the crater had been formed about

(3)

65 million years ago.

Scientists were convinced. An enormous crater had been predicted, and one had been found; _____, the area had much more iridium than would normally occur

(4)

on Earth. _____, many scientists felt that they had strong support for the

(5)

claim that one meteor was responsible for the extinction of the dinosaurs, and the single-meteor hypothesis became widely accepted. There was certainly a lot of evidence in favor of it. _____, many scientists were not convinced.

(6)

C Show the relationship between the underlined sentences by adding the correct conjunctive adverb from the box. One adverb will be used twice. Use correct punctuation. Follow the example.

also	however	thus
nevertheless	~~in addition~~	therefore

Dr. Axel: I just don't understand why you don't accept the single-meteor hypothesis.

(1) There's iridium in the area of the crater in Yucatan. *In addition,* The crater is from the same time period as the extinction of the dinosaurs.

Dr. Ross: (2) I admit that there's an enormous meteor crater in Yucatan. I admit that there's iridium at the site. (3) In fact, I accept all your data. I don't accept the claim that the meteor wiped out the dinosaurs.

Dr. Axel: (4) Why not? An enormous meteor hit 65 million years ago, and the dinosaurs died right afterwards. We can conclude that the meteor was responsible for the death of the dinosaurs.

Dr. Ross: (5) The events certainly coincide. There's some evidence that the dinosaurs did not die out until 300,000 years after the meteor hit. (6) Other species that became extinct at the same time took several hundred thousand years to die off. The arguments for a single-meteor hypothesis haven't convinced me yet.

Dr. Axel: (7) I know the data you're talking about. I think they can be explained without abandoning the single-meteor hypothesis.

Dr. Ross: I guess we'll just have to agree to disagree until more information and evidence become available.

D GROUP WORK In class, conduct a formal debate on what caused the extinction of the dinosaurs. Remember to use conjunctive adverbs whenever appropriate.

1. Have different speakers choose a point of view that each wants to represent. During the debate, speakers take turns making their statements to the class. Each speaker should have no more than 3 minutes.
2. Then, the speakers can rebut, or argue against, the ideas and evidence presented by the other speakers. The rebuttals should last no more than 1 minute each.
3. After the rebuttals, speakers can engage in a freestyle debate, or discussion.

PART THREE	More Conjunctive Adverbs

A Reread the passage on page 150. Put a wavy line under all of the following conjunctive adverb phrases in the reading: *on the other hand, in fact, on the contrary.* Check your answers with a partner. If you need help, use the chart below.

More Conjunctive Adverbs	
Sample Sentences	**Notes**
The single-meteor hypothesis is very convincing; **on the other hand**, the multiple-impact hypothesis is also quite persuasive.	*On the other hand* and *at the same time* are used to show a contrast. They mean "viewed in another way."
Paul didn't miss class today; **in fact**, he arrived early.	*In fact* is used to reinforce a previous statement (often one which corrects a prior misunderstanding).
Dinosaurs were not killed by a meteor; **on the contrary**, extreme volcanic activity caused them to die.	*On the contrary* means "the opposite of what has been said is true."

Notes:
- In the above sentences, the two main clauses are separated by a semicolon, and the adverb is followed by a comma.
- These adverbial phrases can also appear at the beginning of a sentence. When they do, they should still be followed by a comma.

B Read the following conversation. Try to guess the missing conjunctive adverb phrases. Then listen to the recording and check your answers.

CD2,TR7

Mark: Dr. Ross was telling our class that she prefers a multiple-impact explanation to the single-meteor explanation for the disappearance of the dinosaurs.

Paul: What evidence did she give?

Mark: She said it's possible that dinosaurs died out in a week or a year, as the meteor hypothesis predicts; _____on the other hand_____ **(1)**, the evidence is not precise, and it may have taken them several thousand years to die. In addition, not all of the life forms that became extinct died at the same time; _____ **(2)**, some survived for hundreds of thousands of years after the impact of the Yucatan meteor. And, she told us that the Yucatan meteor was not the only huge meteor that fell around that time. _____ **(3)**, there are a number of other very large meteor craters throughout the world that are the same age as the Yucatan crater.

Paul: Wow, that sounds pretty convincing. _____ **(4)**, the single-meteor hypothesis had me convinced, too. What do you think?

Mark: I'm not sure which I accept. _____ **(5)**, I'll defend the multiple-impact explanation on any tests she gives.

C Put the following sentences in order so that they form two coherent paragraphs. Write a numeral next to each statement to show the correct order. Follow the example and discuss your order of sentences with a partner.

Paragraph I:

_____ Finally, one researcher, Gerta Keller, complained so strongly that she received a reasonable sample.

_____ In addition, when he did distribute the samples, they were very small.

_____ However, there were problems.

___1___ Several years ago, samples from the walls of the Yucatan meteor crater were obtained and given to a researcher, Jan Smit, to distribute to interested researchers.

_____ In fact, they were so small that they were useless for research.

_____ For a year, Smit did not distribute the samples.

Paragraph II:

_____ On the other hand, others still accept the single-meteor hypothesis.

_____ In addition, at about the same time, more meteor craters from the same time period were discovered.

_____ On the contrary, her analysis showed that many of the life forms that became extinct 65 million years ago survived for several hundred thousand years after the Yucatan meteor hit.

_____ Now many researchers have accepted Keller's analysis.

_____ Keller's analysis indicated that a single meteor did not eliminate the dinosaurs and other life forms.

___1___ With that sample, Keller was able to perform an in-depth analysis.

_____ Thus, Keller's analysis did not resolve the conflict.

■ **COMMUNICATE**

D **PAIR WORK** Think of a scientific theory you have heard and discuss it with a partner. Contrast your own thoughts and ideas with the ideas related to the theory. Use coordinate conjunctions, conjunctive adverbs, and adverbial phrases whenever possible.

There's a lot of evidence that modern humans first came from Africa. They migrated to Europe hundreds of thousands of years ago **and** replaced the Neanderthals.

On the other hand, some scientists think the Neanderthals never really died out. **In fact,** you might even say some of us are descendants of Neanderthals!

GRAMMAR AND VOCABULARY Summarize two of the theories presented in this lesson about the extinction of the dinosaurs. Compare the two theories, discussing their strengths and weaknesses. Use as many of the following words and phrases in your summary as possible:

Vocabulary	Conjunctions and Conjunctive Adverbs	
asteroid	also	on the contrary
climate	and	on the other hand
dinosaur	but	or
disaster	however	so
extinct	in addition	therefore
fossil	in fact	thus
hypothesize	nevertheless	yet
meteor		
theory		

PROJECT What's the difference between a paleontologist and a paleobotanist? Form groups, and find out about one of the special disciplines within paleontology. Take notes on its purposes, theories, methods, and discoveries. Tell the class what you found.

 INTERNET Did any dinosaurs live in your area millions of years ago? If so, which ones? Use the Internet to find them. Conduct a search using "dinosaur" and the name of your country, state, or region. Take notes on what you find, and then share your findings with the class.

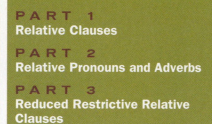

PART 1
Relative Clauses

PART 2
Relative Pronouns and Adverbs

PART 3
Reduced Restrictive Relative
Clauses

Lesson 19

Anthropology: Body Art and Tattooing

■ CONTENT VOCABULARY

Look at the pictures below. What do the pictures have in common? How are they different?

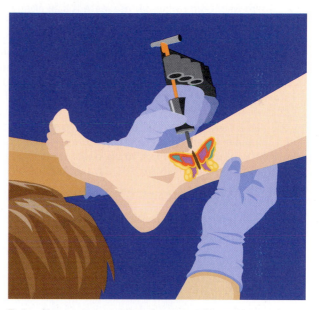

Tattooing is a form of **body decoration** that has been practiced for centuries in many cultures around the world. The Maori of New Zealand, for example, used **tattoos** as a sign of **social status** and **prestige**. Their tribal chiefs wore **distinctive** facial designs, which were applied through the use of a bone chisel.

Today, Europeans and Americans tend to get tattoos that have some personal **significance** or meaning. A butterfly, for example, might **symbolize** freedom. An electric tattoo machine, which **injects** ink into the skin through a needle, is the most common method of tattooing today.

Read the captions. Look up any words or phrases you don't know. Write each word, its definition, and a sentence that illustrates its use in your vocabulary journal.

■ THINK ABOUT IT

Do you or your friends have a tattoo? Where and what kind? What do they symbolize? What do your parents think about tattoos? Do you think tattoos will still be fashionable ten years from now? Why or why not? Take notes in your writing journal, and then share what you wrote with the class.

■ GRAMMAR IN CONTENT

A Read and listen to Dr. Sunna's lecture on tattooing.

CD2,TR8

Introduction to Tattooing

Tattoos have existed in different societies for hundreds and maybe thousands of years. In each of these societies, tattoos have had different purposes. There were tattoos **that** showed status, kinship, and occupation. Some showed special things about the wearer. Some were the result of religious ceremonies, and some were applied for medical purposes. There were even tattoos **that** experts think were supposed to make an individual more attractive to members of the opposite sex.

There was a time **when** tattoos were a sign of an impetuous youth. Tattoos were worn by men **who** were in the military, in jail, or in the sideshow of a circus. It was unusual for females to have tattoos, although there were some women with tattoos **who** were in sideshows. Today, both young and old have tattoos, but tattoos tend to be a rite of passage for the young **that** marks their transition to adulthood. One young woman **whose** tattoo covered most of her arm (such a tattoo is called a "sleeve") explained that all of her friends had tattoos. She said tattoos weren't just body art or even an act of rebellion. Each one has a special meaning **that** represents something of personal **significance**. A young man **whom** we had interviewed earlier agreed. He said there were very few parts of the world **where** young people didn't have tattoos. I'm not so sure this is true. In fact, many experts say that tattoos are going out of style.

impetuous: done quickly, often without thinking

a rebellion: a fight against the people in power

a sideshow: a performance or show that is not the main attraction at a fair or circus

status: one's position in society in terms of power and importance

B Reread the passage. <u>Underline</u> all of the relative clauses. If you need help, use the chart below. Check your answers with your partner's.

Relative Clauses	
Sample Sentences	**Notes**
In the U.S., people often get **tattoos that symbolize their membership in a particular group.** Many members of the armed forces, for example, have **tattoos that identify the place and years of their service.**	There are two kinds of relative clauses: those that identify (restrictive relative clauses) and those that just give additional information (nonrestrictive relative clauses). Both sample sentences on the left are restrictive.
In the South Pacific, islanders use tattooing instruments **that are made of wood and bone.**	**Restrictive relative clauses** specify *which* noun or *what kind* of noun the speaker is referring to.
The Tahitian word *tatau,* **which means "to tap,"** is believed to be the root of the English word *tattoo.* Tattoos are applied with an electric tattoo machine, **which injects ink through a very fine needle.**	**Nonrestrictive clauses** give additional information about the noun—they don't give information necessary to identify it. Commas are used to separate a nonrestrictive clause from the rest of the sentence.
Tattooing is a form of body decoration. It is practiced in many traditional cultures. ↓ Tattooing is a form of **body decoration that** is practiced in many traditional cultures. I know a tattoo artist. He has a studio near the Mission District. ↓ I know a **tattoo artist who** has a studio near the Mission District.	Relative clauses can be used to combine sentences that would otherwise be too short or choppy. The **relative pronoun** comes directly after the **noun** it modifies. (See Part Two of this Lesson for more information on relative pronouns. See Book 5, Lesson 18 for information on nonrestrictive relative clauses.)

C Read the notes below, which were taken during a lecture on the history of tattooing. Use them to write a paragraph, using as many relative clauses as possible. See the sample below for an example of how to get started.

Martin Hildebrandt
- Immigrated to U.S. from Germany
- Opened first tattoo studio in the U.S.
- Studio was in Washington, D.C.
- First of its kind

Civil War
- Tattoos rare during 1800s
- Hildebrandt tattooed soldiers during Civil War
- Some tattoos symbolized army experience
- Others had names of loved ones

Nora Hildebrandt
- Hildebrandt's daughter
- Known as "the tattooed lady"
- Had tattoos all over her body
- Very rare for women to have tattoos

The first tattoo parlor in the U.S. was established by an immigrant who was from Germany. His name was Martin Hildebrandt, and he opened a studio that was the first of its kind in Washington, D.C.

CD2,TR9

D Listen to the following conversations and then complete each sentence using the information that you heard. Use the relative pronouns *that*, *who*, and *which*. Follow the example.

1. Fatima had her hands decorated with henna, _____which is a natural dye._____

2. Dr. Sunna gave a lecture last week _____

3. Some people in the Amazon rain forest sharpen their teeth, _____

4. Jonelle got a new pair of earrings _____

5. Lyle Tuttle is a tattoo artist in San Francisco _____

E **PAIR WORK** Why do you think people get tattoos? Discuss your ideas with a partner using as many relative clauses as possible.

I think people **that** get tattoos just want attention.

Maybe. But a lot of people get tattoos **that** they never show. They must do it for some other reason.

PART TWO	Relative Pronouns and Adverbs

■ GRAMMAR IN CONTENT

A Find all the relative pronouns and relative adverbs in the reading on page 162, and then study the chart below.

Relative Pronouns and Adverbs	
Sample Sentences	**Notes**
In 1991, a pair of hikers in the Tyrolean Alps discovered the frozen, mummified body of a man **who** had died 5,200 years ago.	Relative pronouns and relative adverbs begin restrictive relative clauses. Relative pronouns include *who, that,* and *whom.* Relative adverbs include *where* and *when.* The relative pronoun *who* is used for human subjects in formal writing. *That* is commonly used in informal conversation to refer to people.
The man **whom** they found came to be known as the "Iceman." Scientists to **whom** we spoke didn't know the cause of the Iceman's death.	The relative pronoun *whom* replaces a human object noun in very formal writing. *Whom* is most frequently used after a preposition to refer to a human object noun in formal writing.
The Iceman, **whose** body had 57 tattoos, may have died in a battle.	*Whose* is a relative determiner and must be followed by a noun. It replaces a human possessive determiner (*his, her,* etc.).
Tattoos were probably common throughout Europe until the Christian era. From that time, they were banned in places **where** Christianity had a strong influence.	*Where* is a relative adverb. It replaces the phrase *in that place;* the name of a place, such as *Washington;* or *there.*
The art of tattooing was rediscovered in the 1700s **when** European explorers came back with tattoos they had gotten during their travels in the Pacific.	The relative adverb **when** replaces the phrase *at that time;* the actual time, such as *at 3 o'clock;* or *then.*

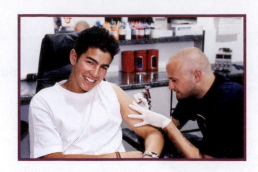

B Use the correct relative pronoun (*who, whom, that*), relative determiner (*whose*), or relative adverb (*where, when*) to fill in each blank.

There are a number of new products _____*that*_____ have come into the marketplace
(1)
as the result of the popularity of tattooing. This is an example of how the types of
changes _____ I mentioned before can move through a society. These products
(2)
are often advertised in magazines, _____ they will be seen by those people
(3)
_____ are most likely to buy them. There are products _____ are used
(4)   (5)
for every stage of the tattooing process. Some, such as numbing wax, can be used at a time
_____ the process is just beginning. "Body positioning tables" are used at a later
(6)
time, _____ the tattoo is being given. There are even products _____
(7)   (8)
can be used at a time _____ the first part of the process is completed. These
(9)
products promise to help heal a tattoo _____ an individual has just received and
(10)
keep it from fading. Judging by the number of advertisements I see in tattoo magazines,
there are many individuals for _____ these types of products fill a need. But
(11)
this should come as no surprise to any of us; we all know people _____ tattoos
(12)
were acquired with a great deal of pain and sometimes even infection, and _____
(13)
tattoos have faded over time.

C Read the following dialog with a partner and together fill in the empty blanks with a relative clause.

Linda: How could anyone ever get a tattoo?

Beto: What do you mean? We both know lots of people _who have tattoos_ .
(1)

Linda: Yeah, but I never would get one. Tattoos last forever.

Beto: That's the point. People want something _____
(2)

Linda: But tattoos change. They fade, and today's "one and only love" is tomorrow's bad memory.

Beto: Sometimes it's a good memory! You can look at your arm and remember the person _____
(3)

Linda: I don't want my husband remembering anyone special from his past.

Beto: Well, I guess you could have it removed by laser.

Linda: I know people _____
(4)
The process leaves an ugly scar.

Beto: I guess you're right. Plus, I suppose a tattoo _____
(5)
isn't going to look quite so fabulous when you're older.

■ **COMMUNICATE**

D **GROUP WORK** Discuss the cultural aspects of tattooing. Where is tattooing practiced, and what purpose does it serve?

Do you know any places **where** tattooing is still common?

Some people in Japan get tattoos **that** cover their body. It's a tradition **that** goes back hundreds of years.

Right. In general, the Pacific is a region **where** tattooing is widely practiced.

■ GRAMMAR IN CONTENT

A **PAIR WORK** Reread the passage on page 162. Work with a partner. Find any relative clauses that can be reduced and reduce them. Explain the steps to a partner. If you need help, use the chart below.

Reduced Restrictive Relative Clauses

Sample Sentences	Notes
A client ~~whom~~ the artist had tattooed wasn't satisfied with the results.	Relative pronouns that replace a direct object can be omitted in a restrictive relative clause. These kinds of omissions result in reduced relative clauses.
People ~~who are~~ planning to get a tattoo should think about it twice. Lyle uses the sketches ~~which are~~ hanging on the wall as models for his tattoos. An exhibit ~~that is~~ at the museum documents the history of tattooing.	The relative pronouns *that, which,* and *who,* when combined with a form of the verb *be,* can be omitted in a restrictive relative clause.
Tattooing has been prohibited during times ~~when~~ it was associated with illegal activity. Are there any places ~~where~~ tattooing is still prohibited?	*Where* and *when* can also be omitted from restrictive relative clauses when they follow very general nouns such as *time(s)* or *place(s)*.

B Look at the following paragraph from a student's essay. He has reduced adjective clauses in five places. Find those places and return the identifying clause to its full form. The first one has been done for you.

People *who are* currently doing original tattoo work usually begin with a color drawing done on paper. However, once the paper is placed on the body of the person getting the tattoo, individual muscles and skin can force the artist to change the design he or she originally envisioned. Even experienced tattooists encounter this problem. Because the final image is not on paper, but rather on an individual living, breathing, and constantly changing, expert tattooists take their time before they begin work that will last a lifetime and change as the person's body changes.

C **PAIR WORK** Read the following text and put the appropriate relative pronoun or adverb in the blank space. If the clause can be reduced, draw a line through the answer. Follow the example.

In many traditional societies, tattooing is or was a social practice _that_ **(1)** has great significance. Among the Maori of New Zealand, for example, tattooing was once a ritual _____ **(2)** signified the transition from youth to manhood. Men _____ **(3)** were preparing for a tattoo ceremony worked with the tattooist to create their own personal designs. The designs _____ **(4)** were applied reflected a young man's new status as an adult member of society. Such tattoos typically covered a man's face and, in effect, became his identity. Before colonization, at a time _____ **(5)** writing did not yet exist in native New Zealand, a man's uniquely personal design could even serve as a signature. In fact, there were some tribal chiefs _____ **(6)** drew their facial designs whenever Europeans asked them to sign legal documents. Tattooists refused to tattoo people _____ **(7)** weren't Maori for these reasons. The Maori rarely practice facial tattooing today, although some Maori may have traditional designs _____ **(8)** are tattooed on other parts of their body. Indeed, foreigners _____ **(9)** are looking for Maori designs can find them at almost any tattoo shop in any part of the world.

■ **COMMUNICATE**

D **PAIR WORK** In recent years, the use of permanent cosmetics has become more common. It is a form of cosmetic "tattooing" in which a specialist applies ink or pigmentation to the eyebrows, eyelids, lips, or other facial features. How is cosmetic tattooing similar to other forms of tattooing? How is it different? Discuss your ideas with a partner, using as many restrictive relative clauses and adverbial relative clauses as possible.

Eyebrows **that** are tattooed are just like any other tattoo, don't you think?

People **who** get them must not want to bother putting on makeup every day.

GRAMMAR AND VOCABULARY Write a short composition on body decoration in your community or home country. Is there a form of body decoration that is common where you come from? If tattooing or other forms of permanent decoration are rare, you might also write about everyday forms of body decoration, such as jewelry and cosmetics. After introducing your chosen topic, address the following questions:

1. Is this form of body decoration practiced by a particular group or class of people? Or is it practiced across a wide range of society?
2. What are the conditions in which it is displayed? Is it displayed publicly or only in private?
3. What is its social significance? In other words, what are the "messages" it conveys to the people who see it?
4. Are there any costs or unwanted consequences associated with it? How do people weigh these consequences against their desire to be decorated?

When writing your composition, remember to use restrictive and adverbial relative clauses as often as possible. Reduce the relative clauses whenever possible as well.

PROJECT Design your own anthropological research project related to the art of tattooing. Write a report that you can circulate among your classmates, or make an oral presentation during class. Use restrictive relative clauses and adverbial relative clauses. Here are some suggestions:

Conduct a survey. Create a list of questions that people can answer anonymously in writing, such as: *Do you have a tattoo? Where is the tattoo located? At what age did you get it? Are you male or female?* Analyze the results of your survey. What conclusions can you draw from this data?

Interview somebody who has a tattoo. Ask open-ended questions that are designed to help your classmates understand the reasons for and consequences of getting a tattoo.

Interview a tattoo artist. Look in your local directory for a tattoo shop in your area and ask a tattoo artist if you may interview him or her about the craft of tattooing.

Create a tattoo photo gallery. Take photos of tattoos on people that you know (or find photos on the Internet) and use the photos to create an exhibit in your classroom.

 INTERNET With a partner or in small groups, use the Internet to learn about other forms of body decoration around the world. Try using the following search terms:

- African scarification
- Balinese tooth filing
- Body painting
- Chinese foot binding
- Henna tattooing (Mehndi)
- Lip plates
- Long-neck women of Chiang Mai

When you are finished, share the information you found with the other groups in your class.

Life Sciences: Genetics and Cell Biology

■ CONTENT VOCABULARY

Look at the diagrams and read the captions. As you read, think about the following question: How can the study of genetics help patients with serious diseases and injuries?

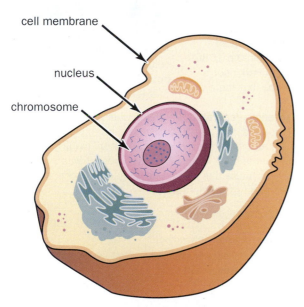

cell membrane

nucleus

chromosome

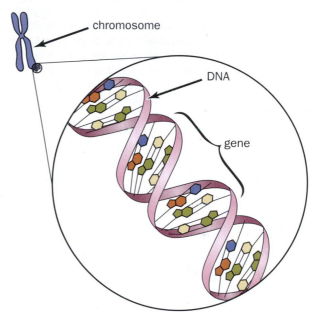

chromosome

DNA

gene

A **cell** is the smallest unit of any living thing. All cells have a **membrane** and a **nucleus**. Inside the nucleus are **chromosomes**, which are long strands of **DNA**. Each strand of DNA contains the code for a **physical trait** or some other **characteristic**. Scientists think that DNA may even contain the code for certain diseases, such as **cancer**.

The code for a certain trait is called a **gene**. How could we use our knowledge of **genetics** to help cure diseases? First we have to know how to read the genetic code for these diseases. Then we have to be able to **reprogram** the cells with that code. Scientists have already made great progress in answering these questions, but there is still a lot of work to do.

Read the captions under the diagrams. Look up any words you don't know. Write each word, its definition, and a sentence that illustrates its use in your vocabulary journal.

■ THINK ABOUT IT

In a group, discuss the following questions: What diseases are (or might be) caused by genetics? What kinds of treatments are available for people diagnosed with these illnesses? When you have finished, summarize the discussion in your writing journal.

■ **GRAMMAR IN CONTENT**

CD2, TR10

A Read and listen to this passage about stem cells and genetics.

Stem Cells and Genetics

Stem cells are special kinds of cells that are found in human embryos. They are unique because they haven't **yet** become specialized; that is, they haven't developed into the cells that form bones, muscles, skin, and so on. **Before** the embryo is fully developed, these stem cells will develop into more than 200 different kinds of specialized cells.

Geneticists believe that the study of stem cells can help patients heal from terminal diseases and serious injuries. In a laboratory, stem cells can be programmed to replace tissue, for example. Scientists can also use the cells to learn about diseases and **then** apply that knowledge to develop new drugs.

Science has **already** made some progress in these areas. Researchers have been interested in stem cells **for** a long time, but interest has increased dramatically **since** the development of sophisticated gene technology in the 1980s. **Until then,** there was little hope for people who were diagnosed with Parkinson's disease or other degenerative diseases. **Now** there is renewed hope, but there are **still** many questions to be answered.

When scientists began to conduct stem cell research, their research generated a considerable amount of controversy, because most stem cells were obtained from embryos. It is **now** possible to create stem cells, however, by injecting skin cells with four different genes. These genes reprogram the skin cells into "blank slates," which can **then** turn into any of the 220 cell types of the human body. **Before** this discovery, it was necessary to destroy an embryo to obtain the stem cells. In the near future this should no longer be necessary and scientists will have unlimited access to stem cells for research and experimentation.

Advancements in stem cell technology could help patients replace tissue that is lost after surgery.

an embryo: an early stage of growth before birth

geneticists: scientists that study genes

degenerative: progressively worse

a controversy: a public disagreement, usually involving strong opinions about an important topic

B **Reread the passage. Look at the time words and then study the chart below.**

Review: Time Words and Phrases	
Sample Sentences	**Notes**
Scientists **first** isolated stem cells in 1998. They have **already** used stem cells to develop a number of life-saving drugs.	Time words tell *when*. Most time words can be used with any tense. They are usually inserted before the main verb and after the first auxiliary if there are any. Important time words include *first, next, then, after, later, finally, before, since, for, still, already, yet, now*.
Scientists had **already** hypothesized the existence of cells **before** they actually discovered them using microscopes.	Time words and phrases are very useful in clarifying the order of events.
Dr. Rivera has been doing this type of research **for** ten years. He has been studying stem cells **since** he came to the university. He and his team are **still** trying to find a cure for cancer.	Time words and phrases can also show how long. *Since* and *for* introduce phrases that are often used with the perfect tenses. *Still* is usually used with present tenses.
Scientists have **already** discovered the cause of cancer, although they haven't **yet** discovered the cure.	*Already* can be used in affirmative statements. *Yet* can be used in negative statements and questions.
Scientists had long suspected that Alzheimer's disease had a genetic basis. **Now** they had proof.	*Now* is often used with the present and present progressive, but it can be used with other tenses to highlight a contrast. Put *now* at the beginning of a sentence or clause when using it for this effect.

C **Use a time word from the chart above to complete each sentence.**

Stem cell research has been in the news

_____*for*_____ quite a while; in fact, researchers
(1)

have been interested in stem cells _____ the
(2)

invention of the microscope. _____ with the
(3)

new gene technology, stem cells are even more interesting.

Stem cell research may hold the key for cures that were

impossible before, but it is _____ very
(4)

Gregor Mendel

controversial. One reason is that a major source of stem cells is human embryos. These

embryos are made up of just a few cells and have only about 40 stem cells. These stem

cells are taken out of the embryo and _____ they are put in a special
(5)

environment so they can reproduce. If the cells continue to divide _____
(6)
many months, the new population of stem cells is called a stem cell line. These stem cells
can be used for research. There aren't many stem cell lines in existence and many of
them were produced using methods that are _____ outdated. Scientists
(7)
say they _____ need new stem cell lines using the latest technology
(8)
for good research. The problem for many research organizations is that they haven't
_____ raised the funds they need to conduct this research.
(9)

D Read the notes that Nelson took during his biology class. Turn the notes into a short
composition using as many time words as you can. Follow Nelson's example.

<u>Gregor Mendel</u>

Born in 1822

Monk, lived in a monastery in Austria

Experimented with peas (1856–1863)

Experimented with honeybees

Discovered that traits are passed from one generation to the next

Died in 1884

Discoveries mostly ignored

His work was rediscovered in early 1900s

Considered "father of genetics"

Gregor Mendel is now considered the "father of genetics,"
although his work was ignored for nearly 50 years after his death.

_____

_____

_____

_____

_____

E **PAIR WORK** Take turns talking and asking each other questions. Tell about your education and personal history. Use time words to help show the sequence of events.

> I was born in Costa Rica. I **first** came to Dallas in 2005.

> **First** I lived in Austin, **then** I moved to Dallas. I've been living here **for** about three years.

PART TWO	Time Clauses

■ GRAMMAR IN CONTENT

A Reread the passage on page 172. Look at the time clauses and then study the chart below.

Time Clauses	
Sample Sentences	**Notes**
Many patients are shocked and distressed **when they discover that they have a terminal illness.** Future patients **will have the option** of gene therapy **when they are diagnosed with a terminal illness.** My father **received** chemotherapy **after he found out that he had cancer.**	**Time clauses** tell when the action or event in the main clause happens. In general, follow these patterns: **Main Clause** **Time Clause** present present or future future present past past or past perfect
Most people who suffer from Alzheimer's don't show symptoms **until they reach their sixties or seventies.**	Time clauses have three parts: **a time word, a subject, and a predicate.**
Some patients improve **after they receive therapy.** Cancer patients may feel sick **as they undergo chemotherapy.** The long-term effects of gene therapy won't be known **until scientists conduct more studies.**	The most frequently used time words for time clauses are *as, since, after, before, until,* and *when.* *As* and *when* can show that two things are happening simultaneously. *Until* clauses can be used with main clauses that make negative statements to show that one thing will *not* happen unless another thing happens.
In a cell, chromosomes copy themselves **before the cell divides.** The cell won't divide **until the chromosomes are lined up and ready to separate.**	*Before, after,* and *until* show a sequence of events. They can also show that one event or action is contingent upon another.
After a cell divides, each new cell has an identical set of genes.	If the time clause begins a sentence, it is usually separated from the main clause by a comma.
Since geneticists mapped the sequence of human genes, many new therapies are being discovered.	*Since* is used to show when the action in the main clause began.

B Look at the diagram. It shows the main stages in mitosis, the process by which cells in the body divide. Then write a short essay about this process, using as many time clauses as possible.

Mitosis

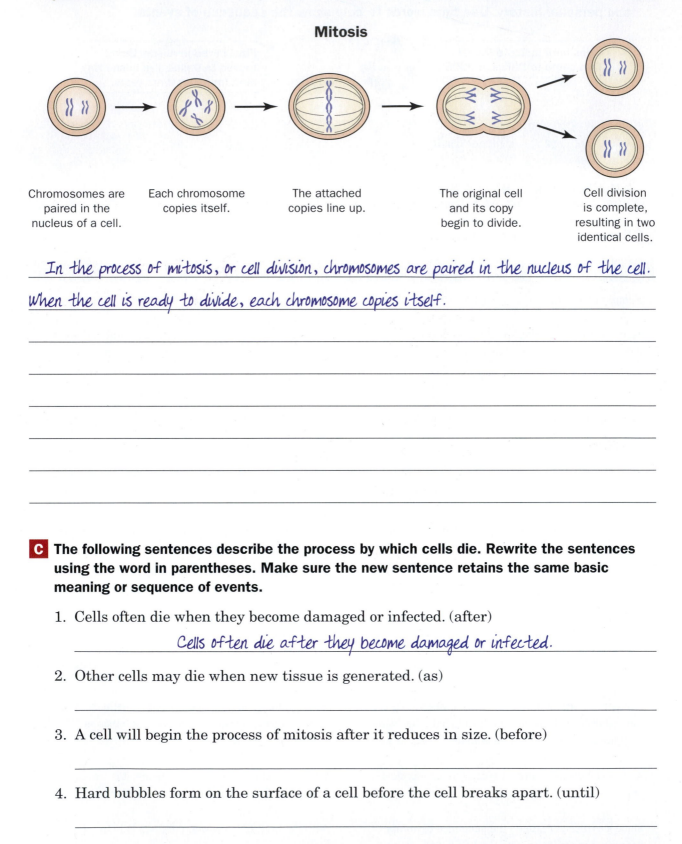

| Chromosomes are paired in the nucleus of a cell. | Each chromosome copies itself. | The attached copies line up. | The original cell and its copy begin to divide. | Cell division is complete, resulting in two identical cells. |

In the process of mitosis, or cell division, chromosomes are paired in the nucleus of the cell. When the cell is ready to divide, each chromosome copies itself.

C The following sentences describe the process by which cells die. Rewrite the sentences using the word in parentheses. Make sure the new sentence retains the same basic meaning or sequence of events.

1. Cells often die when they become damaged or infected. (after)

    Cells often die after they become damaged or infected.

2. Other cells may die when new tissue is generated. (as)

    _____

3. A cell will begin the process of mitosis after it reduces in size. (before)

    _____

4. Hard bubbles form on the surface of a cell before the cell breaks apart. (until)

    _____

5. The cellular fragments are enclosed in membranes when they become separate. (as)

_____

_____

6. The fragments are destroyed by other cells when they become separate. (after)

_____

_____

7. Cancer may develop as large numbers of cells live longer than they should and continue to divide. (when)

_____

_____

Bubbles forming on the surface of a cell

■ COMMUNICATE

D **GROUP WORK** Discuss your own hopes, predictions, and concerns about gene therapy. What are some of the benefits of genetics? What are some of the possible dangers or risks? Use as many time words and time phrases as possible.

Scientists will be able to cure a lot of different diseases **when** they figure out the genetic cause.

Yes, but what about the unknown side-effects? Sometimes new treatments are used **before** researchers know all the consequences. That's a little scary.

I think it's worth the risk. We've **already** found the cure for some diseases. We won't find other cures unless we keep trying.

GRAMMAR AND VOCABULARY Write a composition of at least one page on one of the following topics:

- Do you know somebody who was diagnosed with a serious illness? Write about those experiences from a personal perspective. Tell about the diagnosis and treatment. Write about your own personal thoughts and feelings as a friend or family member.
- Should the government fund research on stem cells and other forms of genetic therapy? Why or why not? What are some of the possible consequences, implications, and responsibilities associated with government funding? If the government doesn't fund this kind of research, who should, and why?
- Are there any ethical or philosophical problems you can think of that are associated with genetic research? Should genetic research be monitored by an independent organization? Why or why not? What, if any, limitations should be placed on this kind of research?

PROJECT In groups, follow these steps to investigate how traits are passed from one generation to the next.

1. Choose a physical trait such as eye color or hair color.
2. To the best of your ability, create a family tree that shows this trait for each member of your extended family.
3. Compare your tree with other members of your group. What kinds of conclusions can you draw?
4. Write down a list of questions that come up during your discussion, then consult outside reference materials and textbooks to help you answer those questions.
5. Summarize your observations and findings in a class presentation.

 INTERNET Using the Internet as a resource, research some aspect of genetics or cellular biology, and present your findings to the class. Try searching for the following terms:

- Alzheimer's disease
- cancer
- cell communication
- cell growth
- DNA
- genetics
- gene therapy
- Parkinson's disease
- stem cells

A **Complete the conversation. Choose from the words in parentheses.**

Sigrid: Hey, that's a cool tattoo you got there! Why did you choose a dinosaur?

Miles: Well, my birthday was last week, and that morning I went to a tattoo artist. We

looked at designs _____*for*_____ (for, since) a while. I didn't want
(1)

a tattoo that was _____ (too, enough) small to see, but I
(2)

didn't want it to be _____ (too, so) big that it covered my arm.
(3)

Sigrid: It's just the right size. And I like the green scales.

Miles: Yeah, I wanted colors that were bright _____ (enough, so)
(4)

to catch people's attention. I looked a long time _____
(5)

(when, before) I found the perfect one—a T. rex!

Sigrid: He's _____ (too, really) eye-catching!
(6)

Miles: _____ (When, Since) I got it, people have been
(7)

complimenting me on the design. In fact, I like it _____
(8)

(so, very) much that I've made an appointment to get another one.

B **Form relative clauses that complete the meaning of the sentence with each of the phrases in parentheses. Follow the example.**

Tom's brother Marv is running for city council. Tom says that because of some

of the negative advertising by Marv's opponent, he has some campaign expenses

_____*that he hasn't been able to cover*_____ (he hasn't been able to cover the
(1)

campaign expenses). The staff _____ (he hired
(2)

the staff) hasn't been able to raise enough money, and he needs to find some donors

_____ (the donors will fund the rest of his
(3)

campaign).

Last night was a big night for Marv. He had dinner with a well-known fund-raiser

_____ (his name his Dr. Alfred Weiss). They talked
(4)

about issues _____ (the issues are important to
(5)

them). Marv feels that Dr. Weiss is a person _____
(6)
(Marv can trust Dr. Weiss).

C Read about the Baker family's summer plans. Choose from the words in parentheses to complete the sentence. When choosing an answer, pay attention to punctuation.

Jan is going to a conference in Tokyo in July. _____ (It's, There's)
(1)
probably going to be hot and muggy. _____, (However, On the
(2)
contrary) Jan doesn't mind the heat. _____, (On the contrary, On the
(3)
other hand) she doesn't like crowds, and she's heard that the streets of Tokyo are always full

of people. _____, (Moreover, On the other hand) there are going to be
(4)
almost 10,000 people at the conference, and the conference hall looks too small. Jan wants

to travel around Tokyo, but she's heard that _____ (it's, there's) often
(5)
very crowded on the trains. Jan's heard that _____ (it, there) are taxis
(6)
that are reasonably priced. _____, (Moreover, On the other hand) taxis
(7)
are readily available, so they are much more convenient than trains.

LEARNER LOG Check (✔) Yes or *I Need More Practice.*

Lesson	I Can Use . . .	Yes	I Need More Practice
16	Intensifiers with Adjectives, Adverbs, and Nouns; *Too* and *Enough* with Infinitive Phrases; *So . . . that*		
17	Non-Referring *It* and Non-Referring *There*		
18	Coordinate Conjunctions and Conjunctive Adverbs		
19	Relative Clauses; Relative Pronouns and Adverbs; Reduced Restrictive Relative Clauses		
20	Time Words, Time Phrases, and Time Clauses		

PART 1
Present Factual Conditionals

PART 2
Past Factual Conditionals

PART 3
Future (or Predictive)
Conditionals

Lesson 21

Economics: Running a Small Business

■ CONTENT VOCABULARY

Look at the picture. What kinds of activities take place at the businesses shown here?

Korean Restaurant | Dry Cleaners | Beauty Salon | MAIL CENTER | Fast Food

Grand Opening

Many small businesses **operate** in small **suburban shopping centers** or **strip malls,** such as the one above. In these shopping areas there is usually a mixture of **privately** owned small businesses and **franchises.** A franchise gives an individual the right to operate a business that has many other locations across the nation or even around the world. These businesses are usually very **competitive:** if one fails, another takes its place very quickly.

Read the description below the picture. Look up any words you don't know. Write each word, its definition, and a sentence that illustrates its use in your vocabulary journal.

■ THINK ABOUT IT

What are some of the small businesses near your home? Is there a cleaner or laundry service? A restaurant? A beauty salon? Describe these businesses. Do you know if any of them are franchises? Which ones do you patronize? Why? Take notes in your writing journal and then share what you wrote with the class.

■ GRAMMAR IN CONTENT

A Read and listen to a lecture on small businesses.

CD2,TR11

Small Businesses

Businesses with 100 or fewer employees are considered small businesses. If individuals want to start a small business, they face a number of challenges. For one thing, they must have enough start-up capital. If they do not, the business may run out of money before it becomes profitable. Also, if the product or service is not priced high enough, the business doesn't make a profit. If the prices are set too high, customers go elsewhere.

So if you want to start a business, you are going to need to plan carefully. If you start with about $200,000 and expect $300,000 profits, you will need to have at least $500,000 in reserve in case something goes wrong. If you provide a high quality product or service, you will build a base of satisfied customers who return. However, if your business is not in a convenient location, you will not attract those customers in the first place, so you will need to advertise effectively. If you have a lot of capital, you might buy a franchise because much of the planning and advertising will be done for you.

A couple of years ago, two students formed an e-business. Amber was a wizard at accounting, and Jason excelled at sales. If a problem came up with finances, Amber solved it. If they needed work on their web page or with customer service, Jason took care of it. The point is, if you don't have the skills, you'll need to hire someone who does.

capital: money, land, buildings, etc.

a franchise: a legal agreement giving an individual or company the right to sell another company's goods or services

an e-business: an organization that conducts business over the Internet

accounting: the keeping of records and providing of information about a company's or a person's money

B Reread the passage. <u>Underline</u> all the *if* clauses in the reading. If the verb in the main clause is present tense, (circle) it. Check your answers with a partner. If you need help, use the chart below.

Present Factual Conditionals	
Sample Sentences	**Notes**
If Helen **makes** a profit, she **invests** in advertising.	Factual conditionals have two parts: an *if* clause that gives conditions, and a result clause that tells what happens if the conditions are met. Both clauses are in the **present tense**.
If one small business fails, another comes along and takes its place.	Present factual conditionals can be used to tell about situations that are commonly accepted as being true.
If I have time before class, I stop at the Student Union for coffee.	Present factual conditionals can be used to tell about a habit or routine.
If your debts exceed your annual income, you are technically bankrupt. = **When** your debts exceed your annual income, you are technically bankrupt. Your debtors can seize your assets **if** you refuse to settle your debts. = Your debtors can seize your assets **whenever** you refuse to settle your debts.	Rules, laws, and unavoidable consequences can be described using present factual conditionals. In these kinds of sentences, **when** or **whenever** can be used instead of *if*.
If a small business does not have enough start-up money, it inevitably fails. = A small business usually fails **if it doesn't have enough start-up money**.	*If* clauses can occur at the beginning or end of a sentence. *If* clauses most frequently start a sentence and when they do, they are followed by a comma.
If a business fails, it's often because the owner **has mismanaged** it.	Present factual conditionals can be used to make an inference.

C Complete each sentence in the following paragraph with a present factual conditional. The completed sentences must make sense within the paragraph.

Smart businesspeople know the importance of advertising. If they need to expand their base of customers, *they hire an advertising firm* . If they don't have enough money to hire
(1)
an advertising firm, _____. With the consultant's
(2)
help, they can identify their target customers. If they want to know what their competitors
are doing, _____. They can also go to trade shows.
(3)
_____, they follow up with a call or an e-mail
(4)
message.

D Listen to Vhan talking about how he markets his beauty salon. Then answer the following questions. Use an *if* clause in your answers.

CD2,TR12

1. What does Vhan do if he needs to increase his customer base?

   If Vhan needs to increase his customer base, he does some research and advertises.

2. If he can't do the market research himself, what does he do?

   _____

   _____

3. What does Vhan do when he needs to design a mailer?

   _____

   _____

4. Why does he visit competitors' websites?

   _____

   _____

■ COMMUNICATE

E **PAIR WORK** Discuss ways of getting money for special events such as vacations. Use present factual conditionals to share your ideas.

> If I need money for a special event, I usually ask my boss for extra work. How about you? What do you do if you need extra money?

> Well, I don't work, so if I need money, I have to borrow it from my parents.

■ GRAMMAR IN CONTENT

A Reread the passage on page 182. Find all of the sentences with *if* clauses in the reading. If the verb in the result clause is in the past, put a <u>double underline</u> under it. Check your answers with a partner. If you need help, use the chart below.

Past Factual Conditionals	
Sample Sentences	**Notes**
If I **made** extra money, I always **saved** it for the business I planned to own. If I **couldn't** save any money from my regular job, I **got** extra work on the weekend.	Past factual conditionals tell about situations that happened (or didn't happen) as a result of certain conditions being met (or not being met).
If a contractor **missed** a deadline, the developer **renegotiated** the contract fees.= The developer **renegotiated** the contract fees if a **contractor** missed a deadline.	Put both the *if* clause and the result clause in the **simple past**. As with present conditionals, the *if* clause frequently comes at the beginning of the sentence. When it does, the *if* clause is followed by a comma.
Kelly was self-employed as a housecleaner for many years. **Whenever** her clients **asked**, she **cooked** and **served** them dinner. Eventually she began to cater for special events. **When** she **catered**, she **charged** double what she made as a housecleaner.	*When* and *whenever* can often be used instead of *if*. Using *when* or *whenever* suggests that the condition and result happened frequently or on a regular basis. The simple past is often used in the result clause, as well as in the *if* clause. Adverbs such as *also, sometimes, never,* and *always* go before the main verb.
At the end of every year, my business partner and I used to balance our accounts. If we **made** a profit, we **divided** it equally. Sometimes we **reinvested** an equal percentage of that profit back into the business.	Once the conditional has been established, subsequent sentences should be in the same time or tense as the result clause (usually the simple past). Doing this shows that the action (or states) in the subsequent sentences are all **results** of the condition established in the previous sentence.

B Arrange the words and phrases in the correct order to create sentences in the past factual conditional. Add commas whenever necessary. Follow the example.

1. after 9 P.M. / there were / if / the owners / closed the restaurant / no customers

   If there were no customers after 9 P.M., the owners closed the restaurant.

2. a profit / if / she made / Mrs. Jackson / her employees / a bonus / gave

   _____

3. a good review / a pay raise / expected / if they got / the employees

   _____

4. tried to add the receipts / if / the clerk / he made / a mistake / too fast

   _____

5. her business / the employer / additional taxes / if / had to pay / made a profit

   _____

6. we met / a small party / if / we had / our sales goals

   _____

C Complete the following paragraph with the correct form of the verb in parentheses.

My aunt owned a small Indian restaurant several years ago. It was hard for her to estimate how much food she needed to buy every day. If she ___bought___ (1) (buy) too much, she ___had___ (2) (have) to throw it away the next day. And, if she _____ (3) (waste) a lot of food, she _____ (4) (lose) money. So she tended to be very conservative in her estimates, and on a few occasions she was caught by surprise. If a crowd _____ (5) (come) when there wasn't enough food in the kitchen, she _____ (6) (go) around the corner to another Indian restaurant. She

_____ (7) (buy) meals for her customers

and _____ (8) (bring) the meals to her restaurant. Eventually, she got better at estimating how much food she needed to buy.

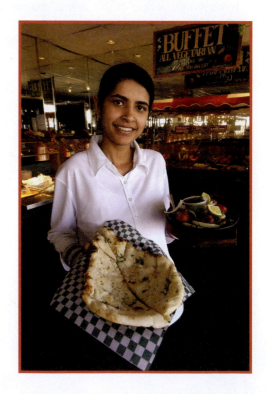

D Use your imagination to complete the sentences below in the past factual conditional. Follow the example.

1. Mark opened a new hair salon and discovered the importance of keeping his clients satisfied. If clients complained about a stylist, _Mark personally did their hair the next time they came in._

2. Barbara worked for many years as a writer, and she sometimes had more work than she could handle. If she had too much work, _____

   _____

3. Tamiya noticed a relationship between advertising and the number of customers that came to her store. If _____

   _____

4. Carlos gave his customers incentives to shop at his online store. If they shopped online, they got a discount. They _____

   _____

■ COMMUNICATE

E PAIR WORK Have you ever had a job? Describe your working conditions to a classmate. What happened if you were late? What happened if you had to miss work? If you needed money, what happened? First write down your answers to these three questions in complete sentences. Then tell your partner about your experience.

> I used to work at a fast-food restaurant. **If** I arrived just five minutes late, they subtracted the money from my pay.

> That's nothing. When I worked at Pizza Palace, **if** employees were late three times, they were fired.

> Wow, that's pretty extreme.

■ GRAMMAR IN CONTENT

A Reread the passage on page 182. Find all of the sentences with *if* clauses in the reading. If the verb in the main clause is in future time or contains *should, may,* or *might,* put a wavy line under it. Check your answers with a partner. If you need help, use the chart below.

Future (or Predictive) Conditionals	
Sample Sentences	**Notes**
If the Wares raise enough start-up money, **our company will sponsor them.** = **Our company will sponsor the Wares** if they raise enough start-up money.	Conditionals can be used to make predictions about the future. They show what will or may happen if certain conditions are met. The prediction is in the **result clause**. The order of both clauses can be reversed although the *if* clause is usually first.
If a restaurant **is** not in a good location, it **will not attract** enough customers.	Use present tense in the *if* **clause** and a future form in the **result clause**.
If I start my own business, my father **will** invest in it.	The auxiliary *will* indicates there is a high probability the prediction will come true.
If Cristina decides to start her own business, she **might** be able to get a loan. If loan applicants have a co-signer, their loan **may** be approved more quickly.	The auxiliary *might* indicates that the prediction is weak. *May* is often used in formal contexts, and it expresses a slightly stronger prediction than *might*.

B Complete the following paragraph with the correct future conditional form of each verb in parentheses.

My cousin Shereen is planning to buy a business. I told her that if she

___*wants*___ (want) to open her own business, but ___*doesn't have*___ (not have) a
    (1)   (2)

lot of experience, she ___*will need*___ (need) to consider a franchise. A franchise
                          (3)

has a number of advantages. If she _____ (buy)
                                              (4)

a franchise, she _____ (not need) to worry about
                          (5)

establishing a base of clients. However, if she _____
                                                          (6)

(decide) to start her own business, she _____ (have to)
                                                  (7)

spend a lot of time on advertising. More importantly, her chances of success

_____ (increase) if she _____
(8)   (9)

(start) her own franchise. If she _____ (buy) a franchising
(10)

license, she _____ (get) a lot of support from the parent
(11)

company in the form of equipment, supplies, and training. Her main concern is

that she _____ (lose) her independence if her business
(12)

_____ (belong) to a chain of other stores.
(13)

C Using your own words, complete the following dialog using the future conditional. Check that your answers make sense within the dialog.

Sarita: I heard your dad's thinking about starting a business.

Shereen: *Yeah, he's going to rent space in the shopping center near our home if he can get a reasonable rent.*

Sarita: What kind of business is he thinking about?

Shereen: _____

_____

Sarita: Why not a restaurant? Everybody has to eat.

Shereen: _____

_____

Sarita: Doesn't he have to be at the laundry full time?

Shereen: _____

_____

Sarita: Knowing your dad, he'll want to be there every day.

■ **COMMUNICATE**

D **PAIR WORK** What kinds of issues and questions come up for somebody who wants to start a business or open a franchise? Brainstorm a list of questions with a partner and talk about possible solutions to those problems.

If you're going to start your own business, you'll probably need to get a loan from a bank.

Right. And if you don't qualify for a loan, you'll have to borrow the money from a friend or relative.

GRAMMAR AND VOCABULARY Write a story about an imaginary small-business owner. Think of the difficulties the owner might have, and how he or she might attempt to solve those problems. Use at least one example each of the present conditional, past conditional, and future conditional. In your conclusion, summarize what lessons people who are thinking of starting their own businesses can draw from your story.

PROJECT In a group, create a plan for a small business that might interest you. Take notes on the following:

- the kind of business you are going to start
- its name
- its location
- your intended market, or customer base
- preliminary budget (estimated expenses and income)
- possible sources of capital and funding
- advertising strategies

When you have finished, select someone from the group to present the plan to the class.

INTERNET How do small businesses get started? Do a search on the Internet to find out. Use the terms "small business," "starting a small business," and "franchise opportunities." Share something interesting that you found with your classmates.

■ CONTENT VOCABULARY

Look at the picture. Before reading the caption, discuss the following questions: What are the chances of getting yellow? What are at least two ways of expressing that probability?

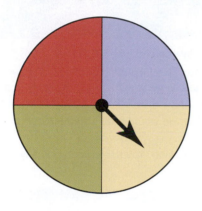

Red	Blue	Yellow	Green
⾧	⾧	⾧	⾧
⾧	⾧	⾧	⾧
l	⾧	l	⾧
			ll

Probability is the **likelihood** or **chance** that something is true or will happen. It is usually expressed as a **ratio** or **percentage**. If you were to spin the arrow on a spinner like the one shown, you would have a 25% chance of getting yellow. In other words, the **odds** of getting yellow would be 1 out of 4. The results of an experiment in probability are often recorded as **data**, which is **analyzed** and **interpreted** by **mathematicians**.

Read the caption. Look up any words you don't know. Write each word, its definition, and a sentence that illustrates its use in your vocabulary journal.

■ THINK ABOUT IT

How are statistics used in daily life? Discuss your ideas in a group and then summarize the discussion in your writing journal.

■ GRAMMAR IN CONTENT

CD2,TR13

A **Albert and José are classmates. Read and listen to their conversation.**

José: Did you do the assignment for statistics and probability?

Albert: Yeah, I decided to calculate the odds of winning at roulette, and I compared that to the payoff.

José: How did you do that?

Albert: A roulette wheel has 38 slots, so the odds of your number coming up are 37 to 1. The casinos pay winners at a rate of 35 to 1. In other words, you'll win once out of every 38 times, and when you do win, your bet will be multiplied by 35. **If** you **did** the math, you **would see** that, for every $100 you bet, you'll get back $95.

José: One time my uncle played roulette in Las Vegas. He won $300, but then he lost $200.

Albert: **If** he **had continued** to play, he **would have** eventually lost everything, including his winnings. **If** it **were** possible for everyone to win on a regular basis, the casinos **would** all **go** bankrupt. But in reality, they make huge sums of money. What does that tell you about the odds? It's called "the house advantage."

José: I **wish** my uncle **had known** all of this before he went to Las Vegas. He **would have saved** himself a lot of money.

Albert: Unfortunately, a lot of people **wish** they **had never** even **gone** to a casino. You know what they say—live and learn.

---

slots: the sections of a roulette wheel

a bet: an agreement that the person in the wrong or the person who loses must give the other something, such as a sum of money; a wager

the house advantage: the practice of a casino (called "the house") paying out at lower odds than the actual odds of the game so that over time, the odds are in favor of the casino

winnings: money that is won in a game of chance

B Reread the dialog on page 192. Look at all the present non-factual conditionals and then study the chart below.

Hypothetical Statements and Questions in the Conditional

Statements in the Main Clause

If	Subject of *If* Clause	Simple Past Verb	Subject of Result Clause	*Would / Wouldn't*	Simple Verb
If	my uncle	**knew** the odds,	he	wouldn't	**waste** his money playing roulette.
If	you	**saved** five dollars a day,	you	would	**have** more than $30,000 in 10 years.
If	a smoker	**stopped** smoking,	his or her chances of developing heart disease	would	**decrease** by 50% within a year.

Yes/No Questions in the Main Clause

If	Subject of *If* Clause	Simple Past Verb	*Would / Wouldn't*	Subject of Result Clause	Simple Verb
If	there	**were** less violence in the media,	would	the crime rate	**be** as high as it is now?
If	a smoker	**stopped** smoking,	would	his or her chances of developing heart disease	**decrease** significantly?

Wh- Questions in the Main Clause

If	Subject of *If* Clause	Simple Past Verb	Question Word + *Would / Wouldn't*	Subject of Result Clause	Simple Verb
If	you	**saved** five dollars a day,	how much **would**	you	**have** in 30 years?
If	researchers	**conducted** a poll,	what **would**	the results	**reveal** about voters?

Notes:

- A hypothetical statement is based on possible ideas or situations instead of actual ideas or situations. Use the simple past in the *if* clause and *would* or *wouldn't* in the result clause.
- The modal **could** can be used in the result clause: *If you had a computer, you could calculate the value of pi.*
- The order of the clauses can be reversed, although the *if* clause usually appears at the beginning. When moving the result clause to the front of the sentence, it is not necessary to have a comma: *My uncle wouldn't waste his money playing roulette if he knew the odds.*
- When results are expressed in successive sentences, continue to use *would* with the simple verb; for example: *If you quit smoking you would save $2,000 in a year. In ten years you would save $20,000.*
- In formal discourse, **were** is the form of *be* used in the *if* clause of a hypothetical statement whether the subject is singular or plural: *If I were you, I'd calculate the odds.* In informal contexts, *was* is often used with *I* and *he/she/it* and third-person singular subjects.

C **Read the following passage, and fill in the blank with the correct form of the verb in parentheses.**

Probability is the measure of how likely it is for something to happen. For example,

if you ___*had*___ (have) a bag with four marbles—one green, one red, one yellow, and one
   (1)

blue—what are the odds you _____ (draw) a marble of a particular
                              (2)

color from the bag? Specifically, if you _____ (reach) into the bag and
                                           (3)

_____ (grab) one marble without looking, what would the chances be
   (4)

of drawing a blue one? Your chances would _____ (be) 1 out of 4, or
                                              (5)

25%. In other words, if you _____ (do) this 100 times, one time out
                               (6)

of every four you _____ (get) blue, and three times out of four you
                      (7)

_____ (draw) some other color. So the probability _____
   (8)   (9)

(be) expressed as 3 to 1, or 75%. If we _____ (complicate) matters, you
                                           (10)

_____ (see) that the math is the same. What if you _____
   (11)   (12)

(have) 6 green marbles, 4 red marbles, and 2 blue marbles in a bag? If you

_____ (remove) one marble without looking, what would the chances be
   (13)

of getting a blue marble? This time it _____ (be) 5 to 1. That means if you
                                          (14)

_____ (pick) a marble at random 12 times, you _____
   (15)   (16)

(not get) a blue marble 10 times, but instead, you _____ (probably get) a
                                                      (17)

blue marble 2 times. So your odds of getting a blue marble _____ (only be)
                                                              (18)

2 out of 12, which can also be expressed as 1 out of 6, or 16.6%.

D Complete the following statements using a past hypothetical conditional. Follow the example.

1. If population growth slowed down, *the world's resources would have more time to renew themselves.*

2. If every citizen voted, _____

_____

3. If weather forecasters had more sophisticated computers, _____

_____

4. If world leaders really wanted to stop climate change, _____

_____

5. If more countries had nuclear weapons, _____

_____

6. If there were intelligent life on another planet, _____

_____

■ C O M M U N I C A T E

E **PAIR WORK** Interview a classmate. Ask him/her these questions. Take notes, and then report your findings to the class.

1. If you won the lottery today, what would you do with the money?
2. If you could talk to any person from history, who would you like to talk to? What would you ask or tell that person?
3. If you were an animal, what kind of animal would you be? Why?

If you won the lottery today, what would you do with the money?

I'd buy my mother a house on the beach.

That's a good question. I guess I'd use some of it to start my own business. How about you?

PART TWO — Past Non-Factual Conditionals

■ GRAMMAR IN CONTENT

A Reread the dialog on page 192. Look at all the examples of past non-factual conditionals and study the chart below.

Past Non-Factual Conditionals				
Affirmative Statements				
If	Subject of *If* Clause	Past Perfect + Complement	Subject of Result Clause	Modal + *Have* + Past Participle
If	the research team	**had collected** more data,	they	**could have reached** more conclusive results.
If	Sonia	**had crossed** the intersection without looking,	she	**might have had** an accident.
If	James	**hadn't left** his house so late,	he	**wouldn't have missed** the train.

Wh- Questions						
Question Word	Modal	Subject of Result Clause	*Have* + Past Participle	*If*	Subject of *If* Clause	*Had* + Past Participle
How	**could**	I	**have known** the answer	if	I	**hadn't had** all the information?
What	**might**		**have happened**	if	nobody	**had tried** to intervene?

Notes:

- Use the past non-factual conditional to talk about unrealized outcomes of hypothetical situations in the past. Use the past perfect in the *if* clause, and a modal with the present perfect in the result clause.
- In formal writing, it is possible to omit *if* and switch the order of the auxiliary and the subject: *Had the officer known the danger, he would have brought a gun.* = *If the officer had known the danger, he would have brought a gun.*

B Read each passage. The <u>underlined</u> sentence at the end of each passage has two errors. Find and correct the errors.

1. A maker of chocolate chip cookies claims that there are 1,000 chips in every bag of cookies. To test this claim, students of a statistics class ordered 275 bags from all over the country. <u>If they ~~buy~~ ^(had bought) all the cookies from the same location, they wouldn't had ^(have) a representative sample.</u>

2. Another group of students wanted to predict the outcome of a local election. To do that, they took a survey of voters who lived in the same neighborhood. The problem was that all the residents of this neighborhood belonged to the same social class. <u>If the students are conducting the survey in several different neighborhoods, they will have got more accurate results.</u>

3. In many states, convicted criminals are now required to give DNA samples. Those samples are entered into a database that contains DNA samples from a backlog of unsolved crimes. <u>Investigators could be solving many of these crimes years ago if they would have had access to this information.</u>

4. Timing technology at the Olympics has become highly sophisticated. Today radar guns and speed photography are used to measure time; in 1896, at the first modern Olympic Games, simple stopwatches were used. <u>If officials then have had the same kind of technology that we have today, they could be calculating times to the 100th of a second.</u>

■ **COMMUNICATE**

C **PAIR WORK** With a partner, talk about a possible chain of events that might have happened if your life had taken a different course. Use the past non-factual conditional.

> When I was a kid, I took piano lessons. I quit after a year and I've always regretted it. If I **had studied** piano all through school, I **might have become** really good. I **might have** even **gone** to a music school. I'm sure I **wouldn't have decided** to study law.

■ GRAMMAR IN CONTENT

A **PAIR WORK** Work with a partner. Reread the passage on page 192. Find all the examples of wishes and then study the chart below.

Wish and *Hope*	
Sample Sentences	**Notes**
Modern science has made it possible for people to know their chances of getting certain inheritable diseases. This knowledge can often be difficult to live with, however. Some people **wish** ~~that~~ they **didn't know.**	Use *wish* to express a desire or regret. Sentences with *wish* are followed by a complement with *that*, although the use of *that* itself is optional. Use the **simple past** in the complement to express a wish about the present.
I felt pressured to place a bet, and I lost everything. I **wish** it **wasn't/weren't** true, but it is.	When expressing wishes, use *were* for all cases; the use of *was* is formally incorrect, although it is acceptable in informal situations.
Brian needed some cash, and so he decided to cash out his retirement account. He **wishes/wished** (that) somebody **had told** him about the tax penalty for doing that.	Use past perfect in the *that* clause to express a wish about the past. The verb in the main clause may be present or past.
A recent poll revealed that 25% of American men and 45% of American women **wish** (that) they **could lose** weight.	Use **would** or **could** with a **simple verb** to express a wish about the future. The *that* is often omitted.
I **wish** I **had** a million dollars. But since the odds of winning the lottery are 13,000,000 to 1, I guess I should keep my job. I just **hope** (that) I **have/will have** enough money to retire by the time I'm 65.	We usually **wish** for things that are or seem impossible; we **hope** for things that are more probable or possible. Whereas *that* clauses after *wish* have past or past perfect tense, *that* clauses after *hope* take present or future verb forms.

B Read each passage, and then complete the last sentence. Follow the example.

1. Celinda found out she was pregnant, so she bought a large and expensive crib. Later, she found out that she was expecting twins. She felt very lucky, since the odds of having twins are only 90 to 1. On the other hand, she wishes _she had bought a smaller and less expensive crib._

2. The Boston Red Sox are one of the oldest teams in professional baseball. Unfortunately, they haven't also been the luckiest. After winning the World Series in 1918, the Red Sox would not win another championship for 86 years. Their losing streak was finally broken in 2004 when they won against the St. Louis Cardinals. The team hopes _____

_____

3. The SETI Institute is dedicated to the search for signs of intelligent life in the universe. It uses advanced radio technology to listen for signals from other distant civilizations. SETI hopes _____

_____

4. Believe it or not, some lottery winners regret being millionaires. William Post, for example, won $16.2 million in Pennsylvania's lottery. He eventually spent all the money and now lives in a trailer. Post says that his life was better before he became a millionaire. In fact, he wishes _____

_____

5. Many criminals leave prison only to commit new crimes. Statistics show that 70% of released criminals are reconvicted within three years of their release. The good news is that counseling and therapy have been proven to cut this figure in half. Many prison officials wish _____

_____

C **PAIR WORK** With a partner, talk about your hopes and dreams for the future. Use conditionals, *wish,* and *hope.* Don't forget to use modals where necessary.

I **wish** that I **spoke** perfect English.

I **would get** a job as an interpreter.

What **would** you do if you **could?**

If I **could speak** English perfectly, I **would** probably **become** an English teacher.

Connection | Putting It Together

GRAMMAR AND VOCABULARY Write a narrative about a situation that "went wrong." Your narrative might be based on personal experience or it could be fictional. Describe the characters' disappointments and regrets. What do the characters wish they had done differently? Use hypothetical statements, past non-factual conditionals, *wish,* and *hope.* Share your narrative with your classmates.

PROJECT In groups, design a research project in statistics and/or probability. Think of a question you would like to have answered, and then discuss methods for collecting data. Present your ideas to the class. If time allows, you can actually do the project with your group afterward.

INTERNET Investigate a topic related to statistics and probability on the Internet. Try combining search terms with a topic that interests you. You might want to find statistics related to sports, for example, or you might want to learn more about experiments in probability. Share what you found in a short oral presentation to your class.

PART 1
Passive Voice

PART 2
Use of Passive Voice

PART 3
Middle Voice

Lesson ㉓

Social Sciences: Demography

■ CONTENT VOCABULARY

Look at the pie chart below. It shows demographic data about the population of the United States. How do you think this information is obtained?

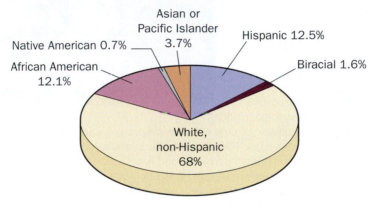

Asian or
Pacific Islander
3.7%

Native American 0.7%

Hispanic 12.5%

African American
12.1%

Biracial 1.6%

White,
non-Hispanic
68%

Source: *U.S. Census*, 2000

Demography is the study of the **characteristics** of a particular human **population** or group. Scientists who study these characteristics, called demographics, are called **demographers**. Demographers deal with questions of **fertility** and **birth**, **health**, **disease** and **death**, **social segregation**, the **distribution of wealth**, and **migration**. Demographic data is often used by governmental, economic, and educational institutions.

Read the description below the chart. Look up any words you don't know. Write each word, its definition, and a sentence that illustrates its use in your vocabulary journal.

■ THINK ABOUT IT

Discuss these questions in a group: How closely does the data in the pie chart reflect the demographics of the town or city where you live? How neatly do people fit into these categories? What new categories would you add? Summarize the discussion in your writing journal.

■ GRAMMAR IN CONTENT

A Read and listen to the following.

CD2,TR14

Demographics

Demographics are the characteristics of a particular human population. As such, they are *population specific*. In other words, they refer to the particular population or group that **is studied,** not to all human beings in general. Scientists who study demographics **are called** demographers. They are concerned with questions of fertility and birth, health, disease and death, social segregation, the distribution of wealth, and migration. Consumer trends in a particular group **are studied** by some demographers. Age, for example, as well as income and self-image, **might all be** studied. Members of the target group **are questioned** about their opinions, habits, and preferences. When this information **is known,** specific populations **can be targeted by marketing companies,** and more effective advertising campaigns **can be designed.**

Demographers must be good statisticians. They use computers and large amounts of data that **are gathered** in the latest census and by private companies to discover and explain trends. Applied demographers use the information that **has been gathered** to make predictions. This information will then **be used by urban planners** to make sound public policy. For example, changes in a population can shift the demands put on public utilities such as water and power, public transportation, telecommunications, roads, and schools. These are services that we don't really think about, yet we expect that they will **be provided.** The planning and development of these services is dependent on the work and expertise of demographers.

to gather: to collect; to bring together

to migrate: to move from one place to another

to segregate: to separate; to pull apart

utilities: basic services such as water and electrical power

B Reread the passage. Look at the passive constructions in boldface and then study the chart below.

Passive Voice

Sample Sentences	Notes
Census takers **are employed by the government** to collect data on the U.S. population. Much of this information **is obtained** through questionnaires that **are sent** to residents in the mail. In some cases, however, residents **are interviewed** by government officials at their places of residence.	The subject of a passive sentence is acted upon by an agent, although the agent isn't always mentioned. Only transitive verbs can be used in passive constructions. Passives are formed by combining a form of the auxiliary verb *be* with a **past participle**.
Census results **are studied** by demographers.	The preposition *by* precedes the agent of the action when the agent is explicitly stated.
The data **is going to be used** to identify issues related to public policy. The results **have been questioned** by critics.	Passives can be used with all tenses, modals, and with perfect and progressive forms.
A poll **should not have been conducted** so early in the election. Homeless people and undocumented residents **are never included** in an official census. Population statistics **are periodically needed** to help plan for growth. The study **will have already been concluded** by the end of this year. The results **should be completely disregarded** because of an error in the method of calculation.	**Adverbs** of negation and frequency come after the modal or auxiliary. Adverbs that modify a verb can appear directly before the main verb.
People who **are born** in foreign countries can become citizens through a process called naturalization.	Certain verbs such as *be born* and *be rumored* almost always occur in passive voice.
The questionnaires **have been sorted** and **processed**.	When two passives refer to the same subject, it is not necessary to repeat the auxiliary verb or verbs.

C Look at the passage below. In each blank space, write the correct form of the verb in parentheses. Include any modals or adverbs given with the verb and put everything in the correct order.

Demographics are an important aspect of public planning. Every ten years, the

population _____*is counted*_____ (count) and the results _____
                    (1)   (2)

(then publish) by the Census Bureau. The first census _____
                                                                      (3)

(take) in 1790, and it _____ (conduct) by U.S. marshals on
                              (4)

horseback. Population statistics _____ (need) so that the nation
                                          (5)

_____ (can divide) into equal voting groups. Over time, more specific
          (6)

questions _____ (add) to the census. The answers to these questions
                  (7)

_____ (now use) to help various governmental agencies draft plans
          (8)

and policies. Many new questions _____ (recently include) so the
                                            (9)

government can identify the kinds of resources that _____ (will
                                                              (10)

need) in the future. If the census shows, for example, that large numbers of children will be

entering school in upcoming years, the necessary funds _____ (should
                                                                  (11)

set aside) for the building of new schools.

■ **COMMUNICATE**

D **PAIR WORK** Listed below are some topics that might be on a census questionnaire. Take turns asking each other questions related to these topics. Use a passive construction whenever possible. You may choose not to answer a question if you find it too personal.

- age
- sex/gender
- race/ethnicity
- education
- address

- socioeconomic status
- income
- employment status
- religion
- marital status

- ownership (home, car, pet, etc.)
- language
- mobility (availability of transportation)

 When and where were you born?

 I was born in the Philippines, in 1989.

■ GRAMMAR IN CONTENT

A Reread the passage on page 202. Make a note of why each passive verb was used. Look at the chart below for help.

Use of Passive	
Sample Sentences	**Notes**
The Spanish language has always had an important role in the culture of New York City. In fact, Spanish **is spoken** as a first language **by** 24% of New Yorkers.	Use the **passive voice** with *by* to make the noun undergoing the action of the verb the subject of the sentence.
The city's population has grown steadily over the last decade. New housing **has been built** in response to the increasing demand.	The agent isn't mentioned when the agent is irrelevant, unimportant, unknown, difficult or impossible to identify, or obvious.
Errors **were made** during the experiment, leading to unreliable results.	The agent can also be omitted to avoid blaming or assigning responsibility for a mistake.
The correct procedures **must be followed** at all times.	Omitting the agent can help to avoid giving direct commands. It is also helpful in avoiding the use of an impersonal pronoun (such as *you*) in formal academic writing.
One problem ~~that is~~ often encountered in face-to-face interviews is a lack of candor.	Passives in identifying clauses can often be reduced. (See Lesson 19.)

B Read the following passage. On a separate sheet of paper, rewrite the passage, replacing the active voice with the passive voice whenever appropriate.

One issue that you should remember when designing and interpreting a survey is that demographics are population specific. Unfortunately, researchers often overgeneralize their results, and they should avoid this temptation. Another problem that you might encounter concerns the nature of the questions. For example, should you take the subject's age into account? Should you consider gender or socioeconomic status? When you omit important factors, you will have biased the results.

C Look at the following entry on the Cumberland Student Underground Blog. Edit the text, eliminating the *by* phrases that are irrelevant or awkward.

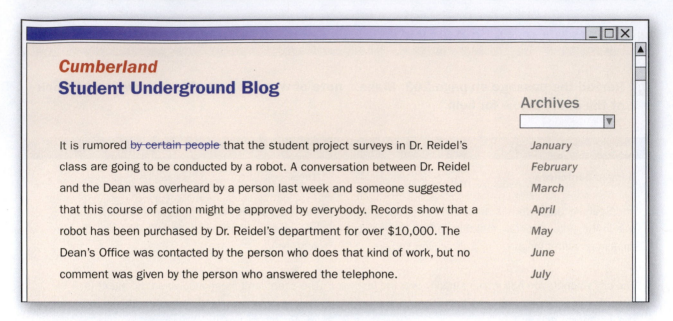

Cumberland
Student Underground Blog

Archives
▼

It is rumored ~~by certain people~~ that the student project surveys in Dr. Reidel's class are going to be conducted by a robot. A conversation between Dr. Reidel and the Dean was overheard by a person last week and someone suggested that this course of action might be approved by everybody. Records show that a robot has been purchased by Dr. Reidel's department for over $10,000. The Dean's Office was contacted by the person who does that kind of work, but no comment was given by the person who answered the telephone.

January
February
March
April
May
June
July

D Rewrite the following sentences in passive voice. Eliminate the *by* phrase whenever appropriate.

1. Technology has transformed American homes.

   American homes have been transformed by technology.

2. Two thirds of all Americans use a computer at home.

   _____

3. Computer makers equip most computers with Internet access.

   _____

4. Americans spend about $36 billion per year on their pets.

   _____

5. The majority of elderly people don't see computers as being necessary.

   _____

6. Single parents head 26 percent of American homes.

   _____

7. Twenty-nine million Americans speak Spanish at home.

   _____

E **GROUP WORK** What kinds of observations have you made about your local culture and society? You might talk about the role of technology in culture, for example, immigration trends, or the family. Share your observations in a group. Use passive constructions whenever possible, including *by* phrases only when necessary.

I think cell phones **are overused** in the United States. They're everywhere!

That's because they're so small and easy to carry. Convenience **is** really **valued** in the United States.

You think cell phones **are used** a lot here? You should go to China!

PART THREE	Middle Voice

■ GRAMMAR IN CONTENT

A Reread the passage on page 202. Put a wavy line under all the middle voice verbs. If you need help, use the chart below.

Middle Voice	
Sample Sentences	**Notes**
Population growth **will have doubled** by the end of the century.	Middle voice describes a state that seems to change by itself. Middle voice has characteristics of both active and passive voice. The verb form is the same as in the active voice; the subject is the same as in the passive voice.
Active: The information changed public opinion. **Passive:** Public opinion was changed by the information. **Middle:** Public opinion changed.	In middle voice sentences, there is no agent. Compare the **middle voice** with the **active** and **passive** voices, in which an agent performs an action. For more comparisons, see Appendix 2.
The population increased as a result of immigration. ~~The population was increased as a result of increased immigration.~~	When the following verbs are used to express a change of state, they typically occur in middle voice: *grow, benefit, move, rise, change, increase, decrease,* and *shift*. For a list of verbs that can be used in active, passive, and middle forms, see Appendix 2.

CD2,TR15

B Listen to the story from a college newspaper, and then answer the questions using complete sentences.

1. How have Cumberland students changed in the last 50 years?

_____

2. What was the educational goal of most Cumberland female students 50 years ago?

_____

3. Has this goal changed or remained the same?

_____

4. Has the number of women students increased or decreased over the years?

_____

5. Have attitudes toward women changed? If so, how?

_____

6. What do you think the male student quoted at the end of the story meant? Why is his comment humorous?

_____

■ COMMUNICATE

C **GROUP WORK** In a group, talk about changes that you have noticed in your community or place of birth. Discuss the benefits and disadvantages, if any, of those changes. Use a variety of active, passive, and middle voice verbs.

The roads **have improved** in my country. When I was a child, the road I lived on was dirt and gravel. Now **it's paved.**

It's the same where I come from. My hometown **has grown** from a small village to a modern city.

The exact opposite happened where I **was born.** It was a farming town, but the **farms closed** and **everybody moved** to the city.

D Look at the chart. It shows data from two demographic surveys that were taken over the course of two years. Use the data to write a narrative summary. Include passive, active, and middle verbs. Do you see any patterns or trends in the data? Draw conclusions about these trends in your summary.

DEMOGRAPHIC SURVEY

City: Boston

Street: Worthington

	2008	2009
Number of Households Interviewed	25	25
Average Number of Residents	4	4
Average Number of Children	3	2
Children Raised by Two Parents	11	7
Children Raised by Single Parent	5	10

The survey was conducted over two years, from 2008 to 2009. Worthington Street, a residential area in the city of Boston, was the focus of the study. Twenty-five households were included in the survey.

GRAMMAR AND VOCABULARY Write a report about language use in your school or community. What languages are spoken? What does the prevalence of these languages reveal about social trends? Use a variety of active, passive, and middle voice verbs in your report.

PROJECT With a group of classmates, design a demographic research project that you can do at your school. Think of a question you want to explore and a method for obtaining data. You might create a questionnaire, for example, or take notes based on observations. Work together to write a summary of your findings (use passive and middle voice). Present your findings to the class.

 INTERNET Use the Internet to assist you in your written report and group research project. Use terms related to your project, and include the search term "demographics." In your written report and class presentation, explain how you used information from the Internet to complete the tasks.

PART 1
Verb + Infinitive

PART 2
Verb + Noun Phrase + Infinitive

PART 3
Passive Verb + Infinitive

Lesson (24)

Nutrition: Diet and Health

■ CONTENT VOCABULARY

Look at the food pyramid. Talk about the foods from each section of the pyramid. What food groups do these sections represent? What are some examples of different foods from each group?

Many people have been trying to become healthy by **supplementing** their diets with foods that have been **enriched** with added **nutrients** such as **vitamins** and fiber. Many **processed foods** claim to have special nutritional value because of the nutrients that have been added to them. Processed foods are made from real food, but they have chemicals and **preservatives** added. Freeze-dried foods, foods with **artificial** sweetener, juice **concentrates**, and dried instant soups are a few examples of processed foods.

Read the text below the food pyramid. Look up any words you don't know. Write each word, its definition, and a sentence that illustrates its use in your vocabulary journal.

■ THINK ABOUT IT

Think about what you eat every day. Do you eat a balanced diet? What kinds of food do you eat most often? Do you ever eat processed food or food cooked with processed fat? Do you supplement your diet with vitamins and energy drinks? In your writing journal, write about at least one of these questions for five minutes.

■ GRAMMAR IN CONTENT

CD2,TR16

A Read and listen to Dr. Lewis's lecture.

Nutritionism and Health

In the 1970s and 1980s, scientists began to publish research indicating that for better health, people needed to eat enough nutrients and to avoid fats. This was the beginning of what is now referred to as nutritionism—a belief that it is the nutrients in foods that are important, not the foods themselves. Advocates of nutritionism sought to discover the ideal balance of nutrients regardless of what foods they were in. As a result of this trend, manufacturers of processed foods began to enrich their foods with nutrients.

Unfortunately, one consequence of this approach to marketing is that individuals now tend to eat more of certain kinds of food, often because these foods claim to provide essential vitamins or fiber. However, many of these foods also contribute to obesity, and some have even been found to be associated with heart disease, cancer, and diabetes.

Many nutritionists are known to have rejected the nutritionism approach to diet. The message that informed nutritionists are trying to spread nowadays is that people need to choose food for its inherent value, not for the nutrients it is supposed to contain. Nutritionists counsel individuals to select foods with a healthy proportion of protein, carbohydrates, and fats. They also advise consumers to eat small portions. Diets with reasonable amounts of fresh foods (rather than processed foods) are believed to be the most effective approach to long-term health. A person who follows such a plan is expected to maintain a reasonable weight and live longer.

to consume: to eat and drink

a carbohydrate: any of a group of nutrients such as sugar or starch that provide the body with energy

diabetes: a disease involving the body's inability to process sugar properly

a proportion: a ratio; a percentage

a trend: an observable pattern

B Reread the passage. <u>Underline</u> all the infinitives in the reading. Make a list of the verbs that precede the infinitives. When you are finished, study the chart below and compare your list with the list at the bottom of the chart.

Verb + Infinitive	
Sample Sentences	**Notes**
Tomoko prefers to eat healthy foods.	An infinitive consists of *to* + **base form of the verb**. Infinitives and infinitive phrases can act as objects of verbs. See the list below.
Aisha's mother doesn't **like to diet**. Personally, I **hate dieting** too.	Some verbs (*like, love, prefer, hate, begin, start, continue, can't stand*) can be followed by an **infinitive** or a **gerund**. Some verbs (*try, remember, forget*) can be followed by an infinitive or gerund; however, the meaning of the resulting sentences is significantly different.
With his new diet, Blas **hopes to improve** his health. With a little luck, he **expects to have lost** five pounds by the end of this month. In any case, his doctor **seems to be surprised** by his progress.	Simple infinitives are most common, but infinitives can also take progressive, perfect, and passive forms.
Marlene likes **to exercise** and **stay** in shape.	When **two infinitives** follow a verb, *to* can be omitted before the second infinitive.

See Appendix 3 for a list of verbs commonly followed by infinitives.

C Complete the sentences in the following passage by providing the correct form of the verbs in parentheses.

Americans ___seem to be eating___ (seem/eat) more. As the population has
(1)

gained weight, more people have _____ (start/experience)
(2)

weight-related health problems. For example, diabetes _____
(3)

(tend/occur) more frequently in heavier people, and weight has also

_____ (prove/be) a factor in some forms of cancer and arthritis.
(4)

In addition, overweight people _____ (tend/snore) more loudly
(5)

when they sleep.

In response to warnings from their doctors, many Americans are now

_____ (try/lose) weight. Some _____
(6)   (7)

(need/follow) a special diet. Others may _____ (want/lose)
(8)

weight more quickly. They may take diet pills or _____
(9)

(arrange/join) a program at a weight loss clinic. Research indicates, however, that

if they _____ (want/maintain) their weight loss, most
(10)

people will _____ (need/control) the number of calories
(11)

they consume, _____ (eat) whole, healthful food, and
(12)

_____ (get) plenty of exercise.
(13)

D Listen to the recording and then complete the sentences with the missing phrases.

CD2,TR17

1. Esther _____ foods with lots of carbohydrates.

2. She _____ fewer processed foods.

3. She _____ sugar,

   but she _____ carbohydrates.

4. She _____ only 2 pounds,

   although she _____ 20 pounds.

5. So far her diabetes doesn't _____.

E **PAIR WORK** What kinds of food do you tend to eat? Tell your partner which foods you like to eat and which foods you try to avoid.

> **I like to eat** noodles. I eat them for breakfast, lunch, and dinner whenever I can.

> That's a lot of noodles. Do you eat the processed ones, too?

> Well, generally I **try to avoid** processed foods, but I will eat the dried noodle soups.

PART TWO	Verb + Noun Phrase + Infinitive

■ **GRAMMAR IN CONTENT**

A Reread the passage on page 212. Look at all the infinitives that you <u>underlined</u> in the reading. If an infinitive is preceded by a noun phrase, (circle) the noun phrase. If you need help, use the chart below.

Verb + Noun Phrase + Infinitive

Sample Sentences	Notes
Sarah **expects her family to be** supportive of her decision to become a vegetarian. ↓ Sarah expects **them to be** supportive of her decision to become a vegetarian.	Some infinitives are preceded by a noun phrase. See below for a list of verbs that can be followed by an infinitive or base form of a verb. Most pronouns in front of an infinitive need to be in object form.
Aisha **is helping me to count** calories. ↓ Aisha **is helping me count** calories.	*Help* can be followed by either an infinitive or the base form of the verb.
Robert **reminded himself to check** the caloric content on the label.	Pronouns before the infinitive need to be in **reflexive form** if they have the same referent as the subject of the sentence.

Some Common Verbs + Noun Phrase + Infinitive

advise	counsel	help	remind
allow	enable	instruct	tell
ask	encourage	like	want
believe	expect	order	warn
cause	forbid	persuade	
consider	force	prepare	

B Read the dialog. Complete the sentences by putting the words in parentheses in the correct order.

Aisha: Hey, Aisha. What's new?

Esther: Well, my mom ___*persuaded me to lose*___ (to lose/me/persuaded)
(1)

10 pounds, and I just got back from getting a diet from my doctor. He

_____ (told/to keep/me) my food intake down to 1,200
(2)

calories a day. I _____ (to prescribe/him/wanted) me diet
(3)

pills, but he wouldn't. So I need _____ (me/you/to help).
(4)

Aisha: How can I help you? You're the one who's dieting.

Esther: Come on. You can _____ (me/to figure out/help) the
(5)

calorie count for my food. You can _____ (warn/me/to
(6)

stop) when I reach my limit.

Aisha: OK, I'm always counting calories. What are you going to have?

Esther: Well, I want to stay motivated, so I'm _____ (myself/to
(7)

eat/allowing) one sweet a day. I just ordered a hot fudge sundae.

Aisha: That's at least 1,000 calories already.

Esther: You've got to be kidding. Are you going to _____ (tell/to
(8)

send/the waiter) it back?

Aisha: No. As your best friend, I'm going to make a huge sacrifice—I'm going to help

_____ (not/to eat/you) too much by eating some of it, too.
(9)

C Complete the passage below with the words in parentheses. Change the form of the verbs as necessary, and add proper nouns or pronouns whenever appropriate.

Esther's doctor has told her that she must control the level of sugar in her blood if she

wants to be healthy. He has ___*warned Esther to cut down*___ (warn/cut down) on processed
(1)

sugar. If she craves something sweet, he has _____ (advise/eat) fruit.
(2)

Esther's roommate has been very supportive. Esther _____
(3)

(persuade/help) with her diet. Now Aisha _____ (forbid/bring) any
(4)

soft drinks or sweets into their dorm room. Esther has also _____
(5)

(promise/stay) on the diet when she eats out.

After 2 months, Esther's blood sugar level is much better, and she's lost 10 pounds.

Aisha _____ (not/expect/lose) weight. However, she didn't realize that
(6)

Esther's diet would affect her, too. Esther's diet has _____ (also cause/
(7)

Aisha/lose) 8 pounds.

■ **C O M M U N I C A T E**

D **PAIR WORK** Role-play a dialog with a partner. One of you has concerns about your diet.
The other one gives advice and suggestions. Use noun phrases with infinitives whenever
possible. When you are finished, switch roles.

My doctor **told me to cut down on** fat, but my cholesterol is still high.

Wow, I've got high cholesterol too. My doctor **advised me not to eat** any fried food.

PART THREE	Passive Verb + Infinitive

■ **G R A M M A R   I N   C O N T E N T**

A Reread the passage on page 212. Find all the verbs preceding the infinitives (these are
the verbs that you listed). Highlight the ones that are in the passive voice. Check your
answers with a partner. If you need help, use the chart below.

Passive Verb + Infinitive	
Sample Sentences	**Notes**
Sami has asked **Chris to help** Marie with her project. ↓ **Chris** has been asked by Sami **to help** Marie with her project. She expects **all her friends to participate.** ↓ **All her friends** are expected **to participate.**	Many verbs with noun phrase (**NP**) + **infinitive** can appear in a passive form. The NP before the infinitive, which was an object in the active voice, becomes the subject of the sentence.

B Read the passage. Using the words in parentheses, fill in the blanks with a passive and infinitive. Use the tense indicated.

There are three types of fat: regular unsaturated, saturated, and unsaturated trans fats. Of the three, trans fats have recently been receiving the most attention. You may recall that trans fats rarely occur in nature, so foods that _have been found to contain_ (present perfect: find/contain) them are generally processed foods. Like saturated fats, trans

fats _____ (present perfect: reveal/cause) changes in the body
that are associated with heart problems. The trans fats _____
(3)
(present: consider/be) particularly dangerous, and patients with heart problems

_____ (present: tell/avoid) foods that contain them. It's not
(4)
always easy to figure out which foods have trans fats. For example, trans fats

_____ (present: know/be) present in commercial baked goods and
(5)
fried foods. However, many unexpected foods are made with trans fats. Patients who need

to avoid trans fats _____ (present: advise/eliminate) from their diet
(6)
any cakes, cookies, and pies that do not include information about trans fat content on their

labels. In addition, they _____ (present: counsel/not eat) any cereals,
(7)
crackers, soups, or even nondairy creamers whose labels do not indicate whether they
contain any trans fats.

C Aisha called her mother, but her mother wasn't home, so Aisha left a voice mail message. As you listen to her voice mail, (circle) the answer to the questions.

CD2, TR18

1. Who gave the warning?	The students	Dr. Lewis
2. Who received the warning?	The students	Dr. Lewis
3. Who is going to avoid trans fats this week?	The students	Dr. Lewis
4. Who said to avoid trans fats?	The students	Dr. Lewis
5. Who is going to read food labels?	The students	Dr. Lewis

D Work with a partner to change each active sentence into a passive.

1. The dietician advised Sara to eat more fresh fruit.

   Sara was advised by the dietician to eat more fresh fruit.

2. The doctor advised Adam to eat more fiber.

   _____

3. The camp allows children to have one snack a day.

   _____

4. The U.S. Surgeon General has warned the public about the dangers of obesity.

   _____

5. Critics have blamed extreme diets for certain health problems.

   _____

E Listen to the lecture and take notes. Then answer the following questions in complete sentences.

CD2, TR19

1. What have doctors begun to study?

   Doctors have begun to study the effects of excess weight on health.

2. What did the doctors initially assume?

   _____

3. What did they find?

   _____

4. Describe the study that the doctors undertook.

   _____

5. What happened to one volunteer?

   _____

6. What did that volunteer claim?

   _____

7. How did Dr. Atkinson explain the anomaly?

   _____

F **PAIR WORK** Take turns talking about health advice you have received from friends, family members, and specialists. Use the passive voice and other constructions with infinitive verbs whenever you can.

> I **was told by** my girlfriend that I should lose some weight, but I'm not worried about it.

> I know what you mean. **I've been told** the same thing, but I **don't want to go** on a diet.

Connection | Putting It Together

GRAMMAR AND VOCABULARY Write a dialog between a nurse or dietician and a patient. Have the nurse give the patient suggestions and advice on how to live a healthy lifestyle and improve his or her diet. Use as many passive constructions as possible.

PROJECT Work with a group. Prepare a report for the class about attitudes toward food and body weight in two or three different countries or regions. Choose countries that you have visited or studied, and share your thoughts and observations with the group. Talk about the body types (thin, heavy, muscular, etc.) that are valued in that culture and their attitudes toward health and diet. Summarize your discussion in a written report. One of the group members can then read the report to the class.

 INTERNET Form several different groups. Using the search term "diet plans," look up different kinds of diets. Each group can take notes on two or three different kinds of diets. Later, the groups can compare the diets and discuss the pros and cons of each with the whole class.

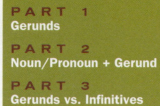

PART 1
Gerunds

PART 2
Noun/Pronoun + Gerund

PART 3
Gerunds vs. Infinitives

Lesson 25

Philosophy: Ethics

■ CONTENT VOCABULARY

Read and discuss the quotations with your classmates.

"You can not make yourself feel something you do not feel, but you can make yourself do right in spite of your feelings."

—Pearl S. Buck, Author

"Ethics is a code of values which guide our choices and actions and determine the purpose and course of our lives."

—Ayn Rand, Author

"To see what is right and not do it is to lack courage."

—Confucius, Philosopher

"If you tell the truth, you don't have to remember anything."

—Mark Twain, Author

"Life is the sum of your choices."

—Albert Camus, Philosopher

"Be the change you wish to see in the world."

—Mohandas Gandhi, Spiritual Leader

"The time is always right to do what is right."

—Martin Luther King, Jr., Civil Rights Leader

One of the concerns of **Ethics**, a branch of philosophy, is the question of **morality** and **proper conduct**. What does it mean to be **moral**? What **constitutes** a **virtuous** life? Is **virtue** a matter of behavior or thought? Are good actions dependent on good **intentions**? What is one's duty to other people and society? **Philosophers** have been asking questions like these for thousands of years.

Read the text below the quotations. Look up any words you don't know. Write each word, its definition, and a sentence that illustrates its use in your vocabulary journal.

■ THINK ABOUT IT

In your writing journal, write for five minutes about one or more of the questions below. When you are finished, share what you wrote with a classmate.

What's your definition of "right behavior"? How can people know that what they are doing is right? Should they even bother asking themselves these questions? Why or why not?

■ GRAMMAR IN CONTENT

A Read and listen to the lecture on ethics.

CD2,TR20

Ethics

Ethics is a branch of philosophy. It tries **to answer** the question: What should I do in any given situation? In other words, is **doing** a particular action right or wrong? **Answering** this question may seem easy, but it isn't if you really think about it. There are many theories that attempt **to define** right actions, but in general, almost all theories of right action can be classified as **being** either End Result theories or Moral Rule theories.

End Result theories say an action is right if it results in the maximum good for those involved. **Defining** "good" is the first step in End Result theories. This is because **doing** what is right depends on **knowing** what is good. Right actions are the ones in which all the people involved in the action experience the most good.

Moral Rule theories are different from End Result theories. These theories say that right actions consist of **following** moral rules. Usually moral rules come from religious books or traditions. The problem with Moral Rule theories is that not all people can agree **to follow** the same religious book or traditions, and sometimes perfectly sound moral rules don't seem **to apply** in every situation. For example, most people would agree that "don't lie" is a good candidate for a moral rule. At the same time, however, most people want **to avoid hurting** people they care about. If **telling** the truth would hurt someone, most people who usually try not **to lie** would at least consider not **telling** the truth.

sound: free from error, fallacy, or misapprehension

B Reread the passage on page 222. Look at all the gerunds in the passage and then study the chart below.

Gerunds	
Sample Sentences	**Notes**
Asking good questions is more important than **knowing** all the answers. Buddhists avoid **harming** animals or **causing** any living thing to suffer. Luisa wasn't happy about **lying** to her friend. **Telling the truth** has always been important to her.	Gerunds, like nouns, can be **subjects** or **objects**. They can also be the **object of a preposition**. Gerunds can do most of the things nouns do.
Doing the right thing isn't always easy or natural. It requires a lot of will power. The alternative, however, is to follow your impulses, and that can be dangerous. **Doing what you want** often leads to unethical behavior.	Sometimes a gerund is an entire phrase or clause consisting of the verb + *-ing* form and words coming after it that complete the thought.

C Edit the passage below, changing nouns and verbs to related gerund forms whenever preferable or necessary. Follow the example.

Deciding
~~To decide~~ on the right course of action is a kind of virtue. Virtues are those dispositions (that is, tendencies or inclinations) that lead to live a good life. Dispositions that do not lead to proper life are vices. Philosophers argue that we can't always tell what promotes good life by to look at a religious book or by imagination the end result. This theory says that to ask an expert is the best way of decision what we should do. For Aristotle, ask an expert means consultation a virtuous person.

D **PAIR WORK** Aristotle observed that virtuous people often avoid excess. This included too much of something as well as too little. For example, both eating too much or eating too little would not be virtuous. Work with a partner and list four other things that Aristotle might think one should avoid.

How about work?

What do you mean?

Well, I think you should avoid working too much as well as working too little.

E **WRITE** In your journal, write a paragraph about things you enjoy and things you don't enjoy. Use gerunds. Read your paragraph to a partner and listen to your partner's paragraph. Report on what your partner does and does not enjoy to the class.

PART TWO	Noun/Pronoun + Gerund

■ GRAMMAR IN CONTENT

A **PAIR WORK** With a partner, reread the passage on page 222. Above each gerund, write its subject. If you need help, use the chart below.

Noun/Pronoun + Gerund	
Sample Sentences	**Notes**
Terry likes **doing** volunteer work. **He** believes in **helping** others.	If the **gerund** is the object of the sentence, the **subject** is usually the one that does the action of the gerund.
Making good decisions is the foundation for a happy life.	If the **gerund** is the subject of the sentence and there is no determiner in front of the gerund, the speaker is usually making a general statement. The subject of the gerund is "people in general."
John's stealing is very unethical.	If there is a **possessive noun** or **determiner** in front of the **gerund**, it is doing the action of the gerund. Nouns or pronouns functioning as the subject of a gerund should be in the possessive form.
Note: In less formal English, especially spoken English, the possessive marker is often omitted in front of the noun; for example: *I appreciate John helping,* rather than *I appreciate John's helping.*	

B Read each of the following questions, then give your opinion. Write a statement using a gerund. Vary your sentence structure so that you use gerunds as both subjects and objects in your sentences.

1. Should wealthier members of society be forced to pay higher taxes than people with low incomes?

   <u>*Yes, they should. Sharing the tax burden according to one's income is fair.*</u>

2. Monica rented a car and found $500 in the glove compartment. She kept the money and didn't say anything about it when she returned the car. Do you think it was OK for her to keep the money?

   _____

   _____

3. John and Alex work at the same company. John accidentally found out Alex's salary, which happens to be much more than his co-workers make. John revealed Alex's salary to his co-workers, and now they all dislike Alex. What do you think of John's gossiping?

   _____

   _____

4. A clothing factory in Southeast Asia employs children and pays them less than $3.00 per day to make silk shirts. A consumer in the United States pays about $75 for one of those shirts. Are these consumers responsible for the working conditions in which the shirts are made?

   _____

   _____

5. Certain states, such as Massachusetts and California, have laws against gambling, and yet some of those same states also hold lotteries. Do you think gambling is ethically acceptable if it's being conducted by the government in the form of a lottery?

   _____

   _____

■ **COMMUNICATE**

C **PAIR WORK** Work with a partner. Sometimes university life requires a roommate. Imagine you have a new roommate. Tell your classmate two things that your new roommate might do that you would find objectionable, and two things that you would enjoy. Use gerunds.

I would object to his playing loud music late at night.

Yeah, I wouldn't like that either.

■ GRAMMAR IN CONTENT

A Reread the passage on page 222. Put a ⟨circle⟩ around the three verbs that can be followed by either a gerund or an infinitive. Put a ☐box☐ around the four verbs that can't be followed by a gerund, but can be followed by an infinitive. Put a ~~wavy line~~ under the two verbs that can only be followed by a gerund. Be careful to mark only verbs that are followed by gerunds or infinitives. If you need help, use the chart below.

Gerunds vs. Infinitives

Sample Sentences	Notes
To err is human. Philosophers attempt **to answer** questions related to ethics and human existence.	**Infinitives**, like gerunds, can be the subject or the object of a sentence.
Some philosophers prefer **not to make** general, categorical statements about ethics and truth. Instead, they tend **to emphasize** the unique circumstances and ethical implications of every situation.	In a negated infinitive, **not** comes before the infinitive.
Buddha warned **against becoming** too attached to results or outcomes.	Only **gerunds** (not infinitives or any other verb form) can follow a **preposition**.
The Greek philosopher Epictetus **recommended living** a life of moderation and self-discipline.	Some verbs, such as *recommend,* must be followed by a gerund.*
Albert Camus suggested that human life is ultimately meaningless. He **refused to accept**, however, that we should resign ourselves to hopelessness and despair.	Some verbs, such as *refuse,* must be followed by an infinitive.*
Mohandas Gandhi, the Indian leader and philosopher, **tried to live** a simple life, and he had very few possessions. Many of his followers **tried giving up** their possessions too. The majority of them, however, found it was almost impossible to live such an austere lifestyle.	Some verbs can be followed by either a gerund or an infinitive, although the meaning differs in some cases.*

*For a list of these verbs, see Appendix 3.

B Fill in the blank to complete each sentence. Use the infinitive or gerund form of the verb in parentheses, as appropriate.

1. Children often enjoy _____*asking*_____ (ask) philosophical questions.

2. Vijay considered _____ (cheat) on the test, but realized he would only be cheating himself.

3. Gloria decided _____ (tell) the truth, no matter what the consequences might be.

4. In spite of his lengthy explanation, the professor only succeeded in _____ (confuse) his students.

5. Most people have at least thought about _____ (take) something that doesn't belong to them.

C Listen to the lecture about the philosopher Immanuel Kant. Then look at the following statements. Would Kant agree or disagree with each statement? Circle "A" or "D."

CD2,TR21

1. A   D   Even if you believe that lying is wrong, it's OK to lie if it will save someone's life.
2. A   D   Pure reason is the best way to determine the morality of an action.
3. A   D   It's difficult to know which rules to follow because the rules change in every situation.
4. A   D   To be immoral, an action must ultimately be irrational.
5. A   D   The best way to determine if an action is moral is to consult religious writings or traditions.

■ **COMMUNICATE**

D **PAIR WORK** Take turns with a partner. Tell each other the following: two things you appreciate; two things you avoid; two things you need to do; two things you hope to do. Use gerunds and infinitives as appropriate.

> OK. Tell me two things you appreciate.

> Well, I appreciate **swimming** on a hot day and **having** a nice cold drink.

Connection | Putting It Together

GRAMMAR AND VOCABULARY Write a short essay giving your views on the difference between right and wrong. What is your personal "code of behavior"? Are there any actions that you find particularly offensive? Why are those actions so objectionable to you? What values guide your own actions? Give a few examples to help illustrate your points. Use as many gerunds and infinitives as you can.

PROJECT Work with small groups. Interview someone from your community: a teacher, a religious leader, a civic leader, or even a student leader. Ask that person how we can know the best way to live. Does the person have an easy rule that we all could follow? Give a panel report to the class on what your group found.

 INTERNET On the Internet, search for one of the following great thinkers (or another that you know of):

- Siddhartha Gautama (Buddha)
- Lao Tzu
- Confucius
- Aristotle
- Plato

- Socrates
- David Hume
- Immanuel Kant
- Albert Camus
- Jean-Paul Sartre
- Simone de Beauvoir

- Friedrich Nietzsche
- Ayn Rand
- Michel Foucault
- Eckhart Tolle
- Deepak Chopra

Take notes on the philosopher's life, work, and major ideas. Summarize your findings in a paragraph, and share your work with classmates.

A Derek has come to Dr. Levy's office to talk to her about his grade in her statistics class. Complete the conversation with the correct form of the verb in parentheses.

Derek: I wanted to apologize for always being late to class. It's because of my job.

If I have to leave early, my boss always ___*needs*___ (need) me to stay
(1)

late. If I _____ (not stay), he reduces my salary. At my
(2)

last job, if I _____ (have) to leave early, my boss always
(3)

_____ (give) me the time off. This job I have now pays so
(4)

well that I can't afford to leave it. If I _____ (quit), I'd have
(5)

to drop out of school.

Dr. Levy: Unfortunately it's affecting your grade. If you _____
(6)

(arrive) on time for your last test, you _____ (get) a much
(7)

better grade. But you were half an hour late, and you didn't finish the test.

And if you _____ (not miss) the lecture on probability
(8)

theory, you _____ (receive) a higher score.
(9)

B Complete the text with the correct form of the verb or verb phrase in parentheses.

Hey Bert,

I've been intending ___*to write*___ (write) you a long note for weeks now,
(1)

but things have been pretty busy. I talked to Mom last week, and she said that you'd

stopped by and asked about me. She told _____ (I, not, put off)
(2)

_____ (write) you any longer!
(3)

Right now I'm trying _____ (apply) to as many colleges as possible.
(4)

The school I really want to go to is reported _____ (accept) only 20% of
(5)

the students who apply. Several of us are hoping _____ (be accepted) by a
(6)

really good school. Dr. Moore is helping _____ (we, write) our applications.
(7)

If you've got any advice on _____ (write) applications to graduate
(8)

school, let me know!

Mehmet

C Doris is writing a report on her internship with a small business this past summer. Complete the report with the correct form (passive or middle voice) of the verb in parenthenses.

Last summer I was an intern at Vitamin King. I really learned a lot about small businesses there. Vitamin King started as a small family business, but in the last few years its business practices had ___*changed*___ (change) a lot, and the business had
_____ (grow) rapidly. In fact, that's why I _____ (hire).
  (2)   (3)
However, the first week I was there, the owners _____ (accuse) of false
  (4)
advertising, and some of their products _____ (take off) the market. There
  (5)
was quite a scandal. Several of the top officials _____ (arrested). And the
  (6)
problems just _____ (increase). It turned out that in addition to the false
  (7)
advertisements, taxes had _____ (not file) correctly, and important legal
  (8)
documents had _____ (destroy).
  (9)
    As a result, the business _____ (shrink) almost overnight. I was
  (10)
afraid I was going to _____ (fire). However, new management took over,
  (11)
and the business _____ (move) to a new location. After a month, the
  (12)
public's attention _____ (shift) to other scandals. Relationships with new
  (13)
customers and suppliers _____ (develop), and in fact, the last month I was
  (14)
there, business had _____ (improve) a lot. I learned a lot more than I had
  (15)
expected.

LEARNER LOG Check (✔) *Yes* or *I Need More Practice.*

Lesson	I Can Use . . .	Yes	I Need More Practice
21	Present Factual Conditionals, Past Factual Conditionals, and Future Conditionals		
22	Hypothetical Statements and Questions in the Conditional; Past Non-Factual Conditionals; *Wish* and *Hope*		
23	Passive and Middle Voice		
24	Verb + Infinitive; Verb + Noun Phrase + Infinitive; Passive Verb + Infinitive		
25	Gerunds; Noun/Pronoun + Gerund; Gerunds vs. Infinitives		

PART 1
Object Noun Clauses with *that*

PART 2
Object Noun Clauses with *if*,
whether, and *wh-* Words

Lesson 26

Technology:
Robotics

■ CONTENT VOCABULARY

Look at the picture. What is the robot doing? What are the advantages of having a robot perform surgery?

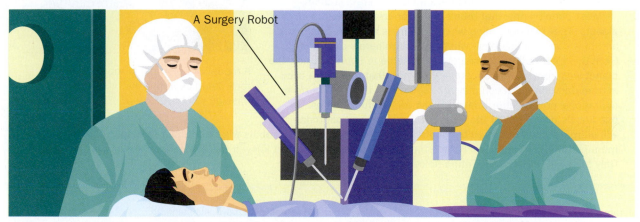

A Surgery Robot

Robots are at work all around us. They are used by hospitals, **manufacturers**, **warehouses**, **law enforcement**, and **private citizens**. Robots perform **surgery**, **dispose** of **bombs** and other **hazardous** material, and **transport** goods from place to place. Robots usually perform tasks that are too dangerous, **precise**, or boring for people to do.

Read the description below the picture. Look up any words you don't know. Write each word, its definition, and a sentence that illustrates its use in your vocabulary journal.

■ THINK ABOUT IT

Discuss the following questions with your classmates: What is the difference between a robot and a machine? What can a robot do that a machine can't do? What is the difference between a robot and a human being? Can a robot think, for example? Give your definition of "thinking" to help explain your answer. Then, summarize the discussion in your writing journal.

■ **GRAMMAR IN CONTENT**

CD2,TR22

A Read and listen to the following.

Robotics

Many people think **that robots are mechanical devices in the form of humans.** However, an engineer will tell you **that robots are really electronic devices operating by remote control.**

You probably know **that robots perform many jobs that are especially dirty, dangerous, or boring.** However, did you realize **that manufacturers are beginning to design robotic pets?** Certain manufacturers have marketed mechanical pets, but it's unclear **whether the general public will have a lot of interest in them.**

Most people know **that robots are often used to explore other planets.** They can determine **whether there is water on a planet,** and they can also establish **what kinds of minerals exist there.** From this information, scientists may be able to figure out **how the planet was formed.** And of course you know **that robots are used in manufacturing.** But you may not realize **that they also perform operations, provide entertainment, and even defuse bombs.** No one knows **how many of the jobs that humans carry out today will ultimately be performed by robots.** Some people believe **that robots will be completely responsible for manufacturing in the future.** For the time being, however, we don't know **if these scenarios are fact or fiction.** Only time will tell **what the future holds for robots.**

A model of Sojourner, a robot that took rock samples during NASA's Pathfinder mission to Mars.

automatic: self-operating, working by itself

a device: an electrical or mechanical machine

electronic: devices controlled or operated by electric currents, for example, electronic mail (e-mail) or electronic keyboards

to establish: to prove, substantiate

remote control: control of a device or machine from a distance

ultimately: in the end

B Find all the *that*-clauses in the reading on page 232, and then study the chart below.

Object Noun Clauses with *that*	
Sample Sentences	**Notes**
Writers of science fiction have predicted **that robots will do more than mere tasks in the future.** They say **that robots will even serve as friendly companions.**	Noun clauses are entire clauses that act like a noun. As a noun clause, they can act as objects of a sentence, and they follow this pattern: main sentence + *that* + verb + complement
Ming: Do you think ~~that~~ most people will have their own robots in the future? **Shawn:** I think ~~that~~ robots are *already* part of daily life.	In conversation and informal discourse, *that* is often omitted.
Most engineers agree **that robots will play an increasingly important role in the future.**	Only certain verbs can take a noun clause as an object. These verbs include *believe, say, think,* and *agree.* For a more complete list, see Appendix 4.

C Read the following dialog. Order the words in parentheses so that they form object noun clauses. Include *that* in some cases, or leave it out for sentence variation.

Salvador: You know, most people expect _that robots will become more prevalent in the_ **(1)** _near future_. (more prevalent in the near future/will become/robots)

Estella: Personally, I don't believe _____ **(2)** _____. (will happen/that/any time soon)

Salvador: Dr. Wagner says the same thing. He worries _____ **(3)** _____. (the public/too much too soon/is expecting) Some people are hoping

_____ **(4)** _____. (available soon/will be/robotic pets)

Estella: A manufacturer already tried to market one, but consumers claimed

_____ **(5)** _____. (it/neither useful nor cuddly/was)

D Listen to the news report and answer the following questions in complete sentences.

1. What did designers at RoboTech demonstrate today?

   <u>Designers at RoboTech demonstrated that a lightweight robot may soon be available</u>
   <u>to help keep American homes clean.</u>

2. When do the developers believe they will be ready to market the robot?

   _____

   _____

3. When does Robert O'Toole think the company will start taking orders?

   _____

   _____

4. What had skeptics assumed about an effective robot household helper?

   _____

   _____

5. What has RoboTech shown?

   _____

   _____

■ **COMMUNICATE**

E **GROUP WORK** Discuss your predictions about robotics and other kinds of technology in the future. Use object noun clauses as often as possible.

You know, I think **most machines will be able to talk** before long. You'll be able to talk to your computer, for example, or your car.

Yeah, in fact, I've heard **that some cars can already talk to the driver.**

I wouldn't be surprised, but I **hope it's not true.** I worry **that machines will start telling *us* what to do!**

■ **GRAMMAR IN CONTENT**

A **Find all the *if/whether*-clauses in the reading on page 232. Look for the *wh*-clauses as well, then study the chart below.**

Object Noun Clauses with *if, whether,* and *wh*- Words	
Sample Sentences	**Notes**
Q: Are engineers at RoboCorp designing a household robot? A: They won't say. ↓ Engineers at RoboCorp won't say **whether they are designing a household robot.** Q: Are they going to do more market research first? A: They haven't decided. ↓ They haven't decided **if they are going to do more market research first.**	Object noun clauses may begin with *if* or *whether*. *Whether* and *if* are similar in meaning and are often used interchangeably. They are both used to introduce embedded *yes/no* questions. Embed a *yes/no* question into the main clause as shown.
Q: What kind of robot is RoboCorp developing? A: The competition hasn't been able to find out. ↓ The competition hasn't been able to find out **what kind of robot RoboCorp is developing.**	Object noun clauses can begin with *wh*- question words such as *who, what, which, when, where, why,* and *how*. They are used to introduce embedded *wh*- questions. Embed the question as shown.
Q: How did consumers rate the product during market research? A: The marketing report doesn't say. ↓ Incorrect: ~~The marketing report doesn't say how did consumers rate the product.~~ Correct: The marketing report doesn't say **how consumers rated** the product.	Object noun clauses with *wh*- have normal sentence word order within the clause, not question word order. The helping verb does not precede the subject.
Q: Who developed the new robot? A: It's unclear. ↓ It's unclear **who developed the new robot.**	When a question with a *wh*- word functioning as a subject is turned into an embedded question, there is no change in the word order; that is, the embedded question has the same word order as the regular question.

See Appendix 4 for a list of verbs followed by object noun clauses with *if, whether,* and *wh*- words.

B Complete the unfinished sentences in the text below using the corresponding questions in the box. Change the questions to noun clause objects with an initial *whether* for *yes/no* questions or an initial *wh-* word for *wh-* questions. Follow the example.

1. Could such robots be dangerous to society?
2. How easily can large machines injure or kill an inattentive human?
3. What could they do to protect humans from possible problems with these robots?
4. What kinds of laws might protect human beings?
5. Did the laws work?
6. Were there situations in which a robot relying on these laws might make the wrong decision?
7. What circumstances might lead to real-world problems for Azimov's robotic laws?

Since the first robot capable of thought was proposed, scientists and authors of science fiction have been wondering *whether such robots could be dangerous to society*.
                                    (1)

Everyone recognizes _____

_____. If robots begin to move more freely and make decisions, the
                (2)

manufacturers must determine _____
                                  (3)

_____. Isaac Asimov, a biochemist and science fiction writer,

anticipated this problem in his stories about future worlds inhabited by people and robots.

Asimov worked out _____
                              (4)

_____. In Asimov's stories, these laws were programmed into every robot's

brain. In these stories Asimov put his robots in a variety of situations and tested

_____. He wanted to know
                      (5)

_____.
                              (6)

These stories not only show scientists _____
                                   (7)

_____, but also provide very interesting reading.

C Read the following excerpts from an interview with an engineer who designs robots. Then summarize each excerpt using the words in parentheses. Follow the example.

1. **Interviewer:** Can robots perceive their environment?
   Engineer: Yes, they can perceive their environment through mechanical sensors. The sensors gauge the pressure.

   (asked whether) _The interviewer asked whether robots can sense their environment._

   (explained how) _The engineer explained how robots sense their environment._

2. **Interviewer:** When was the first robot invented?
   Engineer: I think it was as early as the thirteenth century, but I'm not sure.

   (asked when) _____

   (couldn't remember when) _____

3. **Interviewer:** How do robots process information?
   Engineer: They process information in the same way a computer does—using microprocessors.

   (wondered how) _____

   (explained how) _____

4. **Interviewer:** Will robots ever be able to think and feel?
   Engineer: I doubt that!

   (wanted to know) _____

   (doubts whether) _____

■ **COMMUNICATE**

D **GROUP WORK** Talk about robots from film and literature (including comics and graphic novels). Use object noun clauses with *that, whether,* or *wh-* words.

Did you ever see *2001: A Space Odyssey?* It's about a space crew and a robot named Hal. The crew didn't know **that Hal wanted to kill them.**

I've noticed **that robot characters are always evil types.** *I, Robot* is another one like that.

Isn't that the one about the army of robots? The main character **finds out what they're planning to do,** and he gets into deep trouble.

GRAMMAR AND VOCABULARY In your opinion, how well are people adapting to new forms of technology? How well are *you* adapting? Address these questions by writing a personal essay on the topic of technology and change. Use object noun clauses with *that, if, whether,* and *wh-*words. Include sentences with as many of the following patterns as you can:

- Many people think that . . .
- It isn't yet clear if . . .
- I've noticed that . . .
- Some people claim that . . .
- I can't explain why . . .
- It's hard to imagine when . . .
- Time will reveal whether . . .

PROJECT Work in a group. Together, think of a task that could be performed by a robot. These kinds of tasks are usually very repetitive, mechanical, and/or boring. Or, you might think of a task that is too dangerous to be safely performed by humans. Then, design a robot that could perform that task. Draw a sketch of the robot, and create a written manual or guide for the robot's user. Present your "blueprint" to the class, explaining what the robot can do.

 INTERNET Search for one of the following robots or agencies, and then share what you found with your class.

Famous Robots
- Cog
- Kismet
- KITT
- ASIMO
- Bigtrak

Institutions and Agencies
- Robotics Institute of America
- Japanese Robot Association
- MIT Robot Museum
- International Standards Organization

PART 1
Reported Speech: Statements

PART 2
Reported Speech: Questions

PART 3
Reported Speech: Orders,
Requests, Advice, Warnings

Lesson (27)

Marketing: Making Responsible Claims

■ CONTENT VOCABULARY

Look at the advertisements shown below. Which advertisement makes a factual claim?
Which one makes a claim that cannot be proven?

Many **advertisements** make **exaggerated claims.** Their **slogans** claim that a particular **product** will make you feel or
look younger, for example. Such ads aren't just **promoting** a product—they are selling something that is intended to
enhance the **consumer's** identity. Some ads make **factual** claims that can be tested or proven, although these ads
often fail to draw attention.

Read the description below the picture. Look up any words you don't know. Write each word,
its definition, and a sentence that illustrates its use in your vocabulary journal.

■ THINK ABOUT IT

Have you ever seen an advertising slogan that made an exaggerated claim? What was the
slogan? What is a good example of a factual claim? Discuss these questions in a group. When
you are finished, write your ideas in your journal.

■ GRAMMAR IN CONTENT

CD2,TR24

A Read and listen to the lecture on advertising.

Truth in Advertising

Marketers sometimes make misleading or false claims in their advertisements. In the early twentieth century, this was particularly true. For example, one advertiser sold a bottle lined with radium and stated **that drinking liquids from this bottle could cure cancer, diabetes, and many other diseases.** In the 1930s, an advertisement for an electric belt said **that the belt would restore people's vital force,** although the advertisement never explained **how the belt would do that.**

Nowadays, the Federal Trade Commission (FTC) has guidelines for marketing. These guidelines state **what marketers can say** and **how strong their claims can be.** If an advertisement is misleading, the FTC will order **the manufacturers of the advertised product to change the ad.** Marketers who have learned to be more careful may use vague or misleading terms. One such term is "natural."

The average American is exposed to over 3,000 ads every day.

Many advertisements imply **that "natural" products are more healthful than "artificial" ones.** However, critics note **that snake venom and many other poisons are natural,** but no one would say **that they are healthful.** These critics warn consumers **to be suspicious of "natural" products.** Another misleading term is "promote." An advertisement may state **that it "promotes" hair growth or better health.** Researchers who examine these claims state **that this term means nothing.** Unless rigorous testing has been done, consumers need to ask themselves **whether a product's claims are really true** or **whether that product might even be dangerous.** They also need to ask themselves **whether they can afford to take a chance.**

a commission: a group of people authorized, usually by a government, to do something

federal: related to the U.S. national government

a guideline: an idea or rule on what to do (or not to do)

a marketer: a person, department, or business that generates advertising to sell goods or services

to restore: to make something look like it did when it was new

B **Reread the passage. Look at all the instances of reported statements in the reading, and then study the chart below.**

Reported Speech: Statements

Sample Sentences	Notes
Dr. Corazon **says**, "**My** medicine **has helped** thousands of people suffering from diabetes." ↓ Dr. Corazon says **that** his medicine **has helped** thousands of people suffering from diabetes.	**Reported speech** reports the content of the original utterance in a noun clause without necessarily repeating the speaker's exact words. Referential items (e.g., pronouns, possessive determiners) in the *that* clause may shift according to who has spoken the words and who is reporting them.
The ad **said**, "Harry's Hair Tonic **restores** hair in just one week." ↓ The ad **said** that Harry's Hair Tonic **restored** hair in just one week.	If the tense of the **reporting verb** is **past** or **past perfect**, the tense or form of the verb in the reported speech may also shift.
The Long Life Company **stated**, "Our vitamins **can** extend your life." ↓ The Long Life Company **stated** that their vitamins **could** extend your life.	If the tense of the **reporting verb** is **past**, the form of a **modal** in a direct quotation may also shift to **past** as well.

Notes:
- *Say* is the most common verb introducing a reporting statement in writing. Others include *answer, argue, claim, explain, recommend, reply, state,* and *tell.*
- If the quotation includes *will* or *can*, these verbs may also change to *would* or *could* in a reported statement after a verb in past tense or past perfect. The modals *must* and *might* do not shift (although *must* can change to *had to* in past constructions).
- In casual conversation, some people might report conversations using forms such as *I'm like, He's all,* or *She goes.* In these situations, the exact words are used in the reported speech.
  Example: *I'm like, "You should really see a doctor," and he goes, "Yeah, but I don't have any money."*

C Read the following paragraph, and (circle) any grammatical errors related to reported speech. Rewrite the paragraph in the space provided, correcting all the errors.

The FTC regulates unfair or misleading commercial practices. One FTC regulation states that claims by marketers (will be) supported by evidence. The FTC also states that advertisers must being able to support their claims. So if consumers complain that a particular tanning salon will make false claims, the FTC will investigate. For example, a tanning salon claimed that ultraviolet light has provided a safe way to get a tan. However, frequent exposure to ultraviolet light can cause skin cancer, so the FTC told the salon that it will warn consumers of this risk. In another ad, a pest control company said that its chemicals are completely safe. Virtually any chemical poses some risk, however, and the FTC ordered the company to modify its claims. Similarly, a drug company asserted that one of its drugs is curing cancer. The FTC told the company that it must to substantiate the claim. Unfortunately, the FTC is not able to investigate every questionable claim, so consumers should be skeptical of claims that are too good to be true.

The FTC regulates unfair or misleading commercial practices. One FTC regulation states that claims by marketers must be supported by evidence.

_____

_____

_____

_____

_____

_____

_____

_____

_____

_____

D Listen to the conversation between Sue and Aaron. Then answer the following questions about what was said, using introductory reporting statements.

CD2,TR25

1. What did Sue say she had just bought?

   _____

2. What did the ad for makeup say?

   _____

3. What did Aaron say he needs?

   _____

4. What did Sue recommend?

   _____

■ COMMUNICATE

E **GROUP WORK** Work in groups of three. The first person says something to the second person very quietly so that the third person can't hear. Then the second person reports softly to the third person what the first person said. Finally the third person announces what she or he heard and checks with the first person for accuracy. The first person disagrees if something was incorrectly reported. Continue until everyone has had at least two chances to be the first speaker.

My parents are coming to visit next week.

That's right.

Juan said that his parents were coming to visit next week.

You said that your parents were coming to visit next week.

■ GRAMMAR IN CONTENT

A Reread the passage on page 240. Look at all the instances of reported questions, and then study the chart below.

Reported Speech: Questions	
Sample Sentences	**Notes**
"Do teeth whiteners really work?" ↓ The patient **wanted to know if** teeth whiteners really **worked.**	Reported *yes/no* questions are introduced by **whether** or **if.** The word order is in statement form, not question word order. The auxiliary verb *do* is left out, but other auxiliary verbs are kept. The comma before the direct quote is deleted.
"**Have** the new herbal remedies **been tested** by the Food and Drug Administration?" ↓ The students **asked** whether the new herbal remedies **had been tested** by the FDA.	As with reported statements, verbs in a reported question often shift when the main verb is past or past perfect.
"**Will** the Federal Trade Commission approve our new ad?" ↓ The clinician **asked whether** the FTC **would approve** the company's new ad.	*Will* may change to *would* in a reported question if the reporting verb is in the past tense. *Can* is often changed to *could.*
"**How** did your team conduct the research?" ↓ The professor **asked how** our team **conducted** our research.	Reported *wh-* questions are introduced by *wh-* question words such as *who, what, which, when, where, why, how.* Reported questions do not have question word order. The subject comes before the verb or auxiliary.
"**Why** isn't the project complete yet?" ↓ The department chair **is asking why** the project isn't complete yet.	When reporting a question, use a reporting verb of asking such as *ask* or *inquire.*
"When are **our** grades going to be posted?" ↓ Students asked when **their** grades were going to be posted.	Referential words in a question may shift depending on who has spoken and who is reporting.

B Rewrite the following text, changing direct speech to reported speech. Remember to delete commas before reported quotations.

"Puffery" refers to advertising claims that are so exaggerated that any reasonable consumer will ignore them. Before a claim is made, marketers need to ask, "Could the claim could be disproved?" or "Might a reasonable consumer take the claim literally?" For example, if a pizza shop wants to say that it sells the world's greatest pizza, the marketer should ask, "Could anyone prove such a claim?" If there is a way to test a claim, then the marketer must use it to compare this pizza to all other pizzas and ask, "Which is best?" This is important information for consumers, too. Before a consumer buys a product that claims to cure the common cold and grow hair, he/she should always ask, "What kind of claim is the manufacturer making?" and "Is it a testable claim or puffery?" If it is puffery, the consumer should disregard it. If it is a testable claim, the consumer should next ask, "Has the manufacturer actually done the required research?" Then the smart consumer needs to follow up and ask, "What were the results of the research?"

"Puffery" refers to advertising claims that are so exaggerated that any reasonable consumer will ignore them. Before a claim is made, marketers need to ask whether the claim could be disproved or whether a reasonable consumer might take the claim literally.

C Read the conversation and then report on the professor's questions by completing the sentences that follow.

Professor: Here is an ad by a tire manufacturer. The first claim is "Vulcan tires last 100,000 miles." The next one is "Vulcan tires never have blowouts." The third one is "Vulcan tires are the best buy in town." Do any of these claims constitute puffery?

Student: The third one does.

Professor: Why?

Student: You can't prove it. "Best" is totally subjective.

Professor: Do any of the other claims have problems?

Student: The second one does.

Professor: Where do you see a problem?

Student: The claim can't be true, but it's stated as a fact.

Professor: OK, can you see any problems with Claim Number One? Answer that question for homework.

1. The professor first asked _____ *whether any of the claims constituted puffery.* _____

2. He followed up that question by asking _____

3. Then the professor asked _____

4. After the student answered, he asked _____

5. Finally, he asked the class _____

■ **COMMUNICATE**

D **GROUP WORK** Show and/or describe an ad or commercial you have seen. Share a question you have about the ad's content, claims, or techniques. When the group has finished, take turns reporting to the class about each other's comments and questions.

> Felipe said that he saw a commercial on TV for cold medicine. The ad **claimed** that the medicine **cured** the common cold. Felipe **wondered** whether they **could make** that kind of claim. According to Felipe, there isn't any medicine that can cure the common cold.

■ GRAMMAR IN CONTENT

A Reread the passage on page 240. Look at all the instances of reported commands, requests, advice, or warnings, and then study the chart below.

Reported Speech: Orders, Requests, Advice, Warnings	
Sample Sentences	**Notes**
Taye said, "Make sure you read the label before taking the medication." ↓ Taye told me **to make sure I read the label before taking the medication.**	Reported orders, requests, advice, or warnings are introduced by *to.*
Rhonda asked, "Could you help me with the new ad?" ↓ Rhonda asked **me** to help her with the new ad.	**Indirect objects** come after the verb that reports an order, request, advice, or warning.
Simon told his research assistant, "You should double-check your data." ↓ Simon **advised** his research assistant to double-check her data.	Common reporting verbs include *tell, order, command, advise, ask, invite,* and *warn.* Use the appropriate verb for greater accuracy and variety when writing.
"You should substantiate **your** claims before printing **your** ad," the lawyer told the company. ↓ The lawyer warned the company to substantiate **their** claims before printing **their** ad.	Make appropriate changes to referential forms such as pronouns and possessive determiners when reporting orders, requests, advice, and warnings.
Ray told the group, "Don't omit any of the steps." ↓ Ray warned the group **not to omit** any of the steps.	For a negative reported command, order, request, invitation, advice, or warning, put *not* before the infinitive.

B Look at the text below. Complete each sentence, using the corresponding quotation from the box. Use verbs related to indirect orders, advice, requests, invitations, and warnings. Follow the example.

1. "Please speak at our conference."
2. "Would you conduct research on the relation between our powdered milk and the health of babies?"
3. "Would you closely analyze the researcher's work?"
4. "Don't publish Dr. Smith's studies because they are unreliable."
5. "Provide the original data on which your research was based."
6. "You have to retire."
7. "Don't use Dr. Smith's research to support any claims."
8. "Conduct new research before making any claims about the effectiveness of your products."

In the early 2000s, a Canadian news group investigated problems with the publications of Dr. James Smith, a well-known scientist. Prestigious journals published Dr. Smith's work, and international organizations _invited/asked him to speak at their conferences._ In the
(1)
1980s, several international milk companies _____
(2)
_____ He agreed and soon began to publish his results.

However, as Dr. Smith's studies began to appear in journals, scientists became worried about his data. Journals that were going to publish his work began to ask specialists in his area _____
(3)
_____ These reviewers _____
(4)
_____ To address this problem, his university _____
(5)
_____

Dr. Smith said that the original data had been lost. At this point, the university lost faith in his work and _____
(6)
_____ The government, which had been following the investigation, warned companies _____
(7)
_____ In the U.S., the FTC told companies that had relied on his research

_____
(8)

C Read the quotations, and report what each person said. Use the name of the person and an appropriate verb (*tell, ask, warn, advise, invite*) to introduce the reported quote. Follow the example.

Ellen, could you help me with my homework?

Marc   **Ellen**

1. _Marc asked Ellen to help him with his homework._

Hey Susan, would you like to take a study break and go out for coffee?

Tara   **Susan**

2. _____

You should study harder for the next test.

Instructor   **Student**

3. _____

Don't take the marketing class until you've taken a course in communication.

Karl   **Isabel**

4. _____

Be sure to turn in your project before the next class.

Miguel   **Jason**

5. _____

D **PAIR WORK** Have you ever received very good advice or a very helpful warning? Write down some good advice that you have received in your life and some helpful warnings. Then tell your partner.

My parents always warned me not to spend money I didn't have. They told me to keep a credit card only for emergencies.

Sounds like good advice.

Connection   Putting It Together

GRAMMAR AND VOCABULARY With a partner, write a script for a television commercial. Read the script aloud for the class. When you are finished, have the class report on the statements and claims that were made in your commercial.

PROJECT With a group, choose a certain kind of product, such as perfume, automobiles, alcohol, cigarettes, clothing, etc. Look through magazines and newspapers to find all the ads related to that kind of product. With your group, examine and analyze the ads. Do you notice any recurrent ideas or images? For example, do cigarette ads from different companies make similar claims and associations? What do all or most automobile ads have in common? In answering these questions, you may find that certain kinds of images, themes, and ideas are associated with different products. Prepare an oral presentation to share what you found with the class.

 INTERNET Locate an online newspaper. Look at stories that interest you from the last week. Find a story that uses both direct and reported speech. Print or copy the story, underlining examples of each type of speech. Think about why the writer chose to use each type of speech.

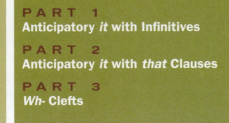

PART 1
Anticipatory *it* with Infinitives

PART 2
Anticipatory *it* with *that* Clauses

PART 3
Wh- Clefts

Lesson 28

Cultural Anthropology: The Anasazi

■ CONTENT VOCABULARY

Look at the picture below. Where do you think it is? Who do you think lived there? What happened to the people who used to live there?

The Anasazi were a Native American group that lived in the American Southwest from around 700 **BCE** to about 1300 **CE**. Originally a **nomadic** group, they **eventually** settled and built large, complex **dwellings** that are still being studied by **anthropologists**. Pueblo Bonito was the largest dwelling in Chaco, one of the Anasazi's ancient cities. What is shown in the picture above is the **remains** of Pueblo Bonito. It is **remarkable** that one building in this tribe's community was four stories high, and had 600 rooms. The **community** at Chaco Canyon was a large, productive one for **centuries**. It is strange that the community disappeared sometime between the twelfth and thirteenth centuries.

Read the description below the picture. Look up any words you don't know. Write each word, its definition, and a sentence that illustrates its use in your vocabulary journal.

■ THINK ABOUT IT

In your journal, write about the following questions: What ancient cultures do you know about? What kinds of remains did they leave behind, and what do we know about them today?

■ **GRAMMAR IN CONTENT**

A Read and listen to the following.

CD2,TR26

The Anasazi

One of the most interesting Native American Indian cultures is the Anasazi. The Anasazi disappeared before the arrival of Europeans in North America, and they had a highly developed culture. **What is perhaps the most interesting aspect of this group** to anthropologists is the structures they left behind. For historians, it has been fascinating **to study the reason for their disappearance.**

Cliff dwellings at Mesa Verde

Two main periods have been identified in the Anasazi culture. During the first period, the Basket-weaving Period, **what distinguished the Anasazi** was the beautiful baskets they wove out of local plants. During this period it was sometimes difficult **to grow many crops in one place**, so it was necessary **to move from place to place in search of food.** However, around 750 CE the Anasazi began relying more on agriculture. This marks the beginning of the second period, the Pueblo Period. It took a long time **to make the shift**, but as the Anasazi settled in one place, they began constructing permanent dwellings. In fact, **what they constructed** were the largest, most complex prehistoric settlements that have been found in the American Southwest. The most famous of these was in Chaco Canyon, in present-day New Mexico.

Sometime before the end of the thirteenth century, the Chaco community collapsed. It is interesting **to speculate about the reasons for the Anasazi's abandonment of Chaco Canyon.** After much research, it has become clear to scientists **that drought was at least one factor in the collapse.** However, it is also possible **that overpopulation contributed to the downfall of this magnificent culture.**

to abandon: to desert; to leave someone or something forever

an aspect: a feature; a part of something

to collapse: to fall into ruin

complex: intricate; involved

a drought: a time of little or no rainfall

B Reread the passage on page 252. Look at all the infinitive phrases and sentences with the anticipatory *it*, then study the chart below.

Anticipatory *it* with Infinitives

Sample Sentences	Notes
To attend the field study program at Chaco Canyon **costs a fortune.** ↓ **It costs a fortune** to attend the field study program at Chaco Canyon.	Some sentences that have an infinitive phrase as subject can move the phrase to the end and replace the subject slot with *it*.
Migrants had to travel a great distance without horses or carts. ~~To carry their belongings on their backs was necessary.~~ **It** was necessary to carry their belongings on their backs.	Moving an infinitive phrase to the end of the sentence avoids an awkwardly long subject and draws attention to the infinitive as new information.
It is **difficult** to know with certainty why the Anasazi chose to live in cliff dwellings.	When a predicate adjective is followed by an infinitive that is not preceded by "for + noun," the noun is usually assumed to be *anyone* or, in some cases, a person or persons referred to previously in the discourse. See below for a list of predicate adjectives that can be followed by a post-posed infinitive subject.

Predicate Adjectives Commonly Followed by Post-Posed Infinitive Subjects

convenient	great	necessary	strange
dangerous	hard	pleasant	surprising
easy	helpful	(im)possible	unusual
essential	important	reasonable	useful
good	interesting	safe	wonderful

C Rewrite the underlined phrases and sentences, using the anticipatory *it* followed by an infinitive.

To learn about the Anasazi's shift from a hunting society to an agricultural society is interesting. From about CE 750, the Anasazi began to abandon a nomadic life of hunting and gathering. To build more permanent buildings and settle into farming took time. However, as small communities were established, to develop leisure activities such as gambling became possible. To live in communities was clearly advantageous. To spend so much time and energy on survival wasn't necessary. As the evidence shows, to relax and participate in sports and games of chance became possible. However, these settlements often did not survive for long. In fact, they often disappeared quickly.

1. *It is interesting to learn about the Anasazi's shift from a hunting society to an agricultural society.*

2. _____

3. _____

4. _____

5. _____

6. _____

D There are five errors in the following e-mail. One error has been fixed. Correct the four other errors in the infinitive phrases.

Hi Mom,

Just a quick note because I wanted to let you know that my computer crashed this week. It was awful. It's

going to cost a fortune ~~to recovering~~ *to recover* my files, but it's really necessary for get them back because my history

paper on the Anasazi is on it. For the rest of my work it's possible to using the computers in the computer lab

on campus, but it's a little scary for being on campus late at night.

Anyhow, I just thought you'd want to know what's happening with your oldest son. By the way, I'll be home for

my birthday in a couple of weeks. It might be nice to received a new computer. Just a thought.

Your devoted son,

Kev

■ COMMUNICATE

G **GROUP WORK** Share what you know and/or think about native peoples in North and Central America such as the Anasazi, Hopi, Pueblo, Maya, Aztec, and Olmec. Use the anticipatory *it* followed by an infinitive whenever possible.

Have you ever heard about the Maya? They lived in southern Mexico and Central America more than a thousand years ago.

Yeah, I read about them in my history class. They had maps of the stars and planets.

Isn't it amazing to know they created those maps without telescopes?

■ **GRAMMAR IN CONTENT**

A Reread the passage on page 252. Highlight the *that* clauses in the reading. Then <u>underline</u> the preceding sentence. <u>Double underline</u> any *it* subject. Check your answers with a partner. If you need help, use the chart below.

Anticipatory *it* with *that* Clauses

Sample Sentences	Notes
That the society disappeared **is well known.** ↓ **It is well known that** the society disappeared.	In some sentences with a *that* clause in the subject position you can move the *that* clause to the end and fill the vacated slot with *it.* In these types of sentences, the subject *it* is usually followed by a predicate adjective and then the *that* clause. See below for a list of predicate adjectives used in such constructions.
That they solve such mysteries **is important to anthropologists.** ↓ **It's important to anthropologists that** they solve such mysteries.	As with the infinitive phrase, moving a *that* clause to the end of the sentence avoids an awkwardly long subject and draws attention to the *that* clause as new information.
It is believed that the Anasazi may have had contact with indigenous people in Mexico.	Passive constructions with *it* can also be followed by a *that* clause. Other verbs that can be used in the passive in this way include *be accepted, be thought, be argued, be claimed, be said, be known.*
It is imperative that nobody touch the walls when visiting the site.	Some predicate adjectives can be followed by the base form of the verb. These adjectives include *critical, desirable, important, imperative,* and *necessary.* Sentences with these adjectives as predicates convey a command, order, or strong request.
It surprises me that you've never heard about the Anasazi.	Emotive verbs—such as *bother, surprise,* and *worry*—can be used with the anticipatory *it* and a *that* clause.

Predicate Adjectives Followed by *that* Clauses

amazing	doubtful	odd	true
apparent	evident	(im)possible	understandable
appropriate	good	ridiculous	(un)likely
astonishing	great	strange	well-known
clear	likely	surprising	wonderful

B Rewrite the following sentences using an anticipatory *it* with a *that* clause.

1. That Chaco Canyon supported an advanced civilization is well-known.

   It's well-known that Chaco Canyon supported an advanced civilization.

2. That such a community could disappear in less than 100 years is amazing.

   _____

   _____

3. That drought caused the disappearance is possible.

   _____

   _____

4. That a neighboring enemy attacked the community is also likely.

   _____

   _____

5. That we will ever know the causes with certainty is doubtful.

   _____

   _____

C Complete all of Franz's and Issa's utterances using the information in parentheses. Use the anticipatory *it* and a *that* clause. Follow the example.

Franz: Did you register for Dr. Clemens's class next semester?

Issa: Oh, darn. I forgot. Now ___*it's likely that the class is already full.*___ (likely/
                                                    (1)
the class is already full)

Franz: _____
                                    (2)
(possible/History Department/has added another section)

Issa: With my schedule, _____
                                                    (3)
(doubtful/I will be able to take it).

_____
                            (4)
(really bothers me/History Department never schedules enough classes)

Franz: _____ (odd/they don't)
                            (5)

Issa: _____
                            (6)
(pretty clear/they don't have enough professors)

D **PAIR WORK** Talk about courses and scheduling at your school. Does anything about the school surprise or bother you? How would you describe the classes? Use the anticipatory *it* with a *that* clause whenever possible.

> **It's kind of surprising that** our school doesn't offer any classes at night. That's a good time for a lot of people.

> **It's possible that** they can't afford to offer more classes. I heard that the school has had some budget cuts.

PART THREE	*Wh-* Clefts

■ **GRAMMAR IN CONTENT**

A Reread the passage on page 252. Draw a <u>wavy line</u> under each of the *wh-* clefts in the reading. Check your answers with a partner. If you need help, use the chart below.

Wh- Clefts	
Sample Sentences	**Notes**
The sudden disappearance of the Anasazi interests historians. ↓ What interests historians **is the sudden disappearance of the Anasazi.**	*Wh-* cleft sentences give special emphasis to the text following the *be* verb that occurs between the *what* phrase and the rest of the sentence.
Historians have studied the old cliff dwellings. ↓ What historians have studied **is the old cliff dwellings.**	The singular form of *be* is used after the *what* phrase, even if a plural noun occurs in the *what* phrase or anywhere else in the sentence.
The artisans didn't make pottery. What they **did was make** baskets.	When the *wh-* cleft contains **does** or **did,** the verb following **is** or **was** is in the base form and does not mark tense. These kinds of sentences often provide a contrast with a previous sentence.

B Read the dialog. In each blank space, rewrite the corresponding sentence from the tinted box as a *wh-* cleft sentence. Follow the example.

1. The pottery and cultural artifacts really attract them.
2. They're made from sandstone and clay.
3. They paint geometric designs.
4. Women make most of the pots because of certain gender roles.
5. They believe that the spirit of Mother Earth lives in the pottery.

A Hopi Pueblo Jar

Kevin: The Southwest is so dry and warm. A lot of

students must come here because of the climate.

Pearl: That may be true for some students. But the archaeology

students have a special interest in the Southwest.

What really attracts them is the pottery and cultural artifacts.
(1)

Kevin: I heard that Southwestern pottery is made from stone. Is that true?

Pearl: In a sense, but not hard stone. _____
(2)

Kevin: Right—and they use animal tails to paint realistic scenes on the pottery.

Pearl: You might be thinking of another region. Southwestern groups use local plants.

_____
(3)

Kevin: And almost all the potters are women because the women are more artistic.

Pearl: Well, you're right—most of the potters are women.

_____
(4)

Kevin: You mean they believe that women are superior?

Pearl: Not exactly. _____
(5)

■ **COMMUNICATE**

C **WRITING** On your own or with a partner, write a dialog about a cultural group you know well. Have one character voice common misperceptions or assumptions about that group. The other character can clarify or correct those misperceptions using *wh-* clefts, as in the above dialog. Read the dialog aloud for your class.

GRAMMAR AND VOCABULARY Write a personal essay about common attitudes and perceptions of a cultural group with which you identify. Use sentences that include an anticipatory *it.* Contrast those attitudes and perceptions with what you know to be true. Share your writing with your classmates.

> I was born in Lebanon and moved to New York City three years ago. I have encountered many misperceptions about Arab people since coming to the United States. For example, it is commonly believed that everybody from the Middle East follows the religion of Islam. What some Americans may not know is that many people from my country are in fact Christians.

PROJECT Find images (online or at your library) showing the ruins or artifacts of an ancient civilization that interests you. Some ancient civilizations you may have heard of include: the Maya, Aztec, Inca, Greeks, Romans, Celts, and Rapa Nui. Prepare a report, including a written description of the images you found. Use the anticipatory *it* in your description. Present the report to your class by showing the images while reading aloud the description you wrote.

INTERNET You can learn more about native peoples of the American Southwest using the following search terms: Anasazi, Hopi, Pueblo, Zuni, Navajo, Western Apache. Choose a website that you think is especially interesting, and share what you learned with your classmates.

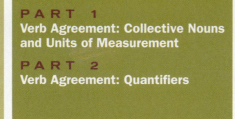
Business: Hotel and Restaurant Management

■ CONTENT VOCABULARY

Look at the picture. What do you know about the occupations shown?

clerk   chef   manager   line cook   waitress

The **manager** of a major restaurant or hotel has to be able to **supervise** a large **staff**. It's a job that requires a special combination of skills and the ability to work under daily pressure. A lot of managers in the **hospitality industry** receive training and degrees at specialized business and **culinary** schools. Associate, bachelor, and graduate degree programs are offered in restaurant management by community colleges, junior colleges, and some universities.

Read the description below the picture. Look up any words you don't know. Write each word, its definition, and a sentence that illustrates its use in your vocabulary journal.

■ THINK ABOUT IT

In your journal, write about the following questions: What are the duties and responsibilities of the jobs and occupations shown above? What skills does a good manager need in order to supervise these employees?

■ GRAMMAR IN CONTENT

CD2,TR27

A Read and listen to the following lecture given by Professor Jones, Dean of Cumberland University's School of Hotel and Restaurant Management. He is talking to prospective students.

Cumberland University offers both undergraduate and graduate programs in hotel and restaurant management. What makes Cumberland's program special is that it is team-based. What I mean by that is that when students enter the program, they are divided into teams. Each team works together for the duration of the program. A number of schools use this method, and a lot of us feel this is a model that all schools, not just HRM schools, could benefit from. There is a lot of information to master in a professional program, and working with a team just makes sense. It's how things happen in the real world. The teams in our school start out by taking classes in culinary arts. After students have mastered the basics, they learn to do every job in a restaurant. The team plans menus, orders supplies, and takes reservations. Each person has the chance to act as host or hostess, wait on tables, and perform the duties of executive chef and line cook; everyone buses tables and washes dishes. We believe that you cannot successfully supervise employees unless you have experience doing their jobs. We also believe that every highly successful hotel or restaurant is a team effort. So in our program, everyone learns to do all of the jobs in a hotel and every job in a restaurant. And everyone learns to be a part of a team.

Graduate students take numerous courses in accounting and marketing, and usually do an internship at a five-star hotel or restaurant. They earn a Master of Business Administration Degree (an MBA) with a specialization in hotel and restaurant management. Graduating from a program like ours gives any career in the hospitality industry a real head start.

culinary arts: high-level skills related to cooking

a reservation: an arrangement whereby a hotel room, a dining table, a plane/train ticket is held for someone at a given date and time

an internship: serving as a learner or an assistant while completing or just after completing one's studies

B Reread the passage on page 262. Put a <u>double line</u> under each collective noun. Draw a line to the verb. Is it singular or plural? If you need help, use the chart below.

Verb Agreement: Collective Nouns and Units of Measurement

Sample Sentences	Notes
The restaurant **staff works** together in drawing up a menu every morning. **They take** pride in choosing the best ingredients. (Each member of the staff personally takes pride in choosing the best ingredients.) **It takes** pride in choosing the best ingredients. (The staff as a whole takes pride in choosing the best ingredients.)	**Collective nouns** name a group of people, objects, or animals. They take a **singular verb**. After naming the group, you can use **plural pronouns and verbs** to refer to or emphasize the individual members. To refer to the group as a single unit, use **singular pronouns and verbs**. See Appendix 5 for a sample list of collective nouns.
The hotel manager goes to the florist every Sunday afternoon to buy a **bouquet of flowers** for the front desk.	Collective nouns that refer to natural or manufactured objects, packages, and fresh produce are formed with **a phrase that includes a group term, the preposition** *of,* **and the name of the object.** See Appendix 5 for a sample list.
The delivery van unloaded **a crate of watermelons, two sacks of potatoes,** and **a box of cherries.**	With groups of **count nouns**, the **number of items** is always **plural**. The **group term** may be **singular or plural,** depending on how many units or packages there are.
The chef decided to restock the kitchen's pantry when she noticed that there **were** only two **pounds of sugar.**	Some collective nouns, packaging, and units of measurement are associated with **noncount nouns.** The verb must agree with **the number of packages or units of measurement,** not the noncount noun. See Appendix 5 for a sample list.
The head waiter puts a fresh **bouquet of flowers** on every table before the restaurant opens. Each **bouquet** ~~of flowers~~ **is** chosen with care. The ~~bouquets of~~ **flowers are** chosen with care.	After a collective phrase has been introduced, avoid repetition by using **either the group term or the name of the object.** The verb must agree with **the number of packages** *or* **the number of items,** whichever you have chosen to use as the subject.

C Read the following short dialogs. Each dialog has two blanks. In blank (a), write a collective noun from the box. In blank (b), choose an appropriate word or phrase from the two choices in parentheses. In some cases, more than one choice may be correct. Be prepared to explain your choices.

book	~~family~~	staff
faculty	mob	team

1. **Wilmer:** My ___family___ is coming to visit next weekend.
   (a)

   Gloria: Lucky you! When _____ (does it/do they) arrive?
   (b)

   Wilmer: Friday night. I'm excited, because I haven't seen them since Christmas.

2. **Hal:** The _____ is having an emergency meeting at noon.
   (a)

   Paula: What _____ (is it/are they) going to talk about?
   (b)

   Hal: I'm not sure. It seems to be a big secret.

3. **Wilson:** There was a _____ at the restaurant last night.
   (a)

   Annie: I know. I was there at about 8:00. _____ (It was/
   (b)
   They were) forming a line around the block to get in.

4. **Amy:** I really like the _____ at our school.
   (a)

   Agnes: I do too. I heard _____ (it is/they are) rated among
   (b)
   the best in the country.

5. **Lois:** That was a great game last night. Too bad our _____ lost.
   (a)

   Eddy: Yeah, _____ (it/they) made a good effort, but the
   (b)
   opposition was just too tough.

6. **Ang:** What was the name of the restaurant we went to last week?

   Eli: I'm not sure, but it's written on a _____ of matches that I took. I'll
   (a)
   look for _____ (it/them) when I get home.
   (b)

D Read each pair of sentences. Look at the collective noun that is boldfaced in the first sentence, and the pronoun that is boldfaced in the second sentence. Explain why the writer chose to use that pronoun.

1. The **staff** quietly waited for the president to speak. **They** were eager to hear what he had to say.

   Reason: *"They" emphasizes that each member of the staff was eager to hear the president's speech.*

2. The **Wilson family** checked into a suite last night. **They** are going to stay through the weekend.

   Reason: _____

   _____

3. The maid put **three bars of soap** in a tray on the bathroom sink. She made sure **they** were stacked neatly on top of each other.

   Reason: _____

   _____

4. The chef melted **two cubes of butter** in a large pot. He melted **it** slowly so that **it** wouldn't burn.

   Reason: _____

   _____

5. **A team** was appointed to plan events for January. **It** will present a list of upcoming events at the next meeting.

   Reason: _____

   _____

■ C O M M U N I C A T E

E **GROUP WORK** Imagine that you are drawing up a shopping list for a restaurant. Take turns naming an item on the list. Each successive person needs to include everything that has already been named. Include as many collective nouns as possible.

We need to buy two bunches of carrots.

We need to buy two bunches of carrots and three cartons of juice.

We need to buy two bunches of carrots, three cartons of juice, and a bouquet of roses.

■ GRAMMAR IN CONTENT

A Reread the passage on page 262. <u>Underline</u> each of the quantifiers (for example, *each*, *every*, and so forth), the noun they modify, and the verb. If you need help, use the chart below.

Verb Agreement: Quantifiers	
Sample Sentences	**Notes**
A lot of furniture in the hotel lobby **is** made of oak.	When a **quantifier** is used with a **noncount noun**, the verb is **singular**.
All of the students in my class **are** planning to work in international hotels.	When the **quantifier** is used with a **plural noun**, the verb form is **plural**.
A number of guests **dine** at the hotel's restaurant. **The number of** guests at our hotel greatly **increases** during the summer.	*A number of* takes **plural verb forms**; *the number of* takes a **singular verb**.
A few of the meals on our menu **are** vegetarian.	*A few of* takes **plural verb forms** and **plural nouns**.
A **little of** the **rice** still **remains**.	*A little of* takes a **singular verb form** and a **noncount noun**.
One half of the hotel **was** closed for remodeling. **Fifty percent** of our guests **have** stayed at our hotel more than once.	**Fractions** and **percentages** take a **singular verb form** when they modify a **singular** or **noncount noun**. They take a **plural verb form** when they modify a **plural noun**.
None of the classes he wanted to take **is** offered this quarter. **None** of the cooking classes **are** offered this quarter.	*None* takes a **singular verb form** when it is used as a subject. In conversation, a **plural verb form** is often used when *none* is combined with a plural noun, especially if the verb immediately follows the noun.
The clerk showed the guests two rooms. **Neither** ~~of the rooms~~ **was** acceptable to them. **Either was** acceptable to them.	*Neither* and *either* take **singular verb forms** when used as subjects.
Every room **has** cable TV and Internet access. = **Each** room **has** cable TV and Internet access.	*Each* and *every* quantify singular subjects and take a **singular verb form**.

B Look at the hotel fact sheet, and then make sentences based on the information given. Follow the example.

Vacation Inn

Fact Sheet

Total Number of Rooms: 100

Single Occupancy	30	Smoking Allowed	20	Internet Access	50	Hot Tub	3
Double Occupancy	70	Smoking Not Allowed	80	Cable TV	100	Pets Allowed	0

1. (thirty percent) _____ *Thirty percent of the rooms are single occupancy.* _____

2. (half) _____

3. (allow pets) _____

4. (don't allow smoking) _____

5. (twenty percent) _____

6. (seventy percent) _____

7. (each) _____

8. (a few) _____

CD2,TR28

C Listen to the radio ad for the International School of Hotel and Restaurant Management (ISHRM). Then, read each of the statements, editing them to correct any errors. Follow the example.

1. ~~A lot~~ ^All of the ISHRM's graduates have the skills needed to be successful in the

   demanding world of hotel and restaurant management.

2. None of the ISHRM's classes is offered online.

3. One half of the coursework is transferable from other schools.

4. Most of the ISHRM's graduates work in well-known hotels around the world.

5. A number of them have even become famous chefs.

D **PAIR WORK** Role-play a dialog between a guest and a hotel clerk or waiter. The customer asks questions about the restaurant or hotel, and the clerk or waiter answers the questions using quantifiers. When you are finished, switch roles.

How many rooms have a view of the ocean?

What's the best room you have?

That sounds perfect. I'll take one of those.

All of the rooms on the top floor have a view of the ocean, but none of those rooms are available now.

I still have a few rooms near the pool.

Connection | Putting It Together

GRAMMAR AND VOCABULARY Write a review of a hotel that you have stayed at or heard about. Give the hotel a rating (from one to four stars) and then provide a written evaluation. Describe the staff, service, and rooms. If the hotel has a restaurant or if it provides room service, evaluate those amenities as well. Use as many collective nouns and quantifiers as possible.

PROJECT In a group, draw up a plan for a hotel. Think of a name for your hotel and write a brief description of it. What makes it special? Is it located in an unusual place? What is unique about its design and architecture? What kinds of guests are likely to stay at your hotel—families with children, businesspeople, newlyweds? Does the staff need any special skills, such as the ability to speak certain languages? Present your concept to the class and answer any questions they may have about it.

INTERNET Search for one or more of the following celebrity chefs, and report to the class about the chef's cuisine, cooking techniques, and the reasons for his or her fame. Use as many collective nouns and quantifiers in your report as possible.

- Lidia Bastianich
- Mario Batali
- James Beard
- Paula Deen
- Bobby Flay

- Emeril Lagasse
- Jacques Pepin
- Wolfgang Puck
- Paul Prudhomme
- Rachael Ray

- Ming Tsai
- Roy Yamaguchi
- Martin Yan

PART 1
Adverbial Clauses

PART 2
Review: Direct Quotations and Reported Speech

PART 3
Hedging with Modals, Adverbs of Frequency, Quantifiers, and Other Expressions

Lesson 30

Writing: Academic Style

■ CONTENT VOCABULARY

Read this essay.

> Duke Kapeolani
> English 100
> Dr. Hendricks
>
> *Punctuation*   *too strong—hedge!*
>
> Dr. Hendricks says Avoid questions in your compositions. She is wrong.
>   *Fragment*
>
> Because sometimes a question can be helpful. I don't usually use
>   *Run-on*   *Cite your source*
>
> questions, I sometimes do. It is well known that good questions are
>   *Avoid rhetorical questions*
>
> appropriate in formal writing. Don't you agree?

Dr. Hendricks has written **comments** in Duke's paragraph that refer to writing errors or problems of **academic style**. Duke must do the following: 1) correct the **punctuation** of Dr. Hendricks's **quotation**; 2) **hedge** a **claim** that is too strong; 3) correct a **sentence fragment**; 4) correct a **run-on sentence**; 5) **cite** a **source** for his claim about questions; and 6) delete or **reformulate** the rhetorical question.

Read the text below the picture. Look up any words you don't know. Write each word, its definition, and a sentence that illustrates its use in your vocabulary journal.

■ THINK ABOUT IT

Write notes that respond to these questions: Do you understand why sentence fragments and run-on sentences aren't usually acceptable in academic English? Why is it important for writers to cite sources of information and of quotations? Compare your answers with a partner's and discuss them.

■ **GRAMMAR IN CONTENT**

A Read and listen to the following.

CD2,TR29

Academic Writing

The characteristics of formal writing vary from one discipline to another. Even though **a number of** differences exist, there are certain similarities across **most** forms of academic text. For one thing, academic discourse **usually** employs sentences that are more complex than the sentences that are typical of spoken English. Academic discourse **can** be difficult for non-native writers because the writing of complex sentences is **often** time-consuming for them. In spite of these difficulties, the ability to write longer, grammatically correct sentences is essential in an academic setting. Non-native students who have not mastered this skill **may** end up with compositions that sound overly simplistic.

Formal writing in English requires students to cite the work of other writers and scholars. Citations **may** take several forms. In a direct quotation, a writer's exact words are shown in quotation marks, and the work in which the statement first appeared is noted in parentheses or at the end of the paper. Students **can** also paraphrase the ideas of another writer in their own words. Paraphrasing is appropriate when the exact words of a writer aren't particularly important. When paraphrasing, care must be taken to present the original writer's intended meaning with accuracy.

Even though **most** students are aware of the need for citations, they **sometimes** neglect to give proper credit to the words and ideas of other writers. This is considered plagiarism, and **most** schools have very strict policies against it. In **some** cases, students who have been found guilty of plagiarism have even been expelled from school.

A final consideration concerns the expression of one's own ideas. **Most** writers of academic English take certain precautions when expressing their own opinions. They **often** avoid generalizations by using a certain technique known as "hedging," which is a way of qualifying a statement. Hedging involves the use of modals such as *might* and *could,* frequency adverbs such as *sometimes* and *often,* and quantifiers such as *some* and *a few.*

discourse: spoken or written communication

a discipline: an academic subject such as history, biology, or literature

a precaution: an action taken to avoid future difficulties or problems

B Reread the passage on page 270. (Circle) all the adverbial clauses in the reading. Check your answers with a partner's. If you need help, use the chart below.

Adverbial Clauses

Sample Sentences	Notes
I use a variety of sentence types **when I write.**	**Clauses of time** provide information on when the main clause occurs with respect to other events. They are introduced by words such as *when, before,* and *after.*
Because academic writing is complex, using a variety of sentence types is important.	**Clauses of reason** provide a reason for the information in the main clause. They are introduced by words such as *because* and *since.*
Your writing will sound simplistic **if you avoid complex sentences.**	**Clauses of condition** provide a condition in which the information in the main clause is true. They are introduced by *if.*
Even though students may understand the structure of complex sentences, they are often unable to produce them when writing.	**Clauses of concession** provide information in spite of which the information clause is true. They are introduced by words such as *although* and *even though.*

Notes:

- An adverb clause must be connected to a main clause. Treating an adverb clause as a complete sentence results in a fragment, which is usually considered an error in academic English writing.
  Fragment: *I got a C on my composition. Because I used fragments.*
  Correct: *I got a C on my composition because I used fragments.*
- Two independent sentences must not be connected by a comma. Connecting two sentences with a comma results in a run-on sentence (sometimes called a "fused sentence" or a "comma splice"), which is usually considered an error in academic English writing.
  Run-On: *I used too many fragments in my paper, I got a C.*
  Correct: *Because I used too many fragments in my paper, I got a C.*
  Correct: *I used a lot of run-on sentences in my paper, so I got a C.*
  Correct: *I used a lot of run-on sentences in my paper. I got a C.*

C Rewrite the following sets of sentences, combining them by using adverbial clauses.

1. Complex sentences are not required for formal writing in some cultures. Students from these cultures often have difficulty with English academic style.

   Because complex sentences are not required for formal writing in some cultures, students from those cultures may have difficulty with English academic style.

2. Instructors may lower a student's grade. He or she used too few complex sentences that were correctly formed.

   _____

   _____

   _____

3. Students make good grades on grammar tests. Instructors may assume that they can use the forms in writing.

   _____

   _____

   _____

4. These students may understand the rules for complex sentences. They may fail to produce them. Complex sentences sound strange to them.

   _____

   _____

   _____

5. These instructors eventually assign a composition to their students. They receive a shock. Even the best students haven't used complex sentences correctly in their papers.

   _____

   _____

   _____

6. Students write in English. They sometimes use the academic writing conventions of their native language. This often causes rhetorical errors.

   _____

   _____

   _____

D Read the following groups of sentences. Identify the problem with each group, checking "Run-On" or "Fragment." Then rewrite the sentences, combining them with adverb clauses.

	Run-On	Fragment

1. Semicolons and colons are rare in Japanese, Satomi's having a hard time punctuating her English compositions correctly.   ✔ ___

   Because semicolons and colons are rare in Japanese, Satomi's having a hard time punctuating her English compositions correctly.

2. Pedro has a tendency to personalize his papers. Because that way of writing was encouraged in his home country.   ___ ___

3. Satomi keeps making Cs and Ds on her papers, she has decided to write shorter sentences with lots of periods.   ___ ___

4. Satomi doesn't have any complex sentences, she won't have any comma errors or run-on sentences.   ___ ___

5. Pedro has warned her that the professor may still lower her grade. Because she won't have enough complex sentences.   ___ ___

■ **COMMUNICATE**

E WRITE In your journal, write four sentences about the writing of compositions and essays in your native language or another language that you know. Use *because*, *if*, *although*, and *when*.

> When I was in high school, my teacher encouraged me to use a very personal style of writing. Even though that way of writing is discouraged in academic English, I still have a tendency to interject my own thoughts and opinions into my papers.

| PART TWO | Review: Direct Quotations and Reported Speech |

■ **GRAMMAR IN CONTENT**

A Review the difference between direct quotations and reported speech by studying the chart below.

Direct Quotations and Reported Speech	
In his book, *Academic English Writing,* Alex Gomez claims, "**Students who intend to write academic prose must master complex sentences.**"	When using another person's ideas, a writer must either quote the author or paraphrase the author's ideas. You must name the author, the title, and the date of the original work. A **direct quotation** gives the exact words of another writer or speaker. The quote is set apart by quotation marks.
According to Gomez, "Internet plagiarism is becoming a huge problem."	The **quoting phrase** (*Dr. Reed says, Hendricks claims, According to Gomez*) is separated from the quotation by a comma.
Dr. Reed claims that **complex sentences are important in academic writing.** We asked whether we needed **to cite him in our compositions.**	Reported speech uses **noun clauses** and **infinitives** to report the words and ideas of another writer or speaker. When reporting a writer's ideas, it is important to cite the source but not to alter the meaning. For a review of direct quotes and reported speech, see Lesson 27.

B Read the following text. Then, in the spaces provided, rewrite the direct quotes as reported speech.

Dr. Reed talked to us about plagiarism this week. He said, "If you plagiarize, you will receive an F." He warned us, "Don't copy an author's words exactly without quotes." Then he told us, "Don't use more than one quotation in your papers." He asked, "Is citing an author and using his or her exact words without quotes acceptable?" Satomi answered, "It probably isn't." He asked us, "What should you do instead?" Pedro said, "We should probably paraphrase." Dr. Reed asked, "What is paraphrasing?"

We told him, "We know what it is, but we don't know how to do it." As a result of our questions, Dr. Reed is going to spend a couple of classes teaching us how to paraphrase.

1. _____ He said that if we plagiarized we would receive an F. _____

2. _____

_____

3. _____

_____

4. _____

_____

5. _____

_____

6. _____

_____

7. _____

_____

8. _____

_____

9. _____

_____

C **GROUP WORK** Discuss your experiences in learning academic English writing. What has been frustrating for you? What have you learned? When you are finished, tell the class what your group discussed.

Sandra said she has learned to back up all her statements with supporting evidence.

PART THREE	Hedging with Modals, Adverbs of Frequency, Quantifiers, and Other Expressions

■ GRAMMAR IN CONTENT

A Reread the passage on page 270. Look at all the modals, adverbs of frequency, and quantifiers used as hedges, then study the chart below.

Hedging with Modals, Adverbs of Frequency, Quantifiers, and Other Expressions	
Sample Sentences	**Notes**
Akira: The professor said that hedging is a way of making a forceful statement. **Uri:** **I think** you **may** be wrong about that. **I believe** it's actually a way of softening a statement.	**Hedging** is a way of softening a statement that sounds too strong or confrontational. Certain expressions such as *I think, I believe, Maybe, It's possible, It seems,* and *Don't you agree* are used to soften claims in spoken English.
Use of an appropriate modal softens a strong claim. ↓ Use of an appropriate modal **can** soften a strong claim.	**Modals** that are frequently used to hedge in conversation and academic writing include *can, could,* and *may.* See Lesson 9 to review other uses of modals.
Strong claims are easier to challenge. ↓ Strong claims are **often** easier to challenge.	**Adverbs of frequency** are adverbs that tell how often something occurs. Adverbs of frequency that are often used to hedge in conversation and academic writing include *usually, sometimes, often,* and *frequently.* See Lesson 3 to review other uses of adverbs of frequency.
ESL students use conversational expressions in their writing. ↓ **Many** ESL students use conversational expressions in their writing.	**Quantifiers** are core determiners that tell how much. Quantifiers that are often used to hedge in conversation and academic writing include *some, much, many, a little, a few,* and *a number of.* See Lessons 12 and 29 to review other uses of quantifiers.

Notes:
• Adverbs such as *maybe* and *possibly* are usually avoided in academic writing.
• Personal expressions such as *I think* or *In my opinion* should be used sparingly in academic writing.

B Edit the following conversation, softening the statements with personal expressions, modals, and adverbs of frequency.

Brad: *I think* ESL students organize their essays differently than native speakers.

Satomi: We put the main idea at the end of the composition, and we use too many questions.

Brad: That kind of style and organization makes your essays difficult for native speakers to follow.

Satomi: Yes. We English students need a lot of help with our writing.

Brad: A good writing class provides that kind of support.

C Selma needs to hedge much more in her composition. Edit her work, providing suitable hedges. One such hedge has been provided as an example.

English language learners' essays differ from native speakers' essays in several ways. First, their sentences are *often* ungrammatical. Verb tense errors are a good indicator of a non-native speaker's problems. For example, ESL learners omit third-person singular endings in their compositions. They also confuse verb tenses. Native speakers don't do this. Furthermore, English language learners don't use modals effectively as hedges. In fact, students don't hedge their claims at all. The result is statements that are much too strong for an English essay.

D PAIR WORK What do you find most difficult in English academic style? Tell your partner. Use hedges.

I sometimes have a hard time beginning a composition with the main idea. I usually like to lead up to it.

I know what you mean. Readers may not feel any need to read further if they already know what your point is.

Connection Putting It Together

GRAMMAR AND VOCABULARY Write a short essay on the topic of plagiarism. Define what it is and describe your school's official policy regarding plagiarism. Conclude the essay by giving your personal opinion on the subject. Avoid using statements such as *I think* or *I believe*, which are generally avoided in academic writing. Instead, use phrases such as *It seems, It appears,* or *One might conclude.*

PROJECT Work in groups of three. Each group member can interview an English writing instructor. What kinds of errors bother this instructor most? Grammar errors? Punctuation errors such as fragments or run-on sentences? Citation errors? Lack of complex sentences? Claims that are not hedged? Later, discuss what you found out with your group. Did all three instructors mention the same errors?

INTERNET Using a search engine, enter the words "plagiarism" and "culture." Explore the links to see how plagiarism is defined in different cultures. Take notes and reflect on what you find. Later, discuss these issues and perspectives with your class.

A **Rewrite the quotations in their correct form in the corresponding blanks.**

1. How did you first decide to study the Incas?
2. What do I want to study?
3. Write a report on the Incas!
4. What effect will this have on my life?
5. Help me!
6. How did the Inca Empire develop?
7. What caused its downfall?
8. Focus on a particular problem!
9. What would you really like to know more about?
10. Did diseases such as smallpox contribute to the weakening of the Inca Empire?
11. There are a number of good references in the library.
12. I enjoyed writing it.
13. Was the paper any good or not?
14. You have written an excellent paper.
15. Come and participate in a colloquium I am presenting.

Let me tell you about ___how I first decided to study the Incas___. Well, I was in
(1)

my last year of college and I didn't know _____.
(2)

I was taking an anthropology class, and the professor told me

_____. I didn't realize at the time
(3)

_____.
(4)

At that time I didn't really know how to do research, so I had to

ask Dr. Willis _____. I wanted
(5)

to investigate _____ and
(6)

_____. Dr. Willis advised
(7)

me _____. He asked me
(8)

_____. I particularly wanted
(9)

to know _____. He told me
(10)

_____.
(11)

Finally, I turned in my paper. I knew _____,
(12)

but I couldn't judge _____. A few days later I got
(13)

an e-mail from Dr. Willis. He told me _____. Then
(14)

he invited me _____.
(15)

B Complete the following text with the correct form of the verb in parentheses. When no choices are given in parentheses, complete the sentence with *it, that,* or *what,* as appropriate.

A team of researchers on the faculty at Evergreen University ____is____ (be) (1) building a new robotic pet. The group _____ (hope) to sell the design to a large (2) manufacturer. All the faculty on the team _____ (be) enthusiastic about the (3) project, and it's easy _____ (see) why. _____ many people want is a (4) (5) pet that doesn't need maintenance. It's well-known _____ people who live alone (6) often keep pets for company, but it's sometimes difficult _____ (care) for a pet. (7) With a robotic pet, it's easy _____ (keep) the pet clean and happy. And it's nice (8) _____ (have) an affectionate dog or cat that doesn't need a lot of attention. In (9) addition, _____ is safe to operate this robot around children. (10)

Unfortunately, members of the group working on the robot often _____ (11) (disagree). In spite of their differences, the team _____ (have) promised to (12) cooperate in finding solutions. They know _____ the project won't succeed unless (13) they overlook their differences.

LEARNER LOG Check (✔) *Yes* or *I Need More Practice.*

Lesson	I Can Use . . .	Yes	I Need More Practice
26	Object Noun Clauses with *that, if, whether,* and *wh-* Words		
27	Statements, Questions, Orders, Requests, Advice, and Warnings in Reported Speech		
28	Infinitives and *that* Clauses with Anticipatory *it; Wh-* Clefts		
29	Verb Agreement with Collective Nouns, Units of Measurement, and Quantifiers		
30	Adverbial Clauses; Direct Quotes; Reported Speech; Hedging with Modals, Adverbs of Frequency, Quantifiers, and Other Expressions		

Separable Phrasal Verbs			
Phrasal Verb	**More Formal, Academic Term**	**Phrasal Verb**	**More Formal, Academic Term**
bring about	cause to happen	pass out	distribute
figure out	interpret, understand	play down	minimize
carry out	accomplish, complete, fulfill	put on	deceive
draw up	write, compose	save up	accumulate
find out	discover	take over	assume control of
hand over	yield control	think up	create, invent

Inseparable Phrasal Verbs			
Phrasal Verb	**More Formal, Academic Term**	**Phrasal Verb**	**More Formal, Academic Term**
catch on to	become aware of	measure up to	meet the standards of
come off as	give the impression of being	move on	make progress, advance
face up to	acknowledge	put up with	tolerate, endure
get over	forget about	see through	cease to believe
look into	investigate	think about	consider, ponder
look out for	protect	turn on	retaliate against
turn up	appear	wake up	to become aware of

Verb	Active Voice Form	Middle Voice Form	Passive Voice Form
accumulate	The bank accumulated debt.	Debt accumulated.	Debt was accumulated (by the bank).
benefit	Exercise benefits memory.	Memory benefits (from exercise).	Memory is benefited (by exercise).
break	My sister broke the cup.	The cup broke.	The cup was broken (by my sister).
change	The coach changed the team's focus.	The team's focus changed.	The team's focus was changed (by the coach).
close/open	The wind closed the door.	The door closed.	The door was closed (by the wind).
continue	The boy continued the work.	The work continued.	The work was continued (by the boy).
develop	The brain developed new neurons.	New neurons developed.	New neurons were developed (by the brain).
drop	The thief dropped the bucket quietly into the well.	The bucket dropped quietly into the well.	The bucket was dropped quietly into the well (by the thief).
empty	The police slowly emptied the theater.	The theater slowly emptied.	The theater was slowly emptied (by the police).
end	The president ended the debate.	The debate ended.	The debate was ended (by the president).
grow	The researchers grew new cells.	New cells grew.	New cells were grown (by the researchers).
form	The students formed a study group.	A study group formed.	A study group was formed (by the students).
freeze/melt	The reaction froze the steel bar.	The steel bar froze.	The steel bar was frozen (by the reaction).
improve	The loan improved our situation.	Our situation improved.	Our situation was improved (by the loan).
increase/ decrease	The changes increased profits.	Profits increased.	Profits were increased (by the changes).
move	The wind moved the curtains.	The curtains moved.	The curtains were moved (by the wind).

rise	Import taxes raised the price.	Prices rose.	The prices were raised (by import taxes).
shift	The debate shifted public opinion.	Public opinion shifted.	Public opinion was shifted (by the debate).
slow	The malfunction slowed the train.	The train slowed.	The train was slowed (by the malfunction).
spread	The media has spread the story.	The story has spread.	The story has been spread (by the media).
start	The instructor started the car.	The car started.	The car was started (by the instructor).
stop	The police stopped the car.	The car stopped.	The car was stopped (by the police).
turn	The wind turned the car around.	The car turned around.	The car was turned around (by the wind).
turn on	The thermostat turned the heater on.	The heater turned on.	The heater was turned on (by the thermostat).

Verbs Followed by Gerunds

admit	deny	go on	practice	resist
anticipate	detest	can't help	put off	resume
appreciate	discuss	imagine	quit	risk
avoid	dislike	involve	recall	can't see
complete	enjoy	keep	recollect	stop
consider	escape	not mind	recommend	suggest
defend	finish	miss	report	take up
delay	give up	postpone	resent	tolerate

Verbs Followed by Infinitives

agree	claim	hesitate	plan	seem
appear	consent	hope	prepare	strive
ask	decide	intend	pretend	struggle
be able	demand	learn	proceed	tend
beg	deserve	manage	promise	threaten
care	expect	mean	refuse	vow
cause	fail	need	regret	want
choose	have to	offer	resolve	

Verbs Followed by Either an Infinitive or Gerund

afford	cease	forget*	love	remember*
attempt*	commence	hate	prefer	start
begin	continue	intend	propose	stop*
can't stand	dread	like	regret*	try*

*Infinitive and gerund objects differ in meaning.

Verbs Followed by Object Noun Clauses with *That*

answer	establish	mean*	report	think*
argue	expect	note	say*	understand
assume*	explain	notice	see*	warn
believe*	find*	point out	show*	worry
claim	guess	promise	state	write
complain	hear	prove	suggest*	
demonstrate	hope	realize*	suppose*	
discover	indicate*	recommend	suspect	
ensure*	know*	reply	swear	

Verbs Followed by Object Noun Clauses with *Whether* and *If*

ask*	determine*	find out*	learn	say*
care	doubt	indicate*	know*	see*
consider*	establish*	investigate*	mind	tell
decide*	explain	judge*	remember	wonder

Verbs Followed by Object Noun Clauses with *Wh-* Words

ask	find out*	realize*	see*	understand*
depend on	can't imagine	recognize	show*	wonder
determine	indicate	remember	tell	
explain*	know*	say	think about	

*Verbs with an asterisk are most common in academic English.

Collective Nouns that Refer to Groups of People

audience	crew	gang	panel
class	crowd	government	staff
committee	faculty	group	team
company	family	mob	troupe

Packages: Count Nouns

bag of coffee beans	bouquet of flowers	bunch of grapes	jar of pickles
basket of strawberries	box of blueberries	carton of eggs	pack of cigarettes
book of matches	bunch of bananas	crate of melons	sack of potatoes

Packages and Units of Measurement: Noncount Nouns

bar of soap	cube of butter	pack of gum	slice of toast
bottle of oil	cup of sugar	pound of rice	tablespoon of pepper
box of cereal	head of lettuce	quart of milk	teaspoon of salt
can of soup	jar of honey	sack of flour	tub of margarine
carton of milk	loaf of bread	six-pack of soda	tube of toothpaste

The irregular verbs in each box contain the same sound change from the basic form (on the left) to the simple past (on the right). You will need to memorize the verbs in each box.

come	came
become	became

bite	bit
hide	hid

get	got
forget	forgot

sell	sold
tell	told

begin	began
sit	sat
swim	swam

stand	stood
understand	understood

drink	drank
ring	rang
sing	sang

shake	shook
take	took

blow	blew
draw	drew
fly	flew
grow	grew
know	knew
throw	threw

lend	lent
send	sent
spend	spent

speak	spoke
steal	stole

feed	fed
feel	felt
keep	kept
leave	left
lead	led
meet	met
read	read*
sleep	slept

* Pronounced "red"

break	broke
tear	tore
wake	woke
wear	wore

drive	drove
ride	rode
write	wrote

cost	cost
cut	cut
hit	hit
hurt	hurt
put	put
quit	quit
shut	shut

bring	brought
buy	bought
catch	caught*
fight	fought
teach	taught*
think	thought

* The spelling is different for these two verbs: -au- not -ou-

APPENDIX 7 Common Irregular Verbs

The following chart gives the past and past participles of some common verbs. You must memorize these forms, because they are irregular.

Base Form	Past Tense	Past Participle
be	was, were	been
begin	began	begun
bite	bit	bitten
break	broke	broken
bring	brought	brought
build	built	built
buy	bought	bought
catch	caught	caught
choose	chose	chosen
come	came	come
cost	cost	cost
cut	cut	cut
do	did	done
draw	drew	drawn
drink	drank	drunk
eat	ate	eaten
feel	felt	felt
find	found	found
give	gave	given
go	went	gone
grow	grew	grown
hide	hid	hidden
have	had	had
hear	heard	heard
keep	kept	kept
know	knew	known
make	made	made
pay	paid	paid
read	read	read
say	said	said
see	saw	seen
speak	spoke	spoken
take	took	taken
teach	taught	taught
tell	told	told
think	thought	thought
write	wrote	written

Do vs. *Make*

When you *do* something, there is an activity, some kind of action. When you *make* something, you <u>create</u> something that did not exist before.

You do exercises, the laundry / dishes (= wash), homework, gardening, a job, what's right, etc.

You make a telephone call, a reservation, a cake, an appointment, plans, a decision, etc.

Hear vs. *Listen To*

When there is a sound or noise, you *hear* it. You have no control over this. This is what your ears do. We call this an involuntary action. When you pay attention to a sound or noise, you *listen to* it.

Be quiet for a moment. I think I hear somebody outside. Who could it be?

I have to give a short speech in class tomorrow. Can you please listen to me while I practice it?

Say vs. *Tell*

When we use the verb *say*, we normally don't mention the person who is listening. When we use the verb *tell*, we must mention the person who is listening. With *tell*, we can also use the infinitive verb.

She said (that) we needed to pay in cash.

She told <u>us</u> (that) we needed to pay in cash. / She told <u>us</u> to pay in cash.

See vs. *Look At* vs. *Watch*

When you open your eyes, you *see*. You have no control over this. This is another involuntary action. When you pay attention to something that is not doing an activity, you *look at* it. When you pay attention to something that is doing an activity, you *watch* it. *Look at* and *watch* are more examples of voluntary actions.

Jim doesn't see well. That's why he wears glasses.

Look at that sunset! I never saw the sun with such a deep orange color.

I like to watch my dogs play with each other in the backyard.

The one exception is *to see a movie.* (You *watch* a television show.)

Talk vs. *Speak*

These verbs have the same meaning ("have a conversation"), but you *talk to* somebody or you *speak to / with* somebody. The only big difference is that you *speak* a language, not *talk*.

Can I talk to you for a minute, Mr. Conklin? / Can I speak to / with you for a minute, Mr. Conklin?

He's amazing. He can speak six languages.

Cardinal Numbers

1	one
2	two
3	three
4	four
5	five
6	six
7	seven
8	eight
9	nine
10	ten
11	eleven
12	twelve
13	thirteen
14	fourteen
15	fifteen
16	sixteen
17	seventeen
18	eighteen
19	nineteen
20	twenty
21	twenty-one
30	thirty
40	forty
50	fifty
60	sixty
70	seventy
80	eighty
90	ninety
100	one hundred
1,000	one thousand
10,000	ten thousand
100,000	one hundred thousand
1,000,000	one million

Ordinal Numbers

first	1st
second	2nd
third	3rd
fourth	4th
fifth	5th
sixth	6th
seventh	7th
eighth	8th
ninth	9th
tenth	10th
eleventh	11th
twelfth	12th
thirteenth	13th
fourteenth	14th
fifteenth	15th
sixteenth	16th
seventeenth	17th
eighteenth	18th
nineteenth	19th
twentieth	20th
twenty-first	21st

Days of the Week

Sunday
Monday
Tuesday
Wednesday
Thursday
Friday
Saturday

Seasons

winter
spring
summer
fall/autumn

Months of the Year

January
February
March
April
May
June
July
August
September
October
November
December

Write the Date

April 5, 2004 = 4/5/04

Temperature Chart

Degrees Celsius (°C) and Degrees Fahrenheit (°F)

100°C	212°F
30°C	86°F
25°C	77°F
20°C	68°F
15°C	59°F
10°C	50°F
5°C	41°F
0°C	32°F
–5°C	23°F

Weights and Measures

Weight:

1 pound (lb.) = 453.6 grams (g)
16 ounces (oz.) = 1 pound (lb.)
1 pound (lb.) = .45 kilograms (kg)

Liquid or Volume:

1 cup (c.) = .24 liter (l)
2 cups (c.) = 1 pint (pt.)
2 pints = 1 quart (qt.)
4 quarts = 1 gallon (gal.)
1 gallon (gal.) = 3.78 liters (l)

Length:

1 inch (in. or ") = 2.54 centimeters (cm)
1 foot (ft. or ') = .3048 meters (m)
12 inches (12") = 1 foot (1')
1 yard (yd.) = 3 feet (3') or 0.9144 meters (m)
1 mile (mi.) = 1,609.34 meters (m) or 1.609 kilometers (km)

Time:

60 seconds = 1 minute
60 minutes = 1 hour
24 hours = 1 day
28–31 days = 1 month
12 months = 1 year

- **Adjective** An adjective describes a noun. Example: *That's a **small** desk.*

- **Adverb** An adverb describes the verb of a sentence or an adjective. Examples: *He is **very** smart. I run **quickly**.*

- **Adverb of Frequency** An adverb of frequency tells how often an action happens. Example: *I **always** go to the library after class.*

- **Affirmative** An affirmative means *yes.*

- **Article** An article (*a, an,* and *the*) comes before a noun. Example: *I have **a** book and **an** eraser.*

- **Base Form** The base form of a verb has no tense. It has no ending (*-s* or *-ed*). Examples: ***be, go, eat, take, write***

- **Clause** A clause is a group of words that has a subject and a verb. Example: ***Harry likes** college.*

- **Comparative Form** A comparative form of an adjective or adverb is used to compare two things. Example: *I am **taller** than you.*

- **Consonant** The following letters are consonants: ***b, c, d, f, g, h, j, k, l, m, n, p, q, r, s, t, v, w, x, y, z.***

- **Contraction** A contraction is made up of two words put together with an apostrophe. Example: ***She's** my friend.* (She is = she's)

- **Count Noun** Count nouns are nouns that we can count. They have a singular and a plural form. Examples: ***book – books, nurse – nurses***

- **Frequency Expressions** Frequency expressions answer *How often* questions. Examples: ***once a week, three times a week, every day***

- **Imperative** An imperative sentence gives a command or instructions. An imperative sentence usually omits the word *you*. Example: ***Open** the door.*

- **Information Questions** Questions that ask *what, when, who, how,* or *which.*

- **Intransitive** Intransitive verbs do not have an object.

- **Irregular Verbs** See Appendix 7.

- **Linking Verb** A linking verb connects the subject of a sentence to a noun, adjective, or prepositional phrase.

- **Modal** Some examples of modal verbs are ***can, could, should, will, would, must.***

- **Negative** Means *no.*

- **Noncount Noun** A noncount noun is a noun that we don't count. It has no plural form. Examples: ***water, money, rice***

- **Noun** A noun is a word for a person, a place, or a thing. Nouns can be singular (only one) or plural (more than one).

- **Object** The object of the sentence follows the verb. It receives the action of the verb. Example: *Kat wrote a **paragraph.***

- **Object Pronoun** Use object pronouns (*me, you, him, her, it, us, them*) after the verb or preposition. Example: *Kat wore **it.***

- **Phrasal Verb** A verb followed by a particle, such as *point out, think over,* and *turn in.*

- **Plural** Plural means more than one. A plural noun usually ends with *-s* or *-es.* Examples: *The books are heavy. The buses are not running.*

- **Possessive Form** The possessive form of a noun has an apostrophe: *the teacher's class, Jupiter's moons.* Possessive pronouns *(my, mine, our, ours, his, her, hers, their, theirs, its, your, yours)* do not use an apostrophe.

- **Preposition** A preposition is a short, connecting word. Examples: *about, above, across, after, around, as, at, away, before, behind, below, by, down, for, from, in, into, like, of, on, out, over, to, under, up, with*

- **Punctuation (. , ' ?)** Punctuation marks are used to make writing clear (for example: periods, commas, apostrophes, question marks).

- **Regular Verb** A regular verb forms its past tense with *-d* or *-ed.* Example: *He lived in Mexico.*

- **Sentence** A sentence is a group of words that contains a subject and a verb and expresses a complete thought.

- **Singular** Means one.

- **Stative Verb** Stative verbs have no action. They do not often take the progressive form. Examples: *love, like, think, own, understand, want*

- **Subject** The subject of the sentence tells who or what the sentence is about. Example: *The water does not taste good.*

- **Subject Pronoun** Use subject pronouns (*I, you, he, she, it, we, they*) in place of a subject noun. Example: *They (= the books) are on the desk.*

- **Tense** A verb has tense. Tense shows when the action of the sentence happened.

    Simple Present: *She occasionally reads before bed.*

    Present Progressive: *He is thinking about it now.*

    Simple Past: *I talked to him yesterday.*

- **Transitive** Transitive verbs have an object.

- **Verb** Verbs are words of action or state. Example: *I go to work every day. Joe stays at home.*

- **Verb of Perception** Verbs related to the senses, such as *look, see, watch, hear, listen, taste, smell,* and *feel.*

- **Yes/No Questions** *Yes/No* questions ask for a *yes* or *no* answer. Example: *Is she from Mexico? Yes, she is.*

Review: Lessons 1–5
(pages 47–48)

A.
1. do you get
2. get off
3. 'm going to go
4. Are you going to go
5. 're going to be
6. 'll be
7. 'm going to be leaving
8. am I going to get
9. 'll ask
10. won't mind

B.
1. never
2. from
3. until
4. Now
5. Usually
6. sometimes
7. until

C.
1. have you been doing
2. 've been working
3. 're
4. do you like
5. have been
6. fell
7. took
8. haven't had
9. 're engaged
10. didn't know
11. 've known
12. 'll expect

Review: Lessons 6–10
(pages 87–88)

A.
1. have been coughing
2. haven't been sleeping
3. haven't gone
4. have

5. had
6. began
7. will have been coughing
8. haven't ever had
9. has been dry
10. have been hurting
11. Did
12. have
13. started
14. hadn't been feeling
15. began
16. Have
17. had
18. don't think
19. Have
20. been
21. received
22. started

B.
1. can't
2. may
3. might
4. should
5. should
6. might

C.
1. wasn't
2. couldn't
3. couldn't/didn't
4. couldn't/didn't
5. couldn't/didn't
6. haven't
7. wasn't
8. don't

Review: Lessons 11–15
(pages 129–130)

A.
1. came across an ad
2. checked them out
3. took down the
   information

4. look into the job
5. find out more about
   animal communication
6. make up new words
7. pass it up
8. take on any new work
9. turn it down

B.
1. their
2. my
3. a
4. him
5. his
6. they
7. his
8. the
9. the/his
10. him
11. my
12. She
13. a
14. she
15. her
16. she
17. each other
18. she
19. his
20. him
21. such
22. these
23. they
24. their
25. That/This
26. it
27. them
28. them

C.
1. young French
2. daring new
3. short leather
4. long silk
5. large round

6. narrow leather
7. belted
8. really popular
9. enthusiastic design
10. six-hour
11. exciting young
12. dazzling New York

Review: Lessons 16–20 (pages 179–180)

A.
1. for
2. too
3. so
4. enough
5. before
6. really
7. Since

B.
1. that he hasn't been able to cover
2. that he hired
3. that will fund the rest of his campaign
4. whose name is Dr. Alfred Weiss
5. that are important to them
6. that he can trust

C.
1. It's
2. However,
3. On the other hand
4. Moreover,
5. it's
6. there
7. Moreover

Review: Lessons 21–25 (pages 229–230)

A.
1. needs
2. don't stay
3. had
4. gave

5. quit
6. had arrived
7. would have gotten
8. hadn't missed
9. would have received

B.
1. to write
2. me not to put off
3. writing
4. to apply
5. to accept
6. to be accepted
7. us to write
8. writing

C.
1. changed
2. grown
3. was hired
4. were accused
5. were taken off
6. were arrested
7. increased
8. not been filed
9. been destroyed
10. shrank
11. be fired
12. moved / was moved
13. shifted
14. developed
15. improved

Review: Lessons 26–30 (pages 279–280)

A.
1. how I first decided to study the Incas
2. what I wanted to study
3. to write a report on the Incas
4. what effect this would have on my life
5. to help me
6. how the Inca Empire developed
7. what caused its downfall

8. to focus on a particular problem
9. what I would really like to know more about
10. whether diseases such as smallpox had contributed to the weakening of the Inca Empire
11. (that) there were a number of good references in the library
12. that I had enjoyed writing it,
13. whether the paper was any good or not
14. that I had written an excellent paper
15. to come and participate in a colloquium he was presenting

B.
1. is
2. hopes
3. are
4. to see
5. What
6. that
7. to care
8. to keep
9. to have
10. it
11. disagree
12. has
13. that

Words in blue are part of the Content Vocabulary section at the start of each lesson.
Words in black are words glossed with the readings in each lesson.
Words in **bold** are words from the Academic Word List.

Index

Credits

Illustrators

InContext Publishing Partners: pp. 102, 274, 277

Alan King/illustrationOnLine.com: pp. 21, 57, 121, 131, 138–139, 141, 149–150, 161, 231, 239, 251, 261

Katie McCormick/illustrationOnLine.com: pp. 1, 11, 16, 81, 101, 109

Precision Graphics: pp. 5, 7, 19, 26, 30, 36, 43, 52, 62, 63, 69, 79, 86, 100, 107, 119, 126–127, 139 (bottom), 143–144, 147, 153, 155, 164, 171, 174, 176–177, 181, 191, 201, 205–206, 209, 249, 255, 260, 267, 269

David Preiss/Munro Campagna.com: pp. 29, 69, 71, 73, 89–90, 95–96

Scott Wakefield/Gwen Walters Artist Representative: pp. 37, 111, 116–117

Photo Credits